"HAVE YOU GOT Y(

Yvonne Peters

Mrs Y. D. Peters
35 Avenue Gardens
HORLEY
Surrey RH6 9BS

01293-782129

For

Keith Randell
My good friend and editor
1943 - 2002

"HAVE YOU GOT YOUR IRONS?"
It's a Waaf's Life

YVONNE PETERS

GREENRIDGES PRESS

ISBN
1 90201907 5
First published July 2004

© Yvonne Peters 2004

The moral right of Yvonne Peters to be identified as the author of this work has been asserted by her in accordance with the Copyright, Designs and Patents Act 1988

All rights reserved. No part of this publication may be reproduced, stored in a retrieval system, or transmitted in any form by any means, electronic, mechanical, photocopying, recording or otherwise, without the prior permission of the copyright owner.

British Library Cataloguing in Publication Data.
A catalogue record for this book is
available from the British Library.

Mr. & Mrs. J. Loader

Published by
Greenridges Press
13 Vale Road, Hartford
Northwich, Cheshire CW8 1PL
Great Britain
Tel: 01606 75660; fax 01606 77609
email: anne@leoniepress.com
websites: www.leoniepress.com
www.greenridgespress.co.uk

Printed by Anne Loader Publications
Collating and binding by B & S Swindells Ltd, Knutsford
Cover lamination by The Finishing Touch, St Helens

AUTHOR'S NOTE

I was born in 1923. Discipline at home and at my Convent School was strict. Father's secure job in the Civil Service shielded us from the poverty due to unemployment during the Depression in the early Thirties. As a child I was content with my safe world: as a teenager I longed to be free of its restrictions. When World War II broke out in 1939 it affected everyone's life immediately, including mine. I wrote the book to try and recapture the flavour of wartime life as I knew it, in civvy street and in the WAAF.

However, sixty years is a long time and while some memories come back to me pin-sharp, others are hazy and may not always be accurate. It is the same with conversations. Some echo across the years as clear as if they had taken place yesterday; others have had to be reconstituted, as only the gist of them remains. I have changed the names of some of the characters, partly to protect their identities, and partly because in some cases I have forgotten their real ones!

Yvonne Peters
May 2004

ACKNOWLEDGEMENTS

Firstly a special thank-you to my husband Patrick. Without his help and encouragement this book would never have been written.

My grateful thanks also go to my brother David Golton, Helen Franklin, Fiona Leaper, Eric and Dorothy Richman, Ruth Martin, Stanley Rowland, Robert Gregson, Joyce May, Simon Golton, Mary Franks, Denise Wraight, Leslie Bushill, Patricia Clark, and Jack Kenworthy, all of whom helped me in so many different ways.

I would also like to thank Sqn Ldr Beryl Escott for permission to use the list of 'Personal Issue of Clothing and Necessaries' and the 'Layout of WAAF Kit (For Kit Inspection)'; also "After the Battle" for permission to use the photograph of a Blenheim Mk IV taken by Chris Burkett.

CONTENTS

Chapter 1 - Turning point	1
Chapter 2 - War	13
Chapter 3 - The Uncivil Service	30
Chapter 4 - Marking Time	44
Chapter 5 - Think of a Number	51
Chapter 6 - "Sprogs"	65
Chapter 7 - Getting Down to Basics	76
Chapter 8 - Welcome to Blackpool	87
Chapter 9 - Stepping Out	104
Chapter 10 - Moving On	114
Chapter 11 - The real Air Force	126
Chapter 12 - Nights and Days	138
Chapter 13 - Winter	154
Chapter 14 - Springtime 1943	167
Chapter 15 - High Summer	179
Chapter 16 - Autumn	193
Chapter 17 - The End of the Year	205
Chapter 18 - Growing Up	219
Chapter 19 - Leaving Bicester	230
Chapter 20 - The Home Front	241
Chapter 21 - Whitehall	259

WAAF recruiting poster

Chapter 1

Turning Point

I WATCHED the list being passed along the rows of desks with growing tension. Some girls added their name, some didn't. What was I going to do when it got to me? I sat at the back of the class. It would be several minutes before I finally had to make up my mind: had I the courage to defy my father? I thought of the alternative and felt sick with misery. The list came nearer, reached the back row and was handed on to me by the girl on my left. I sat staring at it blankly. My mind had ceased to work. The girls on my right were growing restive, leaning forward over their desks and looking towards me, asking what the hold-up was. I picked up my pen to sign, then put it down again. I couldn't do it. I passed on the list to the girls still waiting, with an unsteady hand.

It was early 1939 and I had just turned sixteen. In the coming July I would take my School's Leaving Exams, hopefully get my Certificate, and then I would be free. Free to leave the Convent School, St Michael's, where I had been a day girl since I was five years old. Free to lead my own life instead of always having to do as I was told. The prospect was exhilarating. However, there were difficulties to be overcome first.

It was quite common in those days for fathers to choose their children's careers for them, or at least tell them where they could or could not work. From about the age of ten I had known, without ever having been told in so many words, that my father intended me to go into the Civil Service. He himself had gone into H.M. Stationery Office straight from school, working as an engineering apprentice in the Printing Department. He had just completed his apprenticeship when war broke out in 1914. He was nineteen. Over six feet in height and broad-shouldered, he was a handsome young man, with dark wavy hair and serious dark brown eyes. All his friends were going off to join the Army and the idea of fighting for his country appealed to him. He volunteered for the Royal Engineers.

Father survived the war virtually unscathed and returned to the Printing Department of HMSO. In 1921 he married my mother and they settled in a three-bedroomed terrace house in North Finchley on the northern edge of London. I arrived in 1923 and my brother David followed me into the world four years later. Some time in the early thirties, with a wife, two growing children and a mortgage to support, he left engineering, which he loved, for a white-collar job in the Accommodation Department at Somerset House. The clerical grades were paid at higher rates than manual workers and he needed the money. My mother was not strong, she had been in hospital several times since they married, and doctors' bills were a constant financial burden.

He was a strict father. As a child I adored him and never thought to question his authority. Gradually, however, as I approached adolescence, I began to find his house rules irksome and to question his judgment, especially in the matter of my future. I had come to realise that I did not want to be a civil servant. The Convent was a sheltered environment, so was the Civil Service. The idea of going straight from one to the other without being given a chance to look round to see what else the world had to offer depressed me. By the age of fifteen my mind was made up. I decided to tell my father outright how I felt. It was summertime, he had been working unusually long hours for some weeks and the opportunity to talk to him did not come until one Saturday afternoon. He was trimming the front hedge and I went out to join him on the pretext of helping him clear up the cuttings. I could think of no way of bringing up the subject except to go straight into it with, "I've been thinking about when I leave school, Daddy."

"Oh?" He sounded absent-minded. This was not encouraging but I took the plunge. "I don't want to go into the Civil Service."

"Why not?"

I had more of his attention now. "It's so impersonal. I want to work with people, not spend my life filling in forms."

To my surprise he told me curtly that I was too young to know what I was talking about. I would feel differently when I was older. He went through the gate to do the outside of the hedge, making it clear he considered the conversation at an end.

He had never treated me so dismissively before and I was hurt. I left him to clear up his own cuttings and went to find my mother. She was dead-heading flowers in the back garden. In an aggrieved voice I told her what had happened.

"You picked a bad time," she too sounded abstracted. "He's got a lot on his mind just now and he's tired."

She showed no more interest in what I wanted to do when I left school than Father had. I wandered off, determined to bring the subject up again as soon as the opportunity arose.

This was the summer of 1938, the year Hitler annexed the Sudetenlands in Czechoslovakia, claiming they were really part of Germany. The wireless talked of 'the seriousness of the situation'; newspapers ran headlines asking, 'Are We Heading For Another War?' Pictures appeared of our troops filling sandbags to stack outside public buildings as protection against bomb blast. Trenches were dug in the parks for use as air raid shelters should they ever be needed. It was all rather exciting to those of us who were too young to remember the Great War. However, Prime Minister Neville Chamberlain travelled to Munich in the September to meet Hitler personally. He returned with the famous Agreement that promised 'peace in our time', and the crisis was over.

"Thank God," said Mother. "Another war would be unthinkable."

I brought up the subject of my future again as soon as I could, and this time Father listened to what I had to say. I thought I was making him understand how I felt, but I was wrong. His response was to try and make me change my mind. He spoke of the advantages of being a civil servant: the reasonable working hours and the paid holidays; the security of having a job for life with a comfortable pension when I retired. I was appalled. A job for life? A comfortable retirement? I said I hoped to be married long before then. Father said supposing I wasn't? I pointed out that Mother's younger sister, Aunt Evelyn, wasn't married and she wasn't in the Civil Service, but she had done all right. Father said she was the exception that proved the rule – whatever that meant.

Aunt Evelyn was personal assistant to some bigwig in a large firm in the City. When I asked her what she did she told me about her work, her face alive with enthusiasm. She earned a good salary and went abroad for holidays (something not many people could afford to do in those days). If I asked Father about his work his face looked closed and he answered in a flat voice, "I'm a clerk." The phrase 'job satisfaction' had not then been coined, but I recognised that Aunt Evelyn had it and Father did not. Repeated discussions did not change my mind and at some point along the line discussion turned into argument and we ended up at loggerheads.

"You keep on telling us what you don't want, but what exactly is it you do want?" demanded my father once in exasperation. Beyond saying 'something to do with people', as I had already told him many times, I couldn't answer his question. I didn't know what there was available. I wanted the chance to find out. That was the whole point.

Mother was weary of listening to us. "Why must you keep arguing with your father?" she asked one evening as we did the washing-up after supper. "He won't change his mind, you know." And I won't change mine either, I promised myself. But her question made me think. She was right. What was the use of arguing when it could do no good? I kept quiet from then on and let Father think I had given in. But beneath my silence I was getting desperate. The time was approaching when a list would be passed round the class at school. Every girl who wished to take the Civil Service Entrance Exam would add her name to it. What was I to do? I was good at exams and would be expected to pass this one. Apart from failing it deliberately, which went against the grain, there was only one way of ensuring that I did not end up as an unhappy clerk like Father: I could fail to take the exam. I spent restless nights worrying whether I would have the courage not to put my name down when the list came round and wishing the ordeal were over. For ordeal it was. I had never defied my father outright before.

I dawdled home after school that day, feeling guilty and hoping it would not show in my face to give me away. I had to keep my secret until after the closing date for submitting applications had passed. There would be trouble when Father realised what I had – or rather, had not – done, but by then there would be nothing he could do about it. Mentally I crossed days off the calendar. The significant date came and went and still I had not been found out. I hugged myself with relief and covert glee. I had done it. I had avoided becoming a civil servant.

The hour of reckoning came over supper one evening some days later. Father said pleasantly, "When do you take the Entrance Exam?"

I had a forkful of scrambled egg on its way to my mouth. I put it carefully back on my plate before answering; "I'm not taking it. I didn't put my name down."

For some seconds I don't think he took in what I had said. His expression remained unchanged and he finished his mouthful of egg. Then it registered. He put down his knife and fork. I had gone off my supper and sat waiting in trepidation for him to speak. Mother too had stopped eating. Only David, my twelve-year-old brother, continued with his supper, though he looked uneasy.

Father was staring at me in disbelief. He thought he must have misheard me. He had been so sure I would do as he wished it had never crossed his mind that I might rebel. He asked uncertainly, "You didn't put your name down?"

My mouth had gone dry. In a voice only a little above a whisper I said, "No."

"Why not?"

Why not? After all I had said over the past months he still had to ask why not? Stung by this final proof that he had not taken notice of anything I had said, I replied with spirit, "Because I don't want to go into the Civil Service. I did try to tell you."

Father went white to the lips. His voice was ominously quiet. "Go to your room and stay there."

I left the table and did as I was told. I was sure Mother sympathised with my desire to see more of the world than the inside of a Government office, and hoped she would come up later to say goodnight, but she didn't. I therefore surmised that I was out of favour with her too. Or maybe she felt Father might construe it as disloyalty to him and she would not want that. I had never known her take sides against him in any family argument in my whole life.

He did not speak to me about the exam again. In fact he hardly spoke to me at all and if I spoke to him he virtually ignored me. At first I was glad. At least there was not going to be a row. I hoped that when his anger subsided I would be able to talk to him about what I had done and he would listen, really listen to me at last. When there was no sign of this happening I became resentful. Why had he brushed aside all my arguments as being of no account? I came to dread suppertimes. The atmosphere was so tense I had difficulty swallowing. I excused myself from the table as soon as I could and went upstairs to my room, where I stayed until bedtime. Mother followed me up one evening and sat on the edge of my bed, clearly wanting to talk. I was wary, not knowing if she had come to speak on her own behalf or on Father's. "This can't go on," she said. "Why don't you go downstairs and apologise? I'm sure he'll forgive you."

"Forgive me for what? Wanting to choose my own job? Is that a sin?" I demanded angrily. "I don't feel sorry and I won't pretend I do."

"He's only got your welfare at heart," said Mother. "Can't you see that?"

"Then why doesn't he want me to have a job I can enjoy?"

"He thought you would be happy once you'd settled down."

"Then he doesn't know me," I said.

"No," she agreed quietly, "and you don't know him." She stood up, gave me a wan smile, and left me. Too wretched to finish my homework, I lay on my bed and stared at the ceiling.

However, my days were not all misery. I had a very good friend at school called Mollie, on whom I could always rely for sympathy and support. We had known each other nearly all our school lives. Mollie was of medium height and slim. Her hair was light brown and wavy, for which I envied her madly. Outgoing and friendly and always the same, she possessed a self-assurance that I also envied.

Mollie had a boyfriend called Ted. They had met when her elder brother brought him home one evening some six months previously. The attraction had been mutual and strong, but they had to be discreet; Mollie's father did not allow her to have boyfriends. To overcome this difficulty Mollie had devised a stratagem. With me standing by to provide alibis if needed, she had managed to meet Ted fairly regularly on Saturday afternoons, either to go to the pictures or walk in the park. One Saturday afternoon I had gone to the park with them. I liked Ted on sight. A year or two older than Mollie, he was tall and fair, with a wide cheerful grin and an easy manner. We fooled around on the swings like kids and everything made us laugh. I thought these secret assignations were frightfully romantic.

Mollie had put her name down for the exam. She intended to marry Ted as soon as they were old enough and did not mind what job she did in the meantime. The Civil Service was safe and the money regular, so why not enter if she had the chance? She was not attracted to the Service for its own sake and could quite understand my desire to look for more interesting work outside it.

At home the atmosphere remained tense. Father did not speak to me until one evening at supper when he looked across the table and said coldly. "As you don't seem to know what you want to do, you'd better go back to school next term and do the commercial course. I'll write to Sister Patricia and arrange it."

It was the last straw. I had been counting the weeks to my freedom in July. And now he was taking it away without any reference to what I wanted, as usual. That was what really hurt. Without stopping to think, I exploded, "No! I won't go! I'm sick of school. I'm sick of being treated like a child. I want to earn my own money and be independent."

"Doing what?" asked Father, adding, "If you were going into the Civil Service you would be earning your own money."

Always we came back to the Civil Service, as if there was nothing else. I had no answer for him. With hot tears of frustration stinging my eyes, I flung away from the table and fled to my room.

After this the atmosphere at home was worse than ever. Father ignored my existence completely. Or so it seemed to me. I was so miserable it disturbed my sleep. I found it difficult to concentrate at school and my work suffered in consequence. So did my homework. Poor Mother, who could see both sides of the argument but was powerless to resolve it, looked strained and unhappy. Her temper began to fray. Everyone got the rough edge of her tongue, even Father – a phenomenon unknown in the family until then. David, who was a dedicated member of the Boy Scouts, contrived to spend as much time as possible with them as a way of keeping out of the house. But I was my father's daughter. If he could be stubborn, so could I. I refused to give in. Mollie, while still supporting me in my battle with my father, was not so sure she understood my attitude towards the commercial course. She said, "I know he's high-handed, but he's offering you an olive branch in a way. Why don't you take it?" An uncomfortable little voice at the back of my mind said I was being unreasonable, but my pride refused to listen to it. I told myself I was misunderstood and hard-done-by, and the situation remained at stalemate.

It was our headmistress, Sister Patricia, who broke the deadlock in the end. She was a tall woman of commanding presence. A strict disciplinarian, but scrupulously fair, she was regarded throughout the school with respectful affection heavily laced with awe. Woe betide any girl caught breaking school rules. Our headmistress could deliver a formidable reprimand. But with any girl whose work suddenly deteriorated for no apparent reason, or who was thought to be in any sort of trouble, she was a different person. The girl would be invited to take a walk with her in the beautiful convent grounds and there, in the tranquillity of the rose garden, or the seclusion of the wooden summerhouse, she would try to discover what the problem might be, and help the girl to solve it if she could.

I was therefore summoned from class one bright afternoon in spring and told to follow her outside. She set off at a pace too brisk for conversation and we proceeded in silence down the broad path under the lime trees that bordered one side of the grounds. Halfway along she turned down a narrower path that ran beneath a pergola covered in wisteria. The summerhouse, known as the 'Indian hut' because of its round shape and conical roof, stood at the end. The entrance was a wide opening at the front, a wooden bench ran round the wall inside. Sister Patricia went in and sat down, motioning me to sit beside her. She adjusted her veil to her satisfaction and came straight to the point. "Well now, Yvonne. Your marks have been increasingly poor in the last few weeks. I'm sure there is some good reason for this?" She waited for me to answer. When I could not think how to begin she enquired, "Is there trouble at home?"

"Yes, Sister."

Once more she waited, then asked gently, "Is your mother's health giving cause for concern again?"

"No, Sister, she's all right," I said, "it's Father. We quarrelled."

"What about?"

Encouraged by her genuine concern for Mother's health, which somehow put the interview on a more intimate footing, I began to tell her what was wrong. Sister Patricia sat with hands folded in her lap and her head slightly bent, not looking at me but listening intently. I told her about Father's longstanding plan for my future and how I had thwarted him. Haltingly I described what happened when he found out.

There was silence when I finished speaking. I waited nervously for her verdict on my conduct. "I see," she said at last and looked up, altering her position on the bench to turn and watch my face. "How much do you remember of the Depression?"

The unexpected question struck me dumb while I reassembled my thoughts. At length I said. "All I can remember are the queues outside the Labour Exchange." When I was a child I had passed them in the High Road every day on my way to and from school. Long lines of shabbily dressed men who made me feel self-conscious in my spruce convent uniform. "And I can remember the bands," I added.

"Ah yes," she said sadly, "the bands." There was a pause while we both looked back to the groups of dejected men trudging along the gutter in broken shoes. Sometimes they sang, sometimes they played an assortment of strange instruments such as the Jew's harp or a comb and paper. One man would be holding out an old cap with a placard saying: 'Ex-servicemen. Wives and families to support' or something similar.

Sister Patricia shook off the memory and returned to the present. "There was so much unemployment after the war," she said. "Your father was lucky to have a job to come back to. Your family was spared the worst of the Depression because his future was secure."

"I know," I said. Father himself had pointed this out on numerous occasions.

"Why are you so against the Civil Service?" she wanted to know.

This was the question I had found so difficult to answer when Father put it to me. I thought for a moment, then told her about Aunt Evelyn and her enjoyment of her job, and how it contrasted with Father's attitude to his. "I know he wants me to be safe, but it's not enough. And I can't make him understand," I finished hopelessly.

Sister Patricia was noncommittal. She said she fully understood my desire to choose my future for myself, but she sympathised with my father too. I know now that they both realised – as I did not – that there was probably going to be another war, only she did not say so. I can't remember exactly what she did say, but by the end of our talk she had persuaded me that my father was not the tyrant I thought he had become. He was merely an extremely worried man trying to secure his daughter's future. "Make it up with him, if only for your mother's sake. Stop fighting," she advised. "After all, you have made your stand. You are not going to be a civil servant, so what is there to fight about?" I hadn't looked at it like that. "Why not come back in September and take the commercial course?" she went on. "Your father's quite right. You'll need some sort of qualification if you're going out into the business world, and shorthand-typing will come in useful whatever you do."

I knew this made sense. I promised her I would take her advice. I don't think I would have dared do anything else!

When I got home Mother was in the kitchen getting tea. I cut the bread and butter for her and told her of the interview as I did so. She asked, over-casually, "What are you going to do?" and nodded approvingly when I told her. I couldn't eat my tea and I couldn't concentrate on my Latin homework afterwards. I was waiting for the sound of Father's key in the front door. When it came Mother signed to me to stay where I was, sitting at the dining room table, but told David to take his homework out into the kitchen. Then she went to talk to Father while he hung up his hat on the hall stand and took off his overcoat. I heard the murmur of her voice and his low reply. After a few moments that felt like hours she led him into the dining room saying, "Yvonne has something to say to us." I gulped and stood up. Very contritely I said I was sorry for all the trouble I had caused. Which was true, I was genuinely sorry for that, though I could not regret refusing to take the exam. "And the secretarial course?" prompted Mother. I said yes, I would go back to school as he had suggested. There was no big reconciliation scene with hugs and kisses. That was not Father's way. He accepted my apology gravely and said he was pleased I had changed my mind. And that was that. I took my Latin book out to join David in the kitchen. Mother came out and put her arm round my shoulders in a quick hug before going back to lay the dining room table for supper. David looked up from the map he was copying and asked, "Is it all right now?" I nodded. "About time too," said my brother with feeling and went back to his geography homework. Family life returned to normal.

Chapter 2

War

MISS MURPHY, who lived with her mother in an elegant old terraced house in Ballards Lane, had turned the top floor of their home into a dance studio. Here, to records of Victor Sylvester and his strict tempo dance orchestra played on a wind-up gramophone, she introduced gauche adolescents like myself to the delights of ballroom dancing. She charged 6d (2½p) a lesson, which lasted an hour every Friday evening. Once the School's Leaving Exam was out of the way I signed on immediately, even before school broke up, eager to acquire at least one social grace to see me into adult life. Like Mollie, I had not been allowed boyfriends while I was still at school. "There'll be plenty of time for all that sort of thing later," Father had said. "For the time being you have to concentrate on your studies and you have homework to do." And now I was free of studies and homework. The promised 'later' had arrived at last.

"Take your partners for a waltz," ordered Miss Murphy, winding up the gramophone. Dutifully boys and girls paired up, or were pushed into partnership by Miss Murphy. She placed the needle on the record and we stepped carefully round the studio floor murmuring "One, two, three, one two, three," and trying not to step on each other's toes. I was asked to dance by a tall, polite boy called Jeff, who was as unaccustomed to girls as I was to boys. We treated each other with great circumspection, and I was surprised at the end of the second lesson when he asked me diffidently, "Would you like to go to the Golders Green Hippodrome one evening?" Not the 'flicks' but a theatre no less. Here was high living indeed! I said, "Thank you," and we made our arrangements for the following week.

I told my parents of the invitation as soon as I got home. Father said, "Does it have to be an evening performance? Couldn't you go on Saturday afternoon?"

"He's not free then." I explained. "He's an Army cadet at his old school. He spends most of his weekends with them. He's a corporal."

"I see. Is he coming to collect you?"

I had no doubt he wanted to inspect this young man who was proposing to carry off his daughter for the evening. I was relieved to be able to say, "No, he won't have time. He's going straight to the theatre from work. We're going to meet outside."

Father looked dubious and my breath caught. Surely he wasn't going to say I couldn't go? He mustn't! Thinking a group outing might be more acceptable than a twosome, I said hastily, "It's not just us. The others are meeting there too."

"What others?" queried Father.

I named two other couples from the dancing class at random. I didn't dare look at my mother. She could always tell when I was lying and I was afraid she might give me away.

Father asked, "What time will you be back?"

"I don't know what time the show ends." I had to admit, "and then it depends on the buses." The theatre was over half an hour's bus ride away and the buses were often unreliable. "I'll come straight home," I promised hopefully.

"Won't he be seeing you home?" demanded Father.

Trying to sound convincing I said, "Oh, yes. Of course he will," although there was no 'of course' about it. Jeff lived in quite the wrong direction to expect him to see me home before going home himself. There had been no mention of it when he invited me.

"All right then," said Father, "If that's the case, you may go."

Unconsciously I had been clenching my hands with tension. Now I flexed them and relaxed. I thanked him warmly, jubilant that I had surmounted all difficulties for the time being.

It was a Variety bill on at the Hippodrome, and I thought the evening was magic. Not that I remember any of the acts we saw. It was just the fact of being there, and with a boy, that was so entrancing.

Jeff did see me home. I felt embarrassed as he followed me up the path to the front door. I guessed he planned to kiss me goodnight before we parted. But there was a light on behind the front room curtains. Mother and Father were waiting for me. They would have heard the click of the gate; any moment now Father would come to the door, ostensibly to let me in, though he knew I had the spare key with me. I slid it quickly into the lock. Jeff leaned towards me. I thanked him for a lovely evening, lingered just long enough for him to give me a peck on the cheek, and went in, leaving him looking sheepish on the step. Better that than being hauled in for questioning, I thought.

Despite the unsatisfactory ending to his evening, Jeff asked me out the following week, this time to the pictures. Father needed to know something more about my boyfriend before he gave his permission again. How old was he? What was his job? Jeff was eighteen, articled to a firm of accountants in the City. Father approved of that. What did his father do? That stumped me. I had no idea. It was not the sort of question I would think of asking. I couldn't see that it mattered, though I didn't say so. "Is he coming to pick you up?" I used the same excuse as before – he wouldn't have time. Father wasn't happy with this arrangement. He asked if I was going to bring him in afterwards. This was more tricky. The cinema was within walking distance, I could think of no good reason why he could not call in for a few minutes, so I had to say yes.

After the pictures we walked round the block, keeping out of sight of the house, and it was under a tree in the next road that I received my first kiss. This was not as thrilling as I had imagined it would be. I didn't want another one and said I'd better be getting home. I added that Father had suggested he come in with me. Jeff said if he didn't hurry he'd miss his last bus. Father took this better than I expected. I wondered if Mother, who had had to deal with her own strict father in her youth, had been having a quiet word with him in the background.

Jeff and I went out to the pictures a few more times, always during the week, and once we went for a walk after dancing class. It wasn't very exciting. Jeff's main interest was the cadet corps and he talked endlessly about 'the chaps'. I got tired of hearing about them. For his part, he probably wanted a girl who was more enthusiastic about his kisses. He was going off to camp with the cadets for a week in August. Our family was due to go on holiday for a fortnight at about the same time and I was fairly sure the affair – if that's what it was – would not be renewed when next we met. If it had not been for the dancing class I doubted if we would ever meet again.

With my head full of my own concerns I had taken little interest in world news. In a vague way I was aware that German troops were reported to be moving towards the Polish border but Hitler always seemed to be doing something menacing and I took no notice. It was not until I came downstairs to the kitchen rather late one morning that I awoke to the fact that something serious was going on. There was a pile of old curtains on the floor, Mother had filled the copper with water and was pouring in packets of black dye. She lit the gas under the copper and began to stir the water as she waited for it to boil. Curious, I asked, "What's that for?"

"Blackout curtains. I should have done them before," she replied shortly, "and now you're here you can make yourself useful. Come and stir this while I go and fetch the dust sheets."

I helped her feed them into the boiling copper and put them through the mangle when she fished them out. They looked distinctly ominous as they blew dry on the washing line.

A few days prior to our holiday Father came home after work and told us his leave had been cancelled. His department, the Accommodation Department, was making active plans to evacuate the staff of Somerset House if the worst came to the worst and he was deeply involved. There was no question of Mother taking my brother and me away without him; our holiday was off. Mother did not seem at all surprised. David and I were stunned. We could not believe what was happening. Even the hanging of the blackout curtains had not alerted us to the true gravity of the situation. Where were the staff going? We wanted to know. And would Father be going with them? He said the plans had not yet been finalised, he could not answer any questions. Over the following weekend he stuck strips of brown paper in a criss-cross pattern on all the windows to minimise the shattering effect of blast should a bomb fall nearby. I remembered Mother saying once that another war would be unthinkable. Now it looked as if the unthinkable had become more than likely.

When Hitler's troops crossed the border into Poland towards the end of August, Britain issued the historic ultimatum: unless he withdrew his forces by 11 o'clock on the morning of September 3rd a state of war would exist between us. Hitler ignored it. We had not opposed him when he broke the Munich Agreement and annexed the whole of Czechoslovakia earlier in the year; he apparently found it inconceivable that we would dare to fight him over Poland.

September 3rd was a Sunday, a beautiful warm sunny day with cloudless skies. Chamberlain was due to broadcast at 11 o'clock to let the nation know what was happening. As the hour approached we gathered round the wireless, as did every other family in the land, anxious yet fearful to hear the news. The broadcast was quite short. Hitler had not withdrawn his troops. As of now we were once more at war with Germany. David and I were too young to realise the full implications of what we had just heard, but it must have been devastating for our parents, especially

Father. Painfully, the last illusion had been stripped away. His war, the one that was supposed to end all wars, had failed in its ultimate objective. No longer 'the Great War', it was being given a number and relegated to being the first of two. I remember we drifted out to the front gate, to find that most of our neighbours had done the same, as if drawn by some common impulse to stand together. Few people spoke. The old lady next door, who had been widowed and also lost her only son in the First World War, had tears in her eyes. Unexpectedly, the air raid warning sounded. Everyone looked up, scanning the blue sky for enemy planes. No one moved to take shelter. No planes appeared and some time later the 'all clear' sounded. One by one the women drifted back into their houses to attend to the Sunday roast. After a while the men followed them. We younger ones stayed outside, waiting to see if anything exciting was going to happen. David swung to and fro on the garden gate, making the hinges creak. I leaned against the gatepost picking leaves off the privet hedge and cracking them into little pieces, scattering them over the pavement. We waited until the street was deserted, then got bored and followed our parents indoors. Although we knew that something momentous had taken place, we did not know that the world we were growing up in was about to change for ever.

Overnight the country was put on a war footing. In expectation of immediate and massive bombing all cinemas, theatres and places of entertainment closed, including the local dance hall. On a more personal level, Miss Murphy closed her dance studio and my friendship with Jeff died a natural death, probably as much to his relief as to mine.

Windows of all buildings had been blacked out after dark for several nights prior to the declaration of war. Police and ARP (Air Raid Precautions) wardens patrolled the streets to ensure that no light showed from any window anywhere. If so much as a chink could be seen from outside, a warden came banging on the door within minutes to point out that a curtain had been carelessly drawn; the cry of "Put that light out!" greeted anyone thoughtless enough to turn on a light without first drawing their blackouts. Persistent offenders could be prosecuted and fined.

On the streets all lighting was switched off, including traffic lights. Town dwellers had never experienced total darkness before and the result was chaos. Cars crashed into one another; people trying to cross the road were run down by unseen vehicles. The death toll soared alarmingly.

Pavements were also hazardous. Pedestrians walked into trees and lampposts, fell up and down kerbs, and bumped into invisible obstacles – including other pedestrians.

In anticipation of heavy bombing the hospitals had evacuated as many patients as possible to make room for air raid casualties. Now they were crowded with victims of road accidents instead. For after all the intense preparations, the bombers did not come. It was the time of the 'phoney war'.

Within months the Government was forced to relax some of its regulations. Traffic lights were switched on again, but masked. Their red, amber and green lights glowed dimly through slits in their blackout covering. Vehicle sidelights could be used provided they were dimmed. Old stockings were found to be ideal for this purpose, pulled over the lamps like hoods. Pedestrians were permitted to carry small torches to light their way so long as the beam was kept pointing downwards. Batteries for these torches became increasingly hard to find. We used to put our old ones in a warm oven, which prolonged their life, hopefully until the shops had another delivery of new ones.

The Government also allowed cinemas, theatres and other places of entertainment to reopen, though not all availed themselves of the opportunity. Miss Murphy's dance studio and the local dance hall both remained closed. Not that it made much difference to me personally. Ever protective, Father would not allow me out in the dangerous dark unless he accompanied me. And as he was frequently out all night firewatching at the office, and rarely came home early enough to act as my escort on the other nights, I was housebound on most evenings. I did occasionally manage to go to the pictures on a Saturday afternoon with a girl from school who lived nearby, but that was the extent of my social life. Inwardly I cursed the malign fate that had allowed me a small taste of freedom only to snatch it away almost immediately. I consoled myself that when the long light evenings returned I would once more be free to go out on my own.

The commercial course had started a week or two after war broke out. I did not enjoy it. For one thing, I missed my friend Mollie badly. She was now out at work. We had never seen much of one another during the holidays, living too far apart to make visiting easy. Now we had left school we had to keep in touch by letter. (This was before the days of universal telephones; Mollie's family was on the phone, mine was not.) She wrote to say she was working underground in the Westminster area. She was not allowed to say who she was working for and I assumed it was some vitally important hush-hush Government department. I envied her her new status as a businesswoman, I did not envy her the job. Working underground sounded gruesome.

As to the course work, although shorthand came easily to me and I eventually attained a respectable speed of a hundred and twenty words a minute, typing was a chore. My speed never crept higher than a low average and I did not manage to pass a single typing exam. Bookkeeping also defeated me. I had not found arithmetic a problem before, but under my hand columns of figures took on a perverse life of their own, giving me a different total every time I totted them up. My failure to master typing and bookkeeping depressed me. Once more I was counting the weeks until I would be free of school, this time for good.

Father's department had evacuated to Llandudno in North Wales and he was due to join it at the end of the year. He and Mother were pleased he was going to be at home over Christmas. David and I were delighted, though I don't think either of us had ever seriously believed he might not be. Christmas without Father was unimaginable. Mother was even more anxious than usual that everything should go well. Her own mother, Nannie, and Aunt Evelyn had always joined us for the holiday since the death of my grandfather when I was small. In previous years they had arrived in time for supper on Christmas Eve and stayed until the evening of Boxing Day. They lived in Holloway, a bus and tram ride away and this year, to avoid travelling in the blackout they decided not to come until Christmas morning and to leave early on Boxing Day. Mother decreed that we should not open our presents until they arrived. "This rotten war spoils everything," I grumbled. Father said grimly, "If that's the worst thing we have to put up with we'll all be very lucky."

Once Nannie and Aunt Evelyn arrived the celebrations began in earnest. The presents were exclaimed over; Father's toast with the ritual glass of sherry before dinner was the same as always, but the grown-ups obviously found it more significant than usual: "Good health and good luck to us all in the coming year!" The King's speech on the wireless after dinner was listened to in thoughtful silence, the only comment afterwards coming from Nannie. "Poor man, he copes with his stammer very well." Nobody referred to the war. As Mother had done all the cooking, she left the washing-up to the rest of us while she went upstairs to 'put her feet up' for an hour and change her frock for tea. Aunt Evelyn and I were the last two left in the kitchen at the end, putting away the china and generally tidying up. It was the first chance we had had to talk alone. She asked, "How's the course going?"

"Shorthand's all right," I said, "but I hate typing. It's boring. And I'm no good at bookkeeping. I wish I could leave."

"What would you rather be doing?" she enquired.

"I don't know. That's the trouble. All I know is that I want to work with people." Thinking of the Civil Service I added, " I don't want some boring routine job. I want to enjoy my work the way you enjoy yours."

"But, darling," said my aunt, "It's taken me years to work my way up to where I am now. I started out in a typing pool and, believe me, I was bored to tears a lot of the time." Determined to stiffen my spine she continued, "You've got your School Certificate; now concentrate on getting the highest qualifications you can. Don't think about the boredom, keep your eye on the future and you'll stand a good chance of finding what you want sooner or later."

Aunt Evelyn was always good to talk to. I felt a lot more positive about what I was doing, and consequently much happier when the new term started.

Father moved to Llandudno early in 1940 and I had great hopes of being allowed more freedom in the evenings, but not a bit of it. He left strict instructions that I was still not to be allowed out in the blackout on my own. Bitterly I protested to my mother, but to no avail. "You know what your father said." I wanted to shout, "To hell with Father," but knew it would only upset her and do no good. Reluctantly I resigned myself once again to waiting for spring. However, when the light evenings returned the social life I had so looked forward to did not return with them. Miss Murphy never reopened her dance studio; the local dance hall had become an extension of the local government offices, if I remember rightly; the tennis club announced that it had lost so many members to the Forces it could no longer afford to keep the courts in good order, and it too remained closed.

I saw little of Mollie. She was working very long hours and all her free time was devoted to meeting Ted. She still had to be careful about these meetings because, incredibly, her Father still insisted she was too young to have a boyfriend. If Ted saw her home they had to say goodnight a couple of streets away in case they were seen together and her father found out.

One of Mollie's special charms for me – and I imagine for Ted – was her lack of bitterness. She accepted her father's attitude, found a way round his restrictions with her mother's connivance and was happy. She did, however, sound regretful in one letter she sent me. "Ted's expecting to be called up any day. It's such a shame we can't spend his remaining time at home visiting each other's family openly. I'm sure our mothers would get on well together." In her shoes I would have been raging against my father, as I had often felt like doing anyway.

Father had always been very much the head of the house and Mother had taken a back seat. After he went to Llandudno it seemed to me that she changed. It was as if she came out of the shadows and became a person in her own right. When she was young she had been spirited and vivacious according to Nannie, her mother. Her hair had been rich auburn and her eyes a vivid blue. Years of recurring ill-health had muted her vivacity, her hair had become pepper-and-salt, and her eyes had lost some of their brilliance. But nothing had subdued her spirit. Left on her own she looked round for something to do towards the war effort. She had been a secretary before she married and still retained her old skills. They were rusty, but would polish up with use. She volunteered to work for the Citizens' Advice Bureau, a newly formed agency set up to help people cope with all the rules and regulations the Government issued daily. In no time at all it found itself dealing with everything under the sun from housing and financial problems to matrimonial troubles. Mother started by doing the filing, progressed to writing letters and finished up as an interviewer. It was noticeable that she was always more animated and talkative on the days she attended the CAB.

The commercial course ended in July and armed with my School Leaving Certificate together with one from Pitmans for my one hundred and twenty words a minute shorthand speed, I set out to conquer the business world. Competition for vacancies was stiffer than I had anticipated. However, fortune smiled and I was taken on as a junior shorthand typist in the Lady Almoner's office at the Royal Northern Hospital, Holloway Road. The 'Lady

Almoner' was a medical social worker. Her role has now been taken over by the Social Services. My salary was £1.17.6d per week (worth £62.09 today, October 2003, I am told). Not bad for a beginner in those days. Father wrote congratulating me, which gave me great satisfaction. I had fought for what I wanted – an interesting job to do with people – and I had got it. His letter was the seal of approval that finally put an end to whatever echoes still remained of our disagreement.

The Lady Almoner, Miss Freeman, looked elderly to my eyes. Somewhere in her forties, I reckoned. Tall and willowy, with her brown hair done up in a bun at the nape of her neck and a mild manner, she gave the impression of not being able to say boo to a goose. The impression was misleading. In her quiet way she was surprisingly formidable. I was still not a very good typist. I could manage accuracy and I could manage speed, but not the two together. If I ever tried to rush a job and gave her something less than perfect to sign she had no hesitation in returning it and requesting me to re-type it before I went home, no matter how long it was. And her manner made it quite clear that her request was in fact an order. I quickly learned to get things right first time, even if it took a little longer.

Miss Freeman's assistant was quick and efficient in everything she did. Her name was Miss Scott, though I always thought of her as Scotty. She had mousy hair permed into hard waves and curls. Her features were plain, her expression kind.

In September the long-expected bombing began. The hospital filled up with air raid casualties, and the Almoner's office was swamped with an influx of problems. I could have done with a little more time to improve my typing speed; I would have been floundering but for Scotty's patient help. With my mind focused on accuracy I did not always take in the meaning of what I typed, but when I did I found some of it rather depressing.

We were so busy I don't remember being scared when the air raid warning went. Its undulating howl was greeted with irritation more than anything. Time wasted in the shelters provided for staff and patients at the rear of the building usually had to be made up as overtime. It was the only way we could keep up with the workload. Not all the patients could get down to the shelters. Those who were too ill to be moved, together with the nursing staff and doctors in charge of them, had no choice but remain up in the wards. Listening for the throbbing hum of enemy planes overhead, hearing the crump and explosion of bombs as they came nearer and being unable to escape to safety, must have been frightening enough in the daytime; at night it must have been terrifying.

At home we did not possess a shelter, although most of the neighbours had an Anderson. This was a corrugated steel hut with a rounded roof. Sunk into the ground – usually the back lawn – with steps leading down to the entrance, it was blast-proof and impregnable to everything bar a direct hit. When fitted with bunks it would sleep a family of four, but not in comfort, being cold and damp. Mother said if a bomb had her name on it, it would find her wherever she was, so she might as well sleep in her own bed. Despite vociferous protests from the family, she slept upstairs throughout the war. This fatalistic attitude was all very well, but so strong was her influence on us that David and I felt compelled to stay upstairs with her, ignoring her angry injunction to do as she said and not as she did. I can remember lying in bed listening to the drone of planes and the barking of the local anti-aircraft (ack-ack) guns and thinking, "If I can just get to sleep everything will be all right in the morning." And so it was, more or less. Three or four houses nearby were hit, but we were lucky. We suffered nothing worse than broken windows.

Looking back, I think I was in less danger on the nights I went firewatching. Our street had a rota of neighbours who turned out in pairs to keep watch for incendiaries. My partner was a middle-aged high-powered business lady, Miss Maclean, who lived in a very smart block of flats at the bottom of the road. When it was our turn for duty I slept in her spare bedroom. We slept fully dressed, ready to dash into action at the first wail of the siren. Firewatchers usually kept watch from the tops of buildings, but we had no suitable rooftop handy. We ran out to watch from the doorway of a brick shelter the council had built in the road outside her flat. I don't know where the other denizens of the flats went in an air raid. As far as I can recall we always had the shelter to ourselves. Wearing tin hats, with stirrup pump and buckets of water and sand at the ready we mentally rehearsed our drill. If incendiaries fell, our orders were to rush out, hauling our buckets and pump, and douse the fires we could reach. Then Miss Maclean was meant to dash back to her flat and telephone for the Fire Service to come and deal with the others. That was the theory. Mercifully we were never called upon to put it into practice. It was all we could do to haul the heavy buckets between us, rushing anywhere with them was out of the question. "Unless a fire bomb falls at our feet in the road," said my partner, "it would be far more sensible to alert the professionals first, then do what we can to put out the fire while we wait for them to arrive." After a moment's thought she added, "It would be even more sensible for us both to go back to the flat and while I summon the fire brigade you could put the kettle on." I suppose I looked surprised. "Hot sweet tea, and strong, that's what the workers need in a crisis, including us," she assured me. "It's an established tradition." As the junior member of this partnership I was perfectly happy to do whatever she suggested.

As a member of the Boy Scouts, David's contribution to the war effort was far greater than mine. The Scouts were involved in a number of projects and he helped with them all. They collected cardboard and waste paper for recycling, storing it in an empty house just off the High Road. If an incendiary had dropped on the place it would have been ablaze in seconds. It was a wonder the neighbours didn't complain but nobody objected. It seemed to be accepted as just another hazard of war. The Scouts also collected scrap metal – old saucepans and the like – to be turned into Spitfires according to the posters. Another of their projects was helping to erect air raid shelters. The Andersons were delivered in sections, which had to be bolted together when it was sunk into the ground. Digging the hole and hauling the panels into place was heavy work, only undertaken by the bigger boys.

The older Boy Scouts also acted as messengers for the ARP wardens, carrying messages back and forth between their Headquarters underneath the Odeon Cinema in the High Road and individual wardens patrolling the surrounding neighbourhood. Although David was only thirteen years old he looked older. He had shot up during the past year and already topped my height of five foot five by an inch or more. He had Father's broad shouldered physique, serious blue-grey eyes and his voice had broken. To Mother's dismay and Father's pride he had been accepted as one of the messengers, the youngest one in the troop.

North Finchley escaped heavy bombing, but had its fair share of both high explosives and incendiaries. The wardens patrolled during raids, accompanied by their messengers. They were often first on the scene where bombs had fallen, coping with whatever situation they found themselves in. If ambulances or fire fighters were needed, it was the messenger's job to cycle back to alert HQ. With only a tin hat and an ARP armband to protect them, they sped through flying red-hot shrapnel from the anti-aircraft guns, trusting to luck they would not be hit. If further bombs began to fall the boys' instructions were to dive for whatever cover they could find. I asked David once if he was ever scared. He said that if he was he thought of Mother refusing to leave her bed in a raid and that gave him courage.

Occasionally David was attached to the Heavy Rescue Squad (HRS), who were specially trained to deal with all the worst scenes of destruction in a bombing raid. One night a land mine fell about two miles away causing massive destruction. The death toll was high, the number of injured even higher. The local services there were overstretched. They sent an urgent call for help to Finchley and our HRS raced to the scene, followed by David on his bicycle.

On noisy nights Mother always waited up for him to come off duty. Often I waited with her. On this particular night, not knowing what had happened, we sat in the kitchen drinking tea and watching the old alarm clock on the dresser. Midnight, one, two o'clock. He should have been relieved by now. Mother's face was white and stiff with anxiety and fatigue and I was dozing with my head on the kitchen table when his key sounded in the lock. "It was a bad one," he announced as he strode into the kitchen. He had no idea of the time and was oblivious to our vigil. "I had to wait for the Squad to come back." His eyes were bright as he launched into an account of the incident, pacing restlessly about the kitchen.

He said that by the time he got there the dead were already being carried away on stretchers and ambulances were clanging about taking the injured to hospital. The Fire Services were getting the fires under control, but two men were trapped in the wreckage of a large building which was burning fiercely. A Heavy Rescue crew worked frantically, trying to reach them before they were burnt alive. Another Squad was trying to free a man trapped in a cellar. He had taken shelter there but the house had been demolished above him. The chimney stack had crashed down through the house and trapped him, breaking both his legs. He was screaming with pain and swearing.

Mother made a cup of cocoa, sat him down firmly and placed it in front of him on the table. "Now drink this and calm down," she ordered. But he couldn't stop talking, the adrenaline was running too fast. "They got them all out," he said triumphantly. "They were bloody marvellous. The two in the fire were unconscious – but they were alive. The man in the cellar passed out in the end, but he was alive too."

Mother made another attempt to calm him down. "It's nearly

three o'clock in the morning. If you don't need any sleep, I do. So finish that cocoa and go to bed." He seemed to become aware of us for the first time. He drained his cup and stood up. Mother went to the kitchen door and held it open pointedly. As he went through into the hall he bent and kissed her lightly on the cheek. "Sorry, Ma," he muttered, abashed. She was tired out, at the end of her tether, but she smiled at him fondly nonetheless.

David had never seemed unduly disturbed by the scenes he witnessed while on duty. Looking back years later he said that most of the time he found it very exciting, but the night of the land mine was an exception. The sheer size of the incident, the immense scale of the destruction, the fires and the man screaming all affected him deeply. "It was like the medieval pictures of hell," he recalled.

Chapter 3
The Uncivil Service

FATHER WAS coming home for Christmas. We hadn't seen him since he left for Llandudno at the beginning of the year and there was great excitement in the house. Mrs Blake, who had been coming in to help Mother in one capacity or another for so long she was almost one of the family, gave the furniture an extra polish to celebrate the occasion. She was a dour woman with a granite face, but she had a soft spot for Father and it was his homecoming, not Christmas, she was celebrating. The butcher magicked a turkey with our name on it from underneath the counter; Mother had queued for hours to get the ingredients for the pudding; everything was as near pre-war as she could make it. Father arrived home to an exuberant welcome. Nannie and Aunt Evelyn did not join us that year. Several houses in their street had been demolished by bombs in the autumn blitz and many more had been damaged by blast, including hers. She did not wish to leave it unattended over the holiday in case of further trouble. We missed them, but had a very happy Christmas nonetheless. Father returned to Llandudno the morning after Boxing Day leaving a warm glow of good humour behind him.

In mid-January he came home again, this time without warning. He arrived late at night; I had gone to bed and did not see him until the following morning. He was in a strange, withdrawn mood, very different to his frame of mind at Christmas. Mother looked uneasy. Father said he had business to attend to with the

Inland Revenue. He went out immediately after breakfast and did not return until the evening. Neither he nor Mother spoke much over supper. As soon as I had finished eating I excused myself from the table, meaning to go to my room. Father's voice stopped me. "Jut a moment! I have something to say to you," I wondered what on earth I could have done to merit his tone, which sounded ominous. I sat down again and waited. Father said, "There's new legislation coming out in a month or so. Women will have to register for war work unless they're in a reserved occupation." I had seen it in the paper, but had not given it serious thought. I assumed that working for a hospital I would be exempt. I said this to Father, but he shook his head. "You can't be sure of that. You're only a junior and could easily be replaced." I began to feel worried about what was coming next. Father went on, " 'War work' can mean anything, of course, not just the Services. You could be sent to a factory somewhere, anywhere. The best thing you can do is leave your job and get into an occupation we know will be reserved."

My heart started to pound. "Leave the hospital? No! I'd rather stay and take my chance."

"Don't be ridiculous," said Father sharply, "you don't want to risk being sent to a factory, do you?" He took a deep breath and continued, "I have secured a post for you as a Temporary Shorthand-Typist in the local Tax Collector's office. You have an appointment with him next week."

After a stunned second the wave of fury that coursed through me was so strong it nearly choked me. I shrieked, "No!" again, "You can't do that!" I looked at my mother for support, but she refused to meet my eyes and stayed silent. She had known what was coming and been powerless to prevent it. I burst into a storm of tears and fled up to my room to sob my heart out.

My first reaction when the storm had passed was to refuse to keep the appointment, but I had caused so much distress when I refused to take the Entrance Exam, I knew I lacked the courage to defy my father again. I was trapped. 'Temporary' in Civil Service language did not mean short-term. All shorthand-typists were called 'temporary'. It separated them in status from the Clerical Assistants – the clerk – and other Grades who had entered by way of the official exam, though everyone was classed as 'reserved'. This meant they could neither leave nor be called up. Once I was in I would be in for good.

I felt physically sick. The legislation wasn't in yet, surely Father could have talked it over with me instead of taking my future into his own hands without discussion? He knew my feelings about the Civil Service and had ignored them yet again. Lying on my bed in the dark I hated him with all the emotional intensity I had felt when I idolised him as a child.

He left early next morning to return to Llandudno. I heard him go out, but I didn't get up to say goodbye. Bleary-eyed with weeping, my head aching from lack of sleep, I asked my mother miserably over breakfast, "Why did he do it?"

"He had your best interests at heart. He wanted to keep your future safe," she said.

Safe! Safe!! All he ever thought about was 'safe'. But I was not yet eighteen and I wanted to go out and live, not merely be safe.

"But why didn't he talk to me about it first? There must have been other alternatives than the Civil Service. Why didn't he give me a chance to think?"

"Why didn't you tell him you weren't going to take the exam?" asked Mother.

"It would only have meant another argument. I just couldn't face it," I said wearily. I didn't add, "and I knew I would lose."

"That's exactly how he felt about the job."

So, reluctantly, I went to see Miss Freeman as soon as I got in to work. She saw my ravaged face and invited me to sit down, taking off the half glasses she always wore for reading and putting them down on the desk to show I had her full attention. I said, "I have to give notice as from next Friday."

She looked shocked. "May I ask why?"

Haltingly I explained. She made no comment, though I could see she disapproved of what Father had done. All she said was, "Well, thank you for telling me so promptly. It gives me more time to find a replacement." She picked up her glasses and I left her office, greatly relieved that I had got out without shedding more tears.

On the day I left I said a miserable farewell to Scotty before going along to say goodbye to Miss Freeman. After wishing me luck for the future she got up and came round her desk to see me out. At the door she laid a restraining hand on my arm and said gently, "Try not to hate your father, my dear. Hate is such a destructive emotion. Don't let it spoil your life." I thought bitterly that Father was doing that already, but in the face of her kindly concern I could only nod my head and promise.

The interview Father had set up for me with the Collector was a total disaster. Mr Langton was a tall, thin, elderly man with a patrician nose set in an unfriendly face. He eyed me balefully, and the smile I had forced onto my face stiffened to a meaningless grimace. He motioned me to a chair, at the same time handing me a shorthand notebook. The job was mine, he explained, but I would have to take a practical test for the sake of the records. With awful clarity I realised that Father had gone over this man's head and arranged my job without his consent. In other words, I had been foisted onto him, and he resented my being there as much as I did. I could have felt sympathy for him had he not picked up his morning 'Times' and dictated one of the Leaders for the test. It concerned Japanese foreign policy. He took it at a speed well in excess of my hundred and twenty words a minute and after the first few sentences I was lost. I asked him to slow down and he looked at me with contempt. To type it back I was shown into a small room with one desk in it on which stood an ancient solitary typewriter. About a dozen sheets of typing paper lay beside it. There was no rubber, the only means of correction known in those days. The girl who had ushered me in said I had half an hour, no longer, to complete the test. Then I was left on my own.

After typing back the opening sentence of the article I sat staring hopelessly at the meaningless squiggles I had scrawled in the notebook until it was pointless to sit there any longer. I left it beside the typewriter with the almost blank sheet of typing paper, collected my coat from the row of hooks on the cloakroom wall and fled in tears.

Father had to come to London for a meeting some weeks later and someone (Mr Langton?) made sure he was shown the rubbish I had produced at the interview. Hardly able to believe what he saw, he was absolutely mortified.

"What happened?" he asked me when he got home that evening.

"He went too fast." I shrugged indifferently.

"It didn't even look like shorthand," he said, bewildered. "And I had told them all you were so good."

Mr Langton could not have found a better way to get his revenge on Father if he had sat down and thought about it for a month of Sundays. Father had secured my future, as had been his obsession all along, but the price was humiliation for both of us.

The day I started work there, knowing I hadn't qualified and I wasn't wanted, was one of the worst days of my life. I shared a room with two other shorthand-typists, Connie and Grace. Connie was a very pretty young woman in her early twenties, with naturally curly, light brown hair, hazel-green eyes, and a delightful smile. Her habit of opening her mouth and putting her foot in it was disconcerting. Grace was older, in her thirties. She was tall, over six feet on her high heels, with a beautiful figure. All her movements were graceful in a slightly theatrical way. Her blond hair was always carefully arranged with never a hair out of place.

They had both heard about my interview (who hadn't?) and were at first inclined to treat me with reserve. It was Grace who broke the ice. "What made you want to come to a tax office?" she enquired.

With nothing to lose I told them the truth. "I didn't. My Father arranged it."

"So we heard," said Connie, giving the game away.

"Did you hear what he gave me for a test?" I asked.

"No. Just that .... " Connie stopped, embarrassed.

"Just that I couldn't do it." I finished for her. When I told them what the test had been, and the speed at which he had dictated it, they were full of outraged sympathy. "Ooh, he can be mean, that man," said Grace, her eyes narrowing to slits, "but don't let him get you down. We've all suffered at one time or another."

"And don't worry about your shorthand," added Connie, "Nobody ever gives us shorthand anyway."

When I got to know them better I found that Connie was a home-body. She had recently married her childhood sweetheart when he was on embarkation leave. She thought he had gone to the Middle East, but she wasn't sure. Her only concern in life was to see him come home again safely. In the meantime all she asked of her job was that the money should be sufficient for her to save up for her 'bottom drawer'.

Grace, also married, was definitely not a home-body. She and her husband had been amateur ballroom dancing champions before the war. He was also in a reserved occupation. They had no children and devoted all their spare time and energy to giving dancing exhibitions in Naafis and canteens for the troops. Like Connie, Grace didn't care what work she did as long as the hours were reasonable and the money regular.

As I soon found out, the work consisted of typing batches of standard letters, a top with two or three carbon copies, from a book of samples. Each sample letter had a number and we would be asked to type, say, forty of No. 6, and then fill in names, addresses and amounts from lists brought in by the clerks. Typing errors were very difficult to correct. The rubbers provided were hard, and it was only too easy to rub a hole in the paper, which was of poor quality and thin. Carbon copies usually smudged. My typing had improved enormously at the hospital, but the monotony of typing the same letters over and over again made concentration difficult. I made so many typing errors and wasted so much paper that I was ashamed to put it all in the waste paper basket. I used to slip some of it into my lunch case when no one was looking and take it home for scrap.

Shorthand-typists were graded lower than Clerical Assistants in the Civil Service, and Mr Langton made sure we never forgot it. His attitude towards the clerks was reasonably pleasant. To us he merely issued orders. This didn't seem to bother Connie or Grace in the least. They laughed behind his back and referred to him cheerfully as 'Lanky Langton' or 'Old Lanky'. I joined in their laughter, but mine was not genuine. I hadn't forgiven him for the unfair test piece he had set me at my interview.

The clerical staff were quite friendly on the whole, especially the Executive Officer, Mr Deane. He was a small middle-aged man of the obviously-busy type, always striding about with a clutch of papers under his arm, his heels sounding loud on the bare wooden floors. His memory rivalled that of the proverbial elephant and Mr Langton, who was approaching retirement age and freewheeling towards his pension, relied on this quite heavily. To Mr Deane fell the weekly task of reading and digesting the flood of Government directives that ruled the life of the wartime Civil Service. He was a cheery, good-humoured soul, the exact opposite of his chief. I thought at first his friendliness was an attempt to compensate for the Collector's attitude towards us. Grace and Connie said he was keeping in with us because they typed private letters for him, strictly against the rules. I hadn't realised this, as he had never brought any to me. I suspected this was a silent comment on my poor typing.

For three such different characters, Connie, Grace and I got on very well. The laughs we had together were the only thing that made the job bearable. With my social life at such a low ebb, life itself would have been unbearable if I had had no one to laugh with at work. I might have felt differently if I had had a boyfriend, but most of the boys of an age to interest me had disappeared into the Services and I rarely got a chance to meet one.

There was one boy I had my eye on, a tall good-looking young man called Michael. I used to see him in church on Sunday mornings. He did not have a girlfriend so far as I knew and I set my heart on filling the vacancy. I noted that he was always one of the first to leave after Mass, so one Sunday I sat in the back pew and left just before the service ended, determined to be outside the porch when he came out.

He was among the first to appear and my heart soared when he stood off to one side, presumably to wait for a friend. I went to stand near him and, plucking up courage, found an excuse to start a conversation. He looked Irish, with very dark curly hair and blue eyes. But if his ancestors had kissed the blarney stone the effect had worn off by the time he came along. He proved to be a reserved, solemn youth, with little small talk; I had to make the running. I thought my plan was working well, but it suffered a disappointing setback when he said, "Excuse me," and went to join a family who had just emerged from the porch, a middle-aged couple and their daughter Anna.

Anna was a good-looking blonde with a wide smile. She was vivacious and popular at school, possessing all the self-confidence that a rich daddy and an extensive wardrobe could bestow. The family lived in a large house with a tennis court in the back garden. They sometimes drove to church in an outsize motor car. After Mass they would fill it with as many friends as they could pack in and take them back for a lunch party, with tennis in the afternoon, weather permitting. (How this squared with rationing was a matter for speculation by those who had not been invited.)

Despite knowing that Michael was chasing after Anna I continued my Sunday dash from church to talk to him while he waited for her. Once the ice had been broken he was always friendly to talk to in his quiet way, friendly enough to encourage my dream that one Sunday something wonderful would happen. Instead of squeezing into the car or walking home with Anna and her friends, Michael would choose to walk home with me. I was sure Mother would be able to manage one extra for dinner. Beyond that my imagination floundered. Sunday in our house was a very quiet day: David did his homework or disappeared with the Scouts; Mother went upstairs for a rest in the afternoon. Maybe Michael and I could go for a walk if the weather was fine. If it rained perhaps we could sit on the sofa and talk.

He told me one Sunday that he had volunteered for the Air Force and was expecting his call-up papers any day. He thought he would be given about a fortnight's notice of his date of departure. A few Sundays later he did not appear at Mass and someone told me he had gone. I felt sick with shock. He had not told me his papers had arrived when I saw him the previous week. With teenage intensity I felt utterly rejected and unlovable. I tried not to show my pain at home, thankful that my family did not know what a total fool I had been making of myself. David always cycled to an earlier Mass; Mother rarely went to church at all. She said it took all her energy to cook Sunday dinner, never mind walking a mile to church and back as well. I prayed they would remain in ignorance of my pathetic behaviour.

My spirits were at rock bottom when I went to work next day. Unable to concentrate, I made endless typing errors and by lunchtime had so little to show for my disastrous morning that I was in despair. Connie and Grace went out to the shops but I stayed behind. All I wanted was a quiet hour alone to eat my sandwiches and lose myself in my book. However, I had hardly opened it when Mr Deane walked in, holding a draft letter for typing. He came to my desk and held it out, smiling. "I know it's your lunch hour but you couldn't do this one for me, could you? It's only short." I could see the letter was private. On any other day I would have been pleased to do it for him, taking it as a sign he thought my typing had improved, but not today. I snapped out something about not being allowed to eat my lunch in peace, dismayed to find I was nearly crying.

Mr Deane said nothing, though he was clearly taken aback. He pulled out Connie's chair from the next desk and sat looking at me, waiting for an explanation. I couldn't ignore him and read my book, I knew I would have to apologise. As soon as I could trust my voice I said, "I'm sorry". He still didn't say anything or make any move to go. Somewhat unnerved, I started to tell him about my dreadful morning and suddenly found myself spilling out all my grievances. How I had been railroaded into the job and how much I loathed it. "And I can't get out," I wailed.

Having listened in silence, Mr Deane finally spoke. "There is a way out, but I don't know how you'd feel about it. You could volunteer for the Forces."

For a moment I was too astonished even to breathe. "We're reserved," I managed at last. "We can't leave."

"You can if you're going to enlist," he assured me. I stared at him, hardly daring to believe what he had said. At no time had the thought of volunteering entered my head. Father had gone to such lengths to make sure I would not be called up, I did not know if he would agree to my going of my own accord. Mr Deane stood up to go. "Think about it," he said.

Think about it! As if I needed telling! It hovered on the edge of my mind all afternoon. Ironically, now I felt happier my fingers relaxed and found all the right keys of their own accord. I did not catch up completely with the work I should have finished in the morning, but I had quite a respectable pile of letters ready for signature by the end of the afternoon. I had done Mr Deane's as soon as he left me and taken it in to him immediately, which pleased him.

My journey home on the bus took half an hour. Thirty minutes in which to sit and dream and plan. There was no doubt in my mind about leaving the job. It was just a matter of choosing which Service to volunteer for. With no real information to go on, I imagined the WRNS probably had to live in dockyard areas, which sounded dreary. They also wore navy blue, the colour of my school uniform. I was sick of navy blue, which I had never thought suited me. The ATS probably lived in barracks on army camps and they wore khaki. Again not a colour I fancied. The Women's Auxiliary Air Force, on the other hand, wore an attractive shade of blue, and if they were lucky they worked on airfields somewhere in the depths of the country, but hopefully within easy reach of civilisation. I could see myself billeted in a pleasant little market town - or maybe in a farmhouse with a thatched roof, a carthorse and chickens in the yard. I visualised it clearly in my mind, as picturesque as the lid of a chocolate box. Five minutes from home I suddenly wondered how I was going to tell my Mother, and what my Father would say. The farmhouse vanished abruptly, as if someone had clicked a switch inside my head. Instead of dreaming, I concentrated on reality and started putting together the words I would use to convince my parents that they ought to let me go.

When Mother came to the door to let me in she said immediately, "You look very cheerful, what's happened?" My prepared speech totally forgotten I blurted out, "I want to join the WAAF." She went very still, then sighed. "I knew you'd never settle." She sounded resigned. We talked about it for most of the evening. Or rather I did. Mother said little but I felt I had her sympathy. Eventually I said, "I suppose I'd better write to Daddy." For once I was thankful we were not on the telephone; I would not have to speak to him direct. Mother asked, "Would you like me to do it?" I regarded her doubtfully. To my knowledge she had never taken my part in anything that might upset Father. If she had ever disagreed with him it had been in private, neither David nor I had been aware of it. Would she speak forcefully enough on my behalf now? I answered her obliquely, "I can't stay there. I just can't." She nodded, "I know." She evidently understood my doubts for she added, "Don't worry. I know what you want to say."

A very long week went by before I met the postman at the gate as I was dashing off to work one morning. He held out a letter from Father. I almost snatched it from his hand and ran for the bus. I went upstairs, hoping for a seat to myself, and I was lucky. Tearing open the envelope, I read the letter at speed. "..... your Mother tells me ..... naturally disappointed ..... be for the best .... I have only one stipulation ..... must do secretarial work ..... keep in practice for after the war." I wanted to laugh, to shout, to tell the whole bus, "She's done it! He's agreed! I'm going to be a Waaf!" To me it seemed that Mother had performed a miracle in persuading Father to let me leave the Civil Service. Months later it occurred to me that he had probably heard that certain categories of reserved workers were to be released for conscription. If 'temporary' secretarial staff in the CS should be one of those categories, I would be no safer at the tax office than I had been at the hospital. The dreaded factory gates could close behind me yet. By allowing me to volunteer he was ensuring that not only would I enter one of the Forces, I would be able to choose my own trade.

As soon as I reached my desk I typed a formal letter giving seven days notice as from the following Friday. As instructed by Mr Deane, I added that I intended to enlist in the WAAF. Feeling that I had as good as left, I took it straight in to Mr Langton. Who refused to accept it. He said he knew nothing about staff being allowed to volunteer. "Where did you get that idea?" he demanded.

"From Mr Deane," I said brightly.

He threw my letter back across the desk. "I'll have a word with him. In the meantime you cannot leave." He flapped me away with a dismissive hand and went back to reading his morning post. I had intended to resign with dignity, but his manner riled me. I walked to the door and turned round to face him. "I'm going on Friday week," I said defiantly, "you can't stop me." I felt I had struck a blow for freedom and slammed the door as I went out.

I can't remember where I went to volunteer. The WAAF recruiting sergeant (or was it an officer?) pushed a form towards me, the first one I had seen that did not depress me. I filled it in happily, ready to be off as soon as I had worked out my notice. To my consternation she informed me that before they could accept my application they would have to check with the Civil Service that I was free to leave. I started to give her Mr Deane's name and office telephone number but she cut me short. "It has to be in writing." Horrified, I protested, "But that could take months." Cheerfully she agreed, but added as consolation, "Don't worry. We won't forget you".

If there was going to be a delay before I was called up I was going to need a temporary job to bring in some money while I waited. Our local Employment Agency said Manor House Hospital at Golders Green would need temps to do the routine paperwork for their Annual Christmas Appeal, starting at the beginning of October. I applied immediately and was accepted.

Old Lanky spoke to Mr Deane about my leaving, but did not speak to me again. On the Friday my notice expired I spent the day on edge in case he sent for me. Despite Mr Deane's assurance that everything would be all right I still feared the Collector would find some way of blocking my resignation. When nothing had happened by five o'clock I cleared my desk and said goodbye to Connie and Grace. Their farewells were typical of them. Connie, tactless to the last, said, "Perhaps you'll be happier once you get into the Air Force. You've been odd one out here without a boyfriend, haven't you?" Grace counselled, "Watch out for the Brylcreem boys!" – a popular nickname for the fighter pilots, the glamour boys of the Service, who were said to use this preparation on their hair.

I promised to keep in touch, knowing I would only write once or twice at the most. Connie was quite right, we had little in common and were about to have even less.

Before I said goodbye to Mr Langton I went along to Mr Deane's office. He knew the Collector had not given me official permission to leave and gave me a knowing smile. "Do you want me to go and see him for you?" I nodded eagerly. He came back within minutes to say that Mr Langton was engaged but he wished me well for the future. Relief made me light-headed. I could find no words to tell Mr Deane how much I appreciated what he had done for me. I stammered "Thank you," and leaned over and kissed him on the cheek. His smile widened to a big grin. He said, "Get off with you. I hope you'll be very happy."

"I'm sure I will," I said with confidence

Chapter 4

Marking Time

I LAY IN BED on the following Monday morning revelling in my prospects for the future. Having escaped from the Civil Service, I was also about to get away from the boring restrictions of home and lead an exhilarating life in the Air Force. I could already hear the roar of aircraft engines in my imagination. I was almost afraid to believe I was wide awake and not dreaming.

I was not due to start at the hospital for another week and spent the time helping Mother with the housework and shopping. And very boring I found it. Fortunately I had Saturday afternoon to look forward to. Not knowing exactly how long – or short – the waiting period might be until my call-up papers arrived, I had arranged to meet Mollie as soon as possible. I wanted to make sure of seeing her before I went away.

We met in the Gaumont Café, upstairs in the cinema at Tally Ho! Corner. An elderly waitress came over to take our order and we settled down to catch up on each other's news. Mollie looked tired and drawn. She was still working underground in her hush-hush Government department. This had changed over to shift working some months previously. I asked, "How do you like the new hours now you've got used to them?"

"I don't! There never seems to be enough time to settle down to anything properly when I'm off duty. And I'm usually too tired when I get home to want to do anything anyway. And I really hate the late shift. Instead of going home afterwards, we sleep in a spare room in the department. It saves us having to travel home on our own late at night. But it's cold and damp and uncomfortable. I'd leave if I could."

She was trapped in a reserved occupation. I felt really sorry for her, knowing only too well how that felt.

The elderly waitress brought our pot of tea with a slice of austerity sponge cake each. Hoping to lighten Mollie's mood I asked how Ted was getting on. "He's doing fine," she said. "He's been offered a commission." There was pride in her voice and for a moment some of the strain went out of her face and she looked less tired. I asked, "Does your father know about you and Ted yet?"

She gave a wan smile. "I'm not sure. He knows we write to each other, but he hasn't said anything."

We ate our cake. It was a bit dry and tasteless, but not bad for wartime. Mollie asked, "What about you and your father? Still fighting?"

"No. He's disappointed in me for leaving the Civil Service, but at least he didn't try to stop me joining the WAAF."

The Manor House Hospital was small, as hospitals go, and there was an intimate feel about it. There were only two of us in the large room allocated to the Appeal. The other 'temp' was a few years older than me, a slightly built young woman called Madge, with sad brown eyes. As we chatted over our work I learned that her boyfriend had been killed at Dunkirk; the small publishing firm she worked for had been forced to close when the owner was called up, leaving her unemployed; and all three services had rejected her because she suffered from colitis. She was temping while she looked for a permanent job she could take a real interest in and enjoy.

At first our work consisted of typing names and addresses at the top of pre-printed letters and addressing envelopes to match. Very similar to the work I had hated so much at the tax office. The difference being that this time 'temporary' meant what it said, I did not feel trapped. We took the names from a card index of all the people who had donated to the Appeal in previous years, and there were hundreds of them. When the money started coming in there was no more time for chatting. We had to concentrate on what we were doing. Every donation had to be entered on the donor's card. We also had to keep a running total for the Accounts Department. Aware of my inability to tot up figures accurately, I left that part of the job to Madge.

She was not lively company, but she was comfortable to be with and we took to going to the pictures together, sometimes after work. Going to an evening performance was a new freedom for me. Mother no longer insisted on my going straight home. Whether Father knew about this I was not sure. It was easier not to ask. Perhaps even he recognised that now I had been out at work for over a year and was about to leave home altogether, it would have been asking too much to expect me to abide by the old rules while my young brother had complete freedom to come and go at all hours.

It had always riled me that Father's attitude towards David was so different to his attitude towards me. He had wanted both of us to go into the Civil Service but when my brother declined there was no pressure put on him to change his mind as there had been on me. David told him that as soon as he was old enough he intended to enlist in the Royal Navy if the war was still on and Father thoroughly approved the plan. A man should go and fight for his country, as he himself had done in his youth.

While he waited for the time to pass David continued to act as a messenger for the ARP and erect air raid shelters with the Scouts. There were now two types of shelter available, the Anderson, for use out of doors, and the new Morrison. This was designed for indoor use. Most people put it in their living room. It was much smaller than the Anderson, shaped like a table with a thick steel top. Panels of heavy-duty steel mesh enclosed the sides to keep out rubble should the house be hit. The top was too low to allow an adult to sit upright and it was only big enough to sleep two. Again, the shelter had to be bolted together after delivery and again only the bigger boys were strong enough to cope with the weight. By dint of persistent nagging, David finally persuaded Mother to have a Morrison, but she never used it. It stood in one corner of the sitting room covered with a large fancy tablecloth to hide its ugliness, with a green ornamental jug on top.

Father had written to say his department had a rota for Christmas leave. He had had his turn the previous year and would therefore not be home for the holiday this time. Nannie and Aunt Evelyn were not going to be with us either, I forget why. Mother did her best to make the season festive but it was difficult. There was no sherry for our customary toast; a small chicken replaced the turkey of former years and Mother had made the austerity pudding from a recipe cut out of the newspaper. Some of the ingredients needed for the traditional family recipe were no longer available. David and I tried to be jolly, but Christmas 1941 was a sad affair without Father.

It troubled me that I had not received a card from Mollie. I had not heard from her since our meeting at the Gaumont at the end of September, but I had taken it for granted I would hear at Christmas. Mother said the simplest explanation was that a post box or sorting office somewhere had been bombed, but I was still uneasy. With good cause as it turned out. In the New Year she wrote me a brief letter. I groaned when I read it and Mother asked sharply, "What's wrong – what's happened?"

"Mollie's in hospital. She's got TB."

"Oh, no!" said Mother. "Has she got it in both lungs, or only one – does she say?"

"Only one."

"Then she's got a good chance of recovery. It might not be as bad as it sounds."

I hoped Mother was right. I wanted to go and see for myself how she was. Mother said, "Well wrap up warm. TB wards are usually freezing."

Mollie was in Harefield Hospital, out Uxbridge way. The TB ward turned out to be a long, wide covered veranda open to the weather on one side, with a line of beds arranged in conventional hospital style down the other. Before the discovery of modern miracle drugs, fresh air was a major component of the treatment. A brisk and bossy nurse pointed out Mollie's bed half way down the line and warned me that the patient must not become excited, it would send up her temperature. Neither must she be distressed in any way, it was bad for morale. "And don't stay more than half an hour. That's quite long enough."

Expecting to see Mollie lying down and looking ill, it was a pleasant surprise to find her sitting up in bed. She was muffled in blankets against the winter wind. Her face broke into a delighted smile when she saw me. Positioning a chair beside her bed gave me time to readjust my ideas. When I was seated, with my coat tucked round my knees and a scarf pulled up to my ears, Mollie said, "It's great to see you. I was hoping you'd come." She looked much better than when I had last seen her at the Gaumont. She had rosy colour in her cheeks, which I at first mistook for a healthy glow, forgetting that it could also mean she was running a temperature. I sat smiling at her, not knowing what to say. I could hardly ignore her illness, but with the nurse's warning in my ears I was uncertain how much to say about it or how to begin. I settled for the practical approach. "What's it like in here?"

"It's OK, the nurses are lovely."

"And the food?" I was always concerned about food.

"Some of it's all right, but some of it' – " she shuddered, "boiled cod, rice pudding made with water and a blob of red jam on top."

"Yuk!" I pulled an exaggerated face of disgust. This made her laugh, which in turn made her cough. To give her time to recover I looked along the veranda at the other patients. Some were lying down; others were sitting up, muffled in blankets like Mollie; several had visitors sitting quietly beside them. From what I could see of her near neighbours they were about Mollie's age or maybe a bit older. I was glad she had congenial company and was not stuck with a lot of old women.

Her coughing fit over, Mollie reached for a glass of water from the top of her locker. A snapshot of her and Ted taken before he went into the Army was propped up against the water jug. She saw me looking at it and said, "He's on the officers' training course now. When it's over he's coming to see me. With luck I'll be out of here before he's sent overseas." I held up crossed fingers and she did the same.

Turning her attention to me, Mollie asked, "You haven't heard from the Air Force yet?"

"No. I'm getting a bit worried in case they've forgotten me."

"You're still at the hospital?"

"Yes." I couldn't think of much to say about my job that would interest her and conversation flagged. In a way I was not sorry when the bossy nurse started walking down the ward, weeding out the visitors she thought had been there long enough. I did not wait for her to reach Mollie's bed, I stood up. "I'll keep in touch," I promised.

She smiled, "Take care of yourself."

"I sure will." I gave her a big theatrical wink.

Outside the ward I almost gave way to tears. Here was I, about to set out on the most exciting adventure of my life so far, and there was she, forced to live in a depressing world of temperature charts and bedpans. Against all reason I felt I was abandoning her.

When another week passed without my hearing from the Air Force, it occurred to me that one reason for their silence might be that Mr Langton had not answered the Air Ministry's enquiries about whether I was free to enlist. It would be like him to be obstructive. I decided to check up.

The following Monday I left the hospital at lunchtime and went down to a public callbox to ring the tax office, praying that Mr Deane would be available. His chirpy voice in my ear told me my luck was in. He said, "I can guess why you're phoning."

I asked, "Did the Air Force contact you? I haven't heard from them."

"They did. There was some delay in returning the form, but it's been dealt with now and you'll be hearing any day, I should think."

I thanked him, inwardly fuming. It was just as I had suspected, Mr Langton had sat on the form for as long as possible before sending it back. Spiteful old devil!

I received notification of my longed-for call-up date a week or two later.

Chapter 5
Think of a Number

I LEFT HOME on 20th March 1942, six weeks after my nineteenth birthday. My orders were to report to the No 2 WAAF Depot at Innsworth, Gloucestershire. Enclosed with them was a travel warrant from Paddington Station. My father was given a special day's leave from Llandudno to come down and see me off, and for once I was glad of his company. For the truth of the matter was that now the day of departure had at last arrived I was scared stiff. Like a blow to the heart it finally hit me that I was leaving my family and friends, all the familiar scenes I had known all my life and going to some unknown place where I would be surrounded by strangers. Would I like them? Would they like me? In a moment of panic over breakfast that morning I almost regretted volunteering. The excitement that had sustained me since I left the tax office had entirely deserted me. I felt too choked up to eat the bacon and eggs Mother put in front of me – probably her own week's ration as well as mine – but she refused to heed my protests. "Get on with it and don't be so silly," she said firmly, "You'll regret it later if you don't." She also insisted I take a packet of sandwiches with me for the journey. At the last goodbye I clung to her and she kissed me with tears in her eyes. Chick No. 1 was leaving the nest and it was a painful moment for both of us. Unexpectedly painful for me, who had been prepared to leave without a backward glance, so eager had I been to get away. Father, not given to emotional scenes, said briskly, "Come along, or we'll miss the train," and led the way down the front path. He held open the gate for me to pass through, and I felt the gesture was symbolic. He was turning me loose. Freedom and independence were beckoning. All I had to do was follow.

I had not seen my father since I left the tax office. He had arrived home so late the previous evening that I had gone to bed, and it was not until we were on the underground that we had a chance to talk. There should have been plenty to say, but somehow the time passed and we couldn't get started. Perhaps it was just that tube trains are not ideal places for serious conversation. Anyway, all we could manage was small talk. In fact the only thing I can recall of any consequence was the one piece of advice he ever gave me to see me through service life: don't go drinking on an empty stomach. This, from a father who until recently had treated me like a child! I was dumbstruck.

I had never been away from home on my own before and the coming journey worried me. Father would find out which platform I had to go to and see I caught the right train. I knew what station to get out at, but who would tell me what to do and where to go then? My worry was completely unnecessary. SPs (the RAF Special Police) were patrolling Paddington Station; I showed my travel warrant to the nearest one and was directed to the correct platform and told to go to the far end. The train was already in and Father and I walked the length of the platform to where a small crowd of young women had already gathered. A few brave souls had come alone, but most, like myself, had brought someone with them for moral support. More girls and their escorts were arriving every minute, until there must have been over a hundred people there, the girls all weighing each other up furtively and smiling self-consciously if anyone caught their eye. Now that the final moment of parting was imminent I was feeling sick with apprehension and it was a relief and a comfort to know that I was not going to be travelling into my new life on my own.

All the compartments of the carriages at the end of the train were reserved for Innsworth recruits. Some of the girls climbed aboard at once; I was one of those who lingered on the platform, reluctant to leave my father until the last minute, though we still did not have much to say to each other. I was hoping that our mutual reserve might give way to something warmer, and did not like to leave him before it happened. The train suddenly let off a deafening blast of steam, and an RAF sergeant came striding down the platform shouting, "Time to go, ladies. All aboard." Father put an arm round my shoulders, gave me a quick hug and pushed me towards the train. We did not kiss goodbye, for which I was both sorry and relieved. Sorry because I would have liked to kiss him, relieved because if I had done so I feared I would have burst into tears. Carriage doors were being slammed all along the platform. I was among the last to climb aboard the train and I heard the door slam behind me. A whistle blew and as I found an empty seat next to the door to the corridor the train moved with a jerk, nearly throwing me off balance. The girl I was about to sit next to caught my arm to steady me and smiled. I tried to smile back but my face was stiff. I put my small case on the rack with everyone else's and settled in beside her. Slowly the train slid past the end of the platform. Some of the girls crowded to the window to wave to the forlorn gathering we had left behind, but I stayed where I was. If I saw my father receding into the distance I knew I would cry and I would be ashamed. The train picked up speed and headed out of London into whatever awaited us in the future.

At first there was silence in the compartment. Several girls lit cigarettes. The girl next to me offered me one, but I shook my head, "I don't." I had never smoked, I did not know how it would affect me and this did not seem the right moment to find out. But I heartily wished I could have accepted the offer. A cigarette might have helped to soothe the unexpected ache of loss I felt at all I was leaving behind me.

Desultory conversations broke out as the cigarette smoke drifted round our heads but I didn't feel like joining in. I sat in my corner slumped in misery. Which was ridiculous. Wasn't this supposed to be my big day of escape to freedom? Then why didn't I feel like rejoicing? Why was I wishing so fervently that I was back at the hospital? They had been very good, allowing me to stay on until my papers arrived even though the Appeal was all but over. Madge was still there, entering up the last of the donations as they came trickling in, making sure the cards were in correct alphabetical order. At that moment I envied her.

"Take care of yourself," Mollie had said when I left her. But at this moment I did not want to take care of myself, I wanted to be somewhere safe and familiar, being taken care of by my mother.

I was roused from my doleful reverie by the voice of a woman sitting on the opposite side of the compartment near the window. Her voice had a harsh penetrating quality that was difficult to ignore. Everyone else seemed to have fallen silent. The woman looked about thirty years old, with flyaway ginger hair and sharp ice-blue eyes. She was talking to a young girl sitting next to her, though talking at her would be a more accurate way of putting it. The poor girl was looking uncomfortable. They had apparently been discussing holidays and the older woman was in full flow listing all the places she had been to abroad. Switzerland: "If you ever get the chance you simply must go to Lake Lucerne." France: "Paris was lovely, but I didn't like the people." And Germany: "Of course, we went to Berlin" and so on. I, who had never been further than the Isle of Wight, felt overawed by all this sophistication. Not so my neighbour. "Have you ever been to Butlins?" she enquired brightly. The ginger haired woman was put completely off her stroke as one or two girls tittered. Someone said she'd been to the one at Skegness, the girl next to Ginger said, "I've been there," pleased to be able to get a word in at last. They began swapping memories of childhood holidays and the conversation became general. My neighbour turned to me with a grin and my depression eased. I smiled, but it was an effort.

She said her name was Kay. Looking at her properly for the first time I saw she was not conventionally pretty, but she was very attractive. The most striking thing about her was her hair. In contrast to her eyebrows and eyelashes, which were dark, it was silver blond. She wore it dead straight and cut in a bob with a fringe, like a little girl. Her eyes were green and sparkled when she laughed, and she looked as if she laughed a lot. I guessed she was about my own age and wished I had her self-confidence. She murmured, "So much for the travelogue!" and chuckled. It was an infectious sound, and I joined in, my depression lifting.

The talk remained general and became increasingly lively. Whenever the loud-voiced Ginger threatened to monopolise the conversation someone would cut across her monologue and change the subject. An hour or so out of London I felt ravenous despite my big breakfast and took my sandwiches from my case with silent thanks to my mother for insisting I bring them. The others also produced mid-journey snacks, and a spirit of real comradeship was forged as we swapped around - "my bloater paste sandwich for one of your jam." By the time we reached our destination we might all have known each other for years.

I cannot recall going to Gloucester itself. My memory is of a small country station with flowerbeds full of early spring colour. "Remember troops, stick together and we'll be all right." cried Kay as we spilled out onto the platform. Here we were met by a WAAF sergeant with attendant corporals. Our group managed to stay together as we were divided into squads. The sergeant commanded, "Attention everybody. Into two lines. At the double." The train gave a goodbye whistle and went on its way; our last link with our past lives was broken.

I think we must have walked to the camp, about a mile away. I cannot remember transport being provided. The guard on the gate lifted the barrier. We surveyed the uniform rows of bleak huts that were to be our homes for the next few days. There was no one about, the place looked deserted and depressing.

My main thought was that I was starving. Breakfast belonged

to another life, the sandwiches on the train were only a memory. Mercifully we were taken straight to the Mess. This was vast and very noisy. Long plain wooden tables filled the centre of the hall. Squads of Waafs in obviously new uniforms occupied some of them, at others civilians like ourselves were eating hurriedly. Above the echoing din of talk and laughter and the clatter of cutlery on plates, patrolling corporals shouted warnings about taking too long to eat. The WAAF sergeant indicated the tables allocated to our contingent and we left our cases on the benches beside them to mark our territory. The corporals issued us with a knife, fork and spoon each - our 'irons'. These, it was impressed upon us, were to be guarded with our lives. If we lost them we would not be issued with a second set. We would either have to eat with our fingers or go hungry.

Clutching these precious implements tightly, as if they had lives of their own and might try to escape, we collected a plate and lined up at a long counter. Holding out our plates we were served by the cooks with the speciality of the day: some anonymous stew, a mound of potatoes and greens, a slab of sponge cake and a dollop of glutinous bright yellow custard. All on the one plate. Ginger's penetrating voice could be heard despite the noise, "I can see why they call this place the mess." We ate quickly, trying to get to the pudding before the sponge cake soaked up all the gravy. A corporal was shouting, "Parade outside in fifteen minutes." I have never been a fast eater. I was the last to scramble from the table, cramming the final lump of sponge into my mouth as I hurried after the others. Copying them I dumped my plate on the end of the counter, sluiced my irons in a huge vat of once-hot water, shook them dry and ran outside to "Fall in. At the double". Our untidy crocodile was then led to the Admin section to begin the induction procedures.

Admin appeared to be in a state of chaos. Waafs and civilians were coming and going in all directions. Corporals shouted orders, names were called and gradually the confusion resolved itself into queues for various interviews in different rooms, and one which disappeared in batches behind a closed door marked 'M.O.' There was a lot of waiting about. At one point we had to have our height measured. The orderlies dealing with this part of the procedure were evidently trying to speed things up. The one who measured me slammed the height bar down on my head before I had time to straighten up properly. I was therefore officially recorded as being about an inch shorter than I really am. And then, all unsuspecting, we passed through the door marked 'MO.' We soon found out why they kept it closed, and were grateful for it. The medical examination was the most intimate and embarrassing inspection possible. I'm not sure if any of us knew what they were looking for and I was not the only one to emerge reeling with shock. The FFI (Free From Infection) was to be repeated at intervals throughout our service life. It was doubtless a vital precaution against the spread of disease, and while we understood this we never ceased to loathe it.

At some point in the afternoon I signed away my civilian status in exchange for a long number which I was sure I would never remember, but have in fact never forgotten. "Make sure you give it to all your relations and friends if you want to get any mail. Letters without a number on can't be delivered." we were solemnly warned. I was very proud of my number. It represented my acceptance into a new and exciting world, out of reach of parental supervision.

The day seemed endless. Eventually, long after dark, we filed through a large warehouse with counters to collect two sheets and a bolster case each. The last march of the day took us to the dormitory huts. There were about twenty beds to a hut, arranged down each side like a hospital ward. We entered through a small lobby that acted as a light trap in the blackout. This formed a secluded corner where the corporal in charge had her bed, facing down the hut instead of across it. An iron stove in the middle of the floor provided the heating.

During the afternoon our original small party had gradually drifted apart. Chivvied and ordered into different queues we had lost touch with one another, although Ginger's voice could be heard uplifted in caustic comment from time to time. There was only one girl from the group still with me by the time we reached our hut, and by great good fortune that girl was Kay. We grabbed beds next to one another and then stared at them uncertainly. They were very basic, iron frames with strong mesh for a base. Stacked on each bed were three small flat mattresses, two rough grey blankets and a bolster that felt as if it was filled with straw. Our corporal strode to one of beds. "These," she said, pointing to the mattresses, "are known as 'biscuits'." She demonstrated the art of laying them out to form a full-size mattress and making up the bed so that it would not part company with itself during the night. Simple when you knew how.

When we had made up our beds she ordered, "Follow me," and led the way outside. We followed obediently, stumbling along the path in the dark to another hut some distance away. "In here," she said, "are the ablutions."

"The what?" asked puzzled voices.

"The baths, the washbasins and the loos."

"The loos? But they're miles from the hut," someone wailed in consternation. "Supposing we want to go in the night?"

"Thank God it's not raining," said Kay devoutly.

If there were forlorn tears shed in the hut after lights out, I never heard them. I was asleep even before I collapsed into bed, emotionally and physically exhausted. The last thing I remembered was Kay muttering something about mice in the bolsters.

The induction process continued next day with I.Q. and trade tests. I had applied for secretarial work, as stipulated by Father when he gave his consent to my enlisting. I was therefore given a shorthand-typing test. However, the pressure of knowing that it was an exam brought back vivid memories of my nightmare interview at the tax office. I panicked, lost the thread of the dictation and couldn't type it back. At my interview afterwards an RAF officer with a kind, patient face looked up from the page of scribbled hieroglyphics I had produced and inquired, "Why did you apply to be a shorthand-typist?" I explained that my father wanted me to keep in practice for after the war. I was about to explain my exam nerves when he asked, "Who's coming into the Air Force, you or your father?" Taken by surprise, I said, "Well - I am." He nodded and said kindly, "And what do you want to do?"

This was totally unexpected. I had accepted Father's stipulation without question. It had not occurred to either of us that I might, as it were, get the sack before I got the job. I had no alternative trade in mind to suggest. I said, "I don't know. What else is there?" He offered me either photography or cooking. I chose photography. It sounded interesting and glamorous and much more fun than serving up stew and chewy sponge with lumpy custard. He told me I would be sent on a special training course. But first I had to take a trade test to see if I was suitable. This would take place at the RAF Trade Test Centre at West Drayton, near Uxbridge.

"Uxbridge!" exclaimed Kay when I told her in the hut later. "Do you know anything about photography?"

"Not really. But I've got a Kodak Box Brownie." We both laughed uncertainly. I had an unhappy feeling that having just failed one test I was about to fail another one.

"It can't be a practical test, or they'd have asked you about experience," Kay said thoughtfully. "I wonder what they mean by 'suitable'." We both thought about it, to no avail. "Whatever they mean, they must think you've got a chance," Kay said at length. "They'd never send you all that way if they thought you were definitely unsuitable." She gave me her flashing grin. It lifted my spirits, as it had done on the train. Perhaps the test would not be as bad as I feared.

"What about you?" I asked. I knew she had applied for Accounts. "Did you pass?"

"I suppose so. He didn't really say. All he seemed to be interested in was how bookmakers fix the odds on different horses. I used to work for my dad, he's a bookie," she explained. I was instantly intrigued and wanted to know more. She said she had worked for her father since she left school, going with him to the races and looking after the office side of the business as soon as she was capable of assuming the responsibility. She genuinely enjoyed working with figures and could not imagine doing anything else. It sounded an exciting life. I said, "The WAAF's going to seem pretty tame after that, I should think."

"Different, anyway. Dad can be difficult to work for sometimes. To tell the truth I was glad to get away." Someone else trying to shake free of her father! I related the story of my father and the civil service and we laughed together because we had both escaped from home restrictions and, like me, she was revelling in the idea of freedom.

Next morning, still in civvies, I collected a packet of sandwiches in the cookhouse and a travel warrant from Admin and set off to catch a train back to London. "Don't forget your irons," exhorted the corporal as I left. Having been out to visit Mollie at Harefield near Uxbridge only a few weeks earlier, I knew roughly where I was going and sat in the train feeling very much the experienced traveller.

I arrived at West Drayton in the late afternoon. The camp entrance was only a short walk from the station, which was a blessing. At least I could not get lost. I showed my papers to the guard on the gate and was directed to Admin. Their first question was the now familiar "Have you got your irons?" before someone took me to the mess for a very welcome meal. Afterwards I reported back to Admin to be interviewed by an austere looking RAF officer who said my test had been scheduled for 0830 the following morning. I asked if I could go home for the night and come back next day, but he refused permission.

The hut where I was due to spend the night looked dismal in

the fading daylight. Dismal, cold and unoccupied. I wondered what on earth I was going to do with myself all evening if I was going to be on my own. After a few minutes I put my case in an empty locker and went out to look for company, hoping to find a Naafi. Expecting to see nothing but uniforms, I was surprised to walk into a small crowd of civilian girls all heading towards the main gate. Presumably a day shift going off duty. On impulse I followed them. Even in the dusk I could see that the guard hardly glanced at them as they went through, and no one had to show a pass. I tagged along behind them. Nobody took any notice of me. Outside the camp I set off briskly for the railway station. At the time it did not seem strange to me that I, who had spent months looking forward to leaving home, should come dashing back at the first opportunity.

When I rang our front doorbell there was a long wait before I heard movement behind the door and Mother's voice called cautiously, "Who is it?"

"It's me," I called back. A chain rattled, bolts were drawn back. Mother opened the door, pulled me hurriedly inside and shut it quickly behind me. I thought it was because of the blackout, but no. She had made the lightning deduction that I didn't like the Air Force, I had run away, and at any moment the military police would come pounding down the street to drag me back. I managed to convince her all was well (omitting to mention I'd come home without permission). Over a very late scrap supper I told her my news. I had failed the shorthand-typing test and I was hoping to be a photographer. She was not at all happy about this and wondered what Father would say. So did I. However, I had not failed the test deliberately so had no need to feel guilty. I would have kept my promise if I could.

Mother was also none too pleased to learn that I would have to disturb the household hours before dawn if I was to be back on camp in time to take my trade test. But despite my assurance that I would creep out quietly and get breakfast in the mess later, she was up earlier than I was in the morning, bless her, and once more fed me before I left. This time we parted without tears as she muttered something about turning up again like a bad penny.

It was still so early only two people got off the train at West Drayton, myself and the Admin officer who had refused me permission to go home. He gave no sign of recognition as I followed him up the road to the camp and turned in at the gate. I showed my papers to the guard, a different one to the day before, and he passed me through with hardly a glance.

My test lasted less than ten minutes. The examiner, an RAF flight sergeant, had a large grey metal camera on his desk. He opened up the back to show me a spool of film similar in shape to those I used in my Box Brownie only much bigger. He asked, "Do you think you could learn to load and unload this in a darkroom?" I could load my own camera in the dark in the cupboard under the stairs, so I said, "Yes." He wrote something on a slip of paper, while I braced myself for the next question. But when he looked up he handed me the slip, told me to take it to Admin and dismissed me. Outside the door I read that I had passed. I could return to Innsworth immediately.

The Admin Officer still acted as if he did not recognise me. Perhaps he didn't. He authorised the sergeant to issue me with a return travel warrant and dismissed me again. I felt like Alice, bemused in Wonderland. I went over to the mess for a late breakfast, collected my case and once more set off on my travels. Secretly I was bubbling over with glee. I didn't have to be a shorthand typist; I was going to be a photographer.

Two days previously Innsworth had looked bleak and uninviting. Now it was my base, my temporary home. I was back among friends and on top of the world. I reported to Admin and went to the mess for a meal before going to the hut.

As I went through the light-trap the corporal looked out from her corner and called my surname. "You're being re-hutted," she said. "Report to Admin at 0800 hours tomorrow morning."

Having delivered her official message, she relaxed and became human. "The others are going on to Morecambe tomorrow. You are being transferred to the next group to be kitted out." Looking round I saw I was now the only person present still in civvies. My euphoria evaporated. I felt as if I was back at school, being kept down while the rest of the class moved up. I said, "Yes, Corporal," dully. If I'd learned one thing in the last few days, I'd learned that this was the best thing to say in most circumstances. Or "No, Corporal," where appropriate.

Kay had her back to me as I walked down the hut. She was trying to stuff the last of her new kit into her kitbag and swearing. Not just the emphatic "damn" or "blast" my mother permitted in trying circumstances, but language she must have picked up on the racecourse. She stopped when I reached my bed. "You're back!" she exclaimed, looking pleased. I agreed glumly. Kay jerked her head towards the corporal. "She told you we're off tomorrow?" I nodded. "Cheer up! You'll be in Morecambe yourself in a couple of days. I'll keep a look out for you. OK?" I nodded again but I was not OK. I was miserable at the thought of being parted from her.

"So what was the trade test like? Did you pass?" she asked brightly.

"Yes," I said and described it.

"All that way, just to answer one question? Incredible!" she chortled. When I told her about the officer refusing to recognise me, she said shrewdly, "You got back on time, so why bother putting you on a charge? He probably didn't want the paperwork."

She put on her cap and struck a mannequin's pose, "What do you think?"

I gave a rather feeble imitation of a wolf whistle and she took off her cap and threw it at me, laughing. "I feel as if I'm back at school, wearing this lot. Did you have to wear a uniform at school?"

"I certainly did! I went to a Convent school."

"A convent?" Kay was instantly concerned. "You do know what's what, don't you?"

"What's – ?" It took me a moment to catch her meaning. "Oh, yes. I learned all about the birds and the bees from my mother."

"Lucky you! My mum never told me a thing. I found out from a friend of mine who's a nurse. Mum would have a fit if she knew. She'd think I was up to no good."

This was a fairly common attitude in those days when intimate matters were not usually spoken of, even within the family. A mother frequently thought it was time enough to enlighten her daughter on the physical side of marriage on the eve of the girl's wedding – if she told her anything at all. Many girls were left to find out for themselves on their honeymoon.

"My mother believed everyone should be taught the facts of life in school, like any other subject." I said, and laughed.

"What's so funny? It sounds like a good idea to me," said Kay.

"And to me. That's not why I was laughing. I was thinking of the time she told the headmistress what she believed." I expected Kay to laugh with me, but she didn't. She asked seriously, "Did the nun know what your mother was talking about?"

"I'm sure she did, or she wouldn't have been so scandalised."

When Kay was brushing her hair ready for bed, I noticed it was dark at the roots. I ought to have guessed she dyed it from the exotic colour that was so at variance with her eyebrows, but I had not given it a thought. My mother would have called her a 'bottle blonde', in that special tone of voice that implies the young lady was no better than she should be. In Mother's eyes bleached hair was a sign of moral depravity. Was she right? In Kay's case I neither knew nor cared. I knew I was gong to miss her and the knowledge hurt.

Chapter 6
"Sprogs"

"PASSION-KILLERS! Get your passion-killers here!" We were in another warehouse, getting kitted out.. Hidden somewhere in the maze of counters, loaded racks and mountains of bales and boxes, an RAF store clerk and wit shouted his wares like a market trader. I remembered Kay's laughing voice the night before, "You'll curl up when you see the knickers. I've packed mine or I'd show you. I wouldn't be seen dead in them."

I had hardly had time to say goodbye to her when we parted that morning. Breakfast had been a hurried affair. The other girls were dashing off to meet the transport with their kitbags, and I was rushing to get to Admin at 0800 as ordered. As we left the table Kay said, "Look out for us and we'll do the same for you." I nodded with my mouth still full of breakfast and left the mess on the run. Or 'at the double', as the saying went.

From Admin a corporal walked me smartly to my new hut. Had there been more than one of me I would have said we were marched there. A squad in civvies waiting on the path outside the hut eyed me curiously as we went in. The corporal directed me to a free bed half way down the hut, gave me a 'chitty' to collect sheets from the stores and told me to hurry up, I was keeping the parade waiting. I pushed my case into the empty locker and dashed out to join it. The corporal marched us to the clothing store, where a Waaf sergeant took over. She wasn't as raucous as the junior NCOs. I suppose the extra stripe gave her the authority she needed without having to yell for it. With Admin staff posted at strategic intervals around the stores to ensure no one missed a bay and upset the system, we snaked our way round collecting a formidable amount of clothing and equipment en route. One item was a kitbag which we filled as we went along. When full, a kitbag was heavy, very heavy, and carrying it required a certain knack. The trick was to grasp it firmly at the top, then swing and heave it over one shoulder in one continuous movement. As demonstrated by our corporal it looked easy. But she was a well-built muscular young woman who had presumably done it many times before. Our first attempts were pathetic. One slightly built girl mastered the swing but the kitbag nearly knocked her over as it landed on her shoulder. There was no point in the corporal trying to march us back to the hut – it was every girl for herself and the corporal had to help the hindmost. This she did with a look of scorn on her hard, rather bony face. Clearly she regarded us as feeble specimens, unlikely to be any credit to the Air Force.

It is surprising how quickly an iron bedstead in about five by six feet of floor space becomes 'home'. I dragged my kitbag up to my locker, pulled a biscuit off the regulation stack at the head of the bed and flopped down on it to get my breath back. The corporal shouted, "Don't just sit there, get changed." I scrambled up to empty my kitbag and examine my new belongings. The powers that be had provided us with an outfit for every occasion. Waking, sleeping, in the cold and rain, or in a gas attack, we would be dressed appropriately. It had been possible to try on such items as the greatcoat, the two jackets, the cap and the shoes in the stores; for the rest we had been forced to rely on the judgement of the store clerks, male and female. On the whole they had sized us up pretty well, but there were hilarious exceptions. The underclothes were of prehistoric design and caused mirth bordering on hysteria. I could see why Kay had laughed about the knickers. Actually they reminded me strongly of the ones I had worn at school all my life, the sort with legs you tucked your hanky up. I

PERSONAL ISSUE OF CLOTHING & NECESSARIES		
1 Cape, Ground Sheet	1 pr. Slacks	1 Button Stick
1 Greatcoat	1 pr. Canvas Shoes	1 Identity Disk No. 1
1 Respirator	1 pr. Overboots	1 Identity Disk No. 2
1 Steel Helmet	2 prs. Knickers	
1 Cap, with Badge	2 prs. Pantees	1 Kitbag
1 Cap Comforter	2 Vests	1 Ration Bag
2 Jackets	2 Brassières	1 Anti-Gas Cape
2 Skirts	2 Suspender Belts	3 Eyeshields
3 Shirts	2 Corselettes to	1 Curtain (anti-gas for Steel Helmet)
6 Collars ; 1 Tie	women of bust sizes 40, 42 or 44	
1 Cardigan		
1 pr. Gloves	2 Hand Towels	1 Field Dressing
3 prs. Stockings	1 Housewife	2 tins Anti-Gas Ointment
2 prs. Shoes	1 pkt. Sanitary Towels	
1 pr. Laces		1 Hairbrush

Extract from a 1942 list of issue clothing, etc.
(Thanks to Sqn Ldr Beryl E Escott)

had hoped never to see their like again, but here they were, dark blue 'blackouts' for winter and lighter 'twilights' for summer. I wished with all my heart that Kay had been there to laugh with me. The girl on my left hand side was laughing with her other neighbour, and the girl on my right, a serious-looking young woman whom I judged to be in her early twenties, did not seem to find humour in the situation at all.

Between giggles and cries of disbelief – "Will you just look at the length of this skirt! I feel like Old Mother Riley"- we shed our civilian image and were transformed into approximate copies of the girl in the recruiting posters.

Having worn a tie at school I had no difficulty with the knot, but the detached collar and collar studs had proved tricky. The jacket fitted fairly well. The skirt on the other hand felt too long. My serious neighbour, who was tall and slim, looked really smart in her uniform, which could have been made for her. Her short dark curly hair tucked itself neatly underneath her cap. I set my cap squarely on my thick straight hair and regretted there was no full-length mirror in the hut to show me how I looked.

My solemn neighbour caught my eye. Determined to break the ice I said, "It's like going back to school, isn't it?" and gave her my name.

She said, "I'm Judith," and suddenly smiled. She had a particularly sweet smile. It lit up her grey eyes and softened her face, which tended to wear a withdrawn and slightly forbidding expression in repose.

We were all officially ACW2s (Aircraftwomen 2nd Class), the lowest rank in the pecking order of the WAAF. In Air Force parlance brand new Waafs in brand new uniforms were known as 'sprogs'.

The corporal raised her voice, "Right. Let's be having you. Stand by your beds. Atten – shun!" Personal inspection followed combined with personal comment. "That skirt's too short. Have you rolled it up at the waist? Then unroll it." "Is that the best you can do with that tie? Ask someone to show you." And the one we were to hear on numerous occasions in the next few weeks, "Get your hair up off your collar." Inspection over, it was, "Parade outside in five minutes. Bring your irons."

We marched to the mess, looking forward with muted enthusiasm to what we were about to receive. In my mind I completed the old childhood grace "... may the Lord make us truly hungry." Our three square meals a day were filling and they were doubtless nutritious, but only hunger could make some of the food look appetising.

At the end of the afternoon, when we had finished sorting ourselves out and parcelled up our civvy clothes ready to be sent home, some of the girls began to drift towards the door. One of them called out, "We're going to the Naafi. Anyone else coming?" Judith and I were among those who tagged along behind. Apart from mugs of tea and thick slices of plain cake – "char and a wad" – the Naafi sold a variety of goods including toiletries, writing

"SPROGS"

materials, sweets, chocolate and cigarettes. The canteen was fairly busy and we had to queue at the counter. Along with our Pay Books we had been issued with Naafi ration cards for cigarettes, which they sold very cheaply. I watched the girls ahead of me handing over their cards and when my turn came to be served I was unable to resist the temptation. I bought a packet of twenty and a box of matches as well as a mug of tea.

The girls headed for a vacant table and settled down to talk and smoke. I pulled up a chair next to Judith's. Someone asked me why I had only joined the squad that morning. Where had I been until then? I told them about my trade test at West Drayton. This caused hoots of laughter. "That must be the shortest trade test on record," said one girl.

"Maybe, but it set me back two days. The others went on to Morecambe this morning,"

"You'll be missing them," said Judith quietly.

"Yes," I said briefly. I was not going to admit how much. I pulled a cigarette from my packet and put it between my lips while I struck a match, trying to look like an experienced smoker. I don't know what gave me away, but Judith leaned towards me and whispered, "Don't inhale." It was a good thing she warned me. My first intake of smoke half choked me and made my eyes water. I was sorry I had not waited until I was alone before embarking on the venture. One of the girls laughed and said, "Picking up bad habits already?" and I smiled sheepishly.

I did not enjoy my first cigarette. It rasped my throat. But I was hooked on the idea of smoking: the ritual of lighting up, blowing out smoke and the feeling of sophistication it gave me. I persevered until it became a habit, one I could well have done without. Non-smokers could always find a buyer for their unwanted cigarette ration. Alternatively they could swap it for extra sweets or chocolate, which were also on ration cards.

From the canteen I went to the stores to hand in my chitty and collect two sheets and a bolster case. When I returned to the hut I was at once aware that something was going on. The girl in the last bed at the far end of the hut was curled up against her blanket stack crying. The corporal was leaning over her, talking in a low voice. The other girls were carrying on scrappy conversations in subdued tones, obviously very conscious of the little scene being enacted at the end of the hut.

I asked Judith, "What's happening?"

"Jenny's upset about something and the corporal's trying to sort her out," she replied.

Jenny was a very pretty girl. I had noticed her earlier and thought how young she looked. Hardly old enough to have left school, let alone enter the WAAF. She continued to cry as the corporal left her to go and fetch help. She returned with a sergeant, an older woman with a pleasant face, who went to speak to Jenny alone. Not very long afterwards the sergeant left. Jenny had stopped crying and looked a lot happier. She and Eileen, the girl in the next bed, went into a whispered huddle, giggling as at some huge joke. Eventually they shared it with another girl and in no time the story had gone round the hut. Jenny had thought she was pregnant because she had let her boyfriend kiss her goodnight! The sergeant had explained 'everything' and she now knew she had nothing to worry about.

Mother was right, I thought. The facts of life should be taught in school, especially these days. It was dangerous for a girl to enter the Services in such a state of ignorance.

Next morning we had kit inspection. All our new possessions had to be displayed on our beds in a prescribed pattern, ready for inspection by the Duty Admin Officer of the day. Her role was only a charade. The real inspection took place before she arrived, carried out by the corporal. The NCO scrutinised each bed in minute detail to make sure every item of kit was present, correctly folded and set out precisely in its allotted place.

The officer was attended by the sergeant who had talked to Jenny the day before. The corporal shouted, "Stand by your

"SPROGS"

LAYOUT OF W.A.A.F KIT
(FOR KIT INSPECTION)

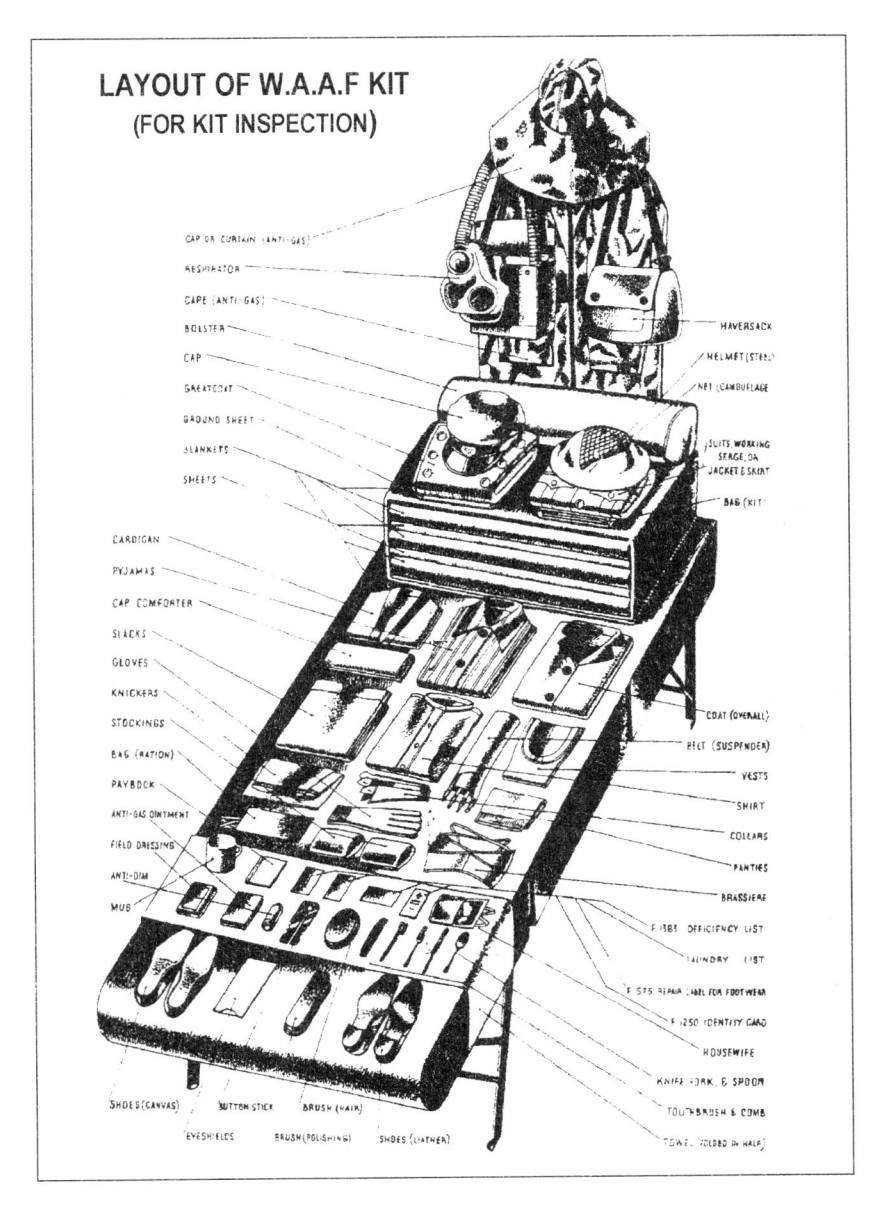

- CAP OR CURTAIN (ANTI-GAS)
- RESPIRATOR
- CAPE (ANTI-GAS)
- BOLSTER
- CAP
- GREATCOAT
- GROUND SHEET
- BLANKETS
- SHEETS
- CARDIGAN
- PYJAMAS
- CAP COMFORTER
- SLACKS
- GLOVES
- KNICKERS
- STOCKINGS
- BAG (RATION)
- PAYBOOK
- ANTI-GAS OINTMENT
- FIELD DRESSING
- ANTI-DIM
- MUG
- SHOES (CANVAS)
- BUTTON STICK
- BRUSH (HAIR)
- EYESHIELDS
- BRUSH (POLISHING)
- SHOES (LEATHER)
- HAVERSACK
- HELMET (STEEL)
- NET (CAMOUFLAGE)
- SUITS, WORKING SERGE, OR JACKET & SKIRT
- BAG (KIT)
- COAT (OVERALL)
- BELT (SUSPENDER)
- VESTS
- SHIRT
- COLLARS
- PANTIES
- BRASSIERE
- F 1383 DEFICIENCY LIST
- LAUNDRY LIST
- F 575 REPAIR LABEL FOR FOOTWEAR
- F 1250 IDENTITY CARD
- HOUSEWIFE
- KNIFE, FORK, & SPOON
- TOOTHBRUSH & COMB
- TOWEL, FOLDED IN HALF

Prescribed layout for service kit, 1944.
Thanks to Sqn Ldr Beryl E Escott)

beds," which we were already doing, and "Atten – shun." The officer walked slowly past the end of each bed, clearly aware there would be nothing amiss for her to find. Having completed her tour of the hut she said, "Carry on, Sergeant." They exchanged salutes and she departed, leaving the sergeant behind.

The sergeant was one of those women who manage to project a motherly image while looking both smart and efficient. I could imagine her in charge of the local Women's Voluntary Service (WVS) headquarters at home. She said something to the corporal who ordered, "Stand at - EASE" in a paradeground voice and "Stand easy," which allowed us to relax. The sergeant walked to the centre of the floor. "Can you all hear me?" she enquired. "Perhaps you'd like to move in closer." Surprised by this novel approach, we gathered round her. "Tomorrow," she began, " you will be going to Morecambe for your basic training. But before you go I would like to give you two pieces of advice. Firstly, never make a close friend of anyone. If either of you gets posted you will break your heart. Secondly, look after No. 1. If you don't, nobody else will".

There was a short silence following this unexpected counsel as we waited to be told officially that we could return to our bed spaces. The sergeant nodded pleasantly to the hut in general, then said, "Carry on, Corporal" and left. The corporal announced, "Parade outside in ten minutes. At the double." Our kit, so carefully and accurately positioned for inspection, now had to be bundled into our lockers before we hurried out for whatever the parade was for this time. I wondered what would happen if just for once we moved at normal speed ('At the single'?) Would Britain lose the war?

We were marched to the parade ground and halted. An RAF sergeant strode towards us, swinging his arms in exaggerated fashion. The ground shook as he stamped to a halt in front of us. "A-a-tten - SHUN!" he roared. We jerked upright. "Blimey!" gasped someone behind me.

"SILENCE IN THE RANKS." He glared at us ferociously. Suitably cowed, we stared ahead, our faces blank. Our first square-bashing session was upon us. We were lined up, tallest on the right, shortest on the left with a good deal of shuffling about in the middle. "Come on, come on," bellowed the sergeant, "We haven't got all day." We learned to 'Right Dress' to straighten up the lines; 'Right Turn', 'Left Turn' and 'About Turn'. When we had grasped all the basic steps he marched us up to the top of the parade ground and, like the Grand Old Duke of York, he marched us down again. Several times. My new shoes rubbed my feet and by the time he handed us over to the waiting corporal I was thoroughly fed up. Back in the hut I eased off my shoes and wiggled my toes to make sure they still worked. Around me others were doing the same. One or two girls were ordered to report to the medical section, their feet were so badly blistered.

There had been no opportunity to think about the Waaf sergeant's little homily after kit inspection. Now I went over it in my mind. I could see that the first piece of advice was good. If I could get so attached to someone after only a few days, as I had done to Kay, and feel so disconsolate when we were separated, what must it feel like to have a close friend for perhaps months and then lose her at the whim of the Air Force? As to the second piece of advice, 'look out for No. 1', I was not so sure. Was she just telling us to stand on our own two feet and not rely on anyone else? Or was she saying it was dog eat dog on a station and we'd best be warned? I asked Judith what she thought. She said, "I expect it's like boarding school. You have to stand up for yourself, that's all."

The corporal emerged from her corner looking purposeful. "Pay attention," she called in ringing tones. "At 0800 tomorrow morning you will report to the gatehouse with your kit. You will be met by transport to take you to Gloucester Station and from there you will travel by train to Morecambe." A buzz of dismay broke out at the notion of having to lug the heavy kitbags across camp to the gate. Rebellious mutters of, "Why can't the transport drive over and pick us up?" were quelled by the corporal. "SILENCE!" The muttering died. She continued, "We always leave the camp as clean as when we found it. You, you and you," choosing three girls at random, "will go to the ablutions and clean the toilets. You four," again her finger pointed, "will clean the bathrooms. And don't forget the wash basins."

"Don't the other huts have to help?" asked one of the bathroom four. "They use the ablutions too."

"The others have been taking turns all week. Now it's your turn," snapped the corporal. "Get moving. AT THE DOUBLE!"

The corporal pointed downwards to the lino-covered floor. "The rest of you. I want this polished until I can see my face in it." She pointed at me. "You will do my bed space." And when we didn't rush to obey, "Go on. Get on with it. The polish won't put itself on."

On investigation we could only find one tin of polish, albeit a large one. We eyed the acres of floor glumly. Someone handed me the tin, "You'd better do hers first, or there'll be trouble." I had never polished a floor before. Mrs Blake did all that sort of thing at home. However, it didn't look difficult. Just wipe the polish on and rub up the shine. Conscious of the other girls waiting for the tin I went down on my knees by the corporal's bed, took a big dollop of polish and started to rub it into the linoleum.

"You're putting on too much," said a sharp-edged voice behind me, "you'll never get a shine on it like that." I looked up. Betty, the girl who had spoken, had sharp features that matched her voice. Her skin was pallid, her eyes pale. She said, "Move over and I'll show you." and dropped down beside me. Spreading the polish as thinly as possible, she began to rub the floor a small patch at a time. She was a skinny girl and looked frail but she was strong. I had a job to keep up with her. The corporal suddenly spotted what was happening and pointed out sharply that I was the one she had detailed to do her corner and nobody else. Betty was ordered back to her own space.

To get a really first class shine there was a heavy 'bumper', a block of wood with a long handle set at an angle, like a broom, to haul it backwards and forwards over the floor. It was an awkward thing to manoeuvre in the confined space in the corner. After a couple of clumsy attempts I gave up and completed the task by hand.

Out on the open floor they were making short work of the polishing, thanks to a girl called Pauline. If Pauline had not been captain of games at school she should have been. She was made for the job. Of athletic build, she was an attractive girl, with a fresh open-air complexion, a cheerful countenance and a very confident manner. She was also a born organiser. Within minutes she had divided the girls into teams, one to help themselves to polish from the tin and spread it over as wide an area as they could manage; the rest to act in concert, pushing and pulling the bumper until the floor shone like glass. We surveyed our handiwork with real satisfaction when we had finished. The corporal could find no fault with it.

Our domestic chores done, we packed our kitbags ready for the morning, then rounded off the evening with a sing-song organised by Pauline.

So much had happened it seemed much longer than two nights ago that Kay and I had sat and talked about our families. Even if I found her in Morecambe I knew it would not be the same. She would have made new friends in her squad and I had Judith in mine. Nevertheless, I hoped very much to come across her again.

Chapter 7
Getting Down to Basics

THE FIRST THING that struck me about Morecambe was the abundance of luscious cream cakes in the bakers' shop windows. We had not seen cakes like that at home for months - years. I can't recall ever buying one and eating it, just standing outside the windows drooling. Otherwise I have little recollection of the town, except where it acted as a backdrop to our training programme. As No. 3 WAAF Depot, it had virtually been taken over by the Air Force. Apart from the many hundreds of Waafs like ourselves, passing through on basic training courses, there was a large permanent staff looking after our welfare, mainly Admin, Medical and Accounts Sections. There were also numbers of airmen passing through.

New WAAF recruits were billeted on local landladies, filling each house to capacity. Judith, Betty and I were among ten or so girls billeted in a tall narrow house with dark echoing stairs winding up to the attics. On the top floor Judith and I were detailed to share a room in what had probably been the servants' quarters when the house was in its heyday. Betty and two other girls were sharing a larger room on the floor below. The bedrooms were furnished with good quality furniture and ancient single feather beds. After the iron mesh bedsteads and solid flat biscuits at the depot they felt like the last word in luxury. We also had the use of a comfortable sitting room.

Our landlady was a friendly, bustling woman aged about fifty. She turned out to be a very good cook and supper was ample by rationing standards. We were lucky. Other members of the squad, including Pauline, Jenny and Eileen, were billeted in a matching house next door, and they were not so fortunate. When the squad formed up outside in the street the following morning Pauline and Co. were most unhappy. During the night several of them had been bitten by fleas. Fleas! The word was passed up and down the ranks in whispered tones of horror. At the first opportunity Pauline organised a delegation comprised of those who had the most bites to show, and led them off to Admin to complain. They reported back that the Waaf sergeant had not been either surprised or impressed, implying that fleas were not uncommon. However, she organised the fumigation of all the beds and bedclothes. The landlady was furious, making angry remarks about sluts who had brought fleas into the house with them. The girls retaliated that there had never been any trouble with fleas at Innsworth, and relations between them deteriorated irretrievably. However, the landlady fed them adequately, if with an ill grace, and as Pauline said, that was really all that mattered once the beds were free of wildlife.

We spent our days square-bashing, doing PT (Physical Training) and attending lectures. The venues for these various activities were widely dispersed throughout the town and wherever we had to go we were marched there and back, whatever the weather. I thought all this marching was in the interests of discipline and fitness. Judith pointed out that it also helped to fill in the time while our documents were being processed and our future postings organised behind the scenes.

For a week or two I kept a lookout for Kay everywhere we went but without success. I never saw her again. At first I mourned the loss of my friend, but gradually she faded into a happy memory, one to enjoy, not grieve over.

Almost the first place we were marched to was the Medical

Section, based for the afternoon in a church hall. Here we were to receive our inoculations. We entered in some trepidation and were surprised to find the hall already part filled with airmen, who were there for the same reason. Our arrival was the signal for much squaring of masculine shoulders and macho posturing. Warriors going into battle could not have looked more heroic. Two tables manned by nurses were set up at one end of the hall. The men were lined up in front of one, the Waafs in front of the other. Orders were given for everyone to remove their jacket, roll up their left shirt sleeve and put their left hand on their hip. Manly voices changed to falsetto cries of "Oh, ducky!" Languid hands drooped from limp wrists all down the RAF line. The Waafs looked on with superior, indulgent smiles. The nurses unsheathed their syringes, an RAF sergeant bawled "Order in the ranks. Advance in single file." and we moved slowly forward. As each nervous victim passed their table a nurse swabbed a patch of bare arm and jabbed it with a syringe. The first few minutes were uneventful. Then an airman slid to the floor. The Waaf line tittered. Another man went down. Outright laughter from the weaker sex, followed by gales of mirth and jeers when a third man fainted. Not one Waaf passed out. We were too busy laughing at the men.

By evening, however, nobody felt like laughing. I forget what the injections were for, but they were powerful stuff. Nearly everyone suffered some sort of reaction. In our billet I think I was one of the least affected. I was unwell, but quite capable of getting out of bed. I can recall going down to the bathroom to fetch drinks of water for Judith, who felt far worse than I did, then crawling back into bed for warmth in the freezing bedroom. A WAAF MO with indifferent eyes toured the billets handing out 'chits' excusing us from duty for twenty-four hours. Several unfortunate girls who were really ill were transferred to a large hotel on the sea front doing wartime duty as a WAAF hospital.

A few days later a lump came up in my left armpit. It was sore but not really painful. I reported sick, the MO painted it with gentian violet and dismissed me. The lump continued to grow until it was about the size of an egg. It made my arm stiff and difficult to swing when we were marching. It was also beginning to throb. I went back to the MO, who repainted it with gentian violet and dismissed me again. As I was walking back to the billet, thoroughly fed up, I passed a row of large, impressive houses. One of them had a doctor's brass plate on the wall beside the gate. It gave the surgery times and there was one in progress at that moment. Without giving myself time to lose my nerve, I pushed open the front door and went in. Across the hall was a door marked Waiting Room. There were few people waiting. Two of them, an elderly man and a woman, stopped their conversation as I sat down and stared at me in hostile silence. I felt I was intruding and my courage wavered. If I had been able to think of anywhere else to go for help I think I would have fled.

The doctor was a heavily-built middle aged man, with a brusque manner. "I can't treat you," he said when my turn came. "You have your own medical facilities,"

"I know. But I've been to the MO twice. She doesn't do anything, and it's beginning to hurt."

Despite his manner he was a kindly man, unable to turn me away without enquiring, "What's the trouble?"

I told him I'd been inoculated, slipped my left arm out of my shirtsleeve and showed him my violet lump. His fingers probed it gently. "Don't worry, it's not serious."

He dabbed it with something icy cold and numbing, placed a kidney-shaped dish underneath it and picked up a scalpel. He said, "Look away," and made a quick movement. I did not feel anything, but I was nauseated when I saw what had spurted out into the bowl. He cleaned the incision, put a dressing on it and told me I could slip my sleeve back on.

"How much do I owe you?" I asked, praying it would not be more than I possessed.

He waved the question aside. "It only took two minutes. If you have any more trouble with it, come back and see me again." He opened the surgery door to show me out, hardly giving me time to thank him.

The cut healed within a day or two and I had no further trouble. But the incident bothered me. If the swelling was so simple to deal with, why hadn't the MO lanced it herself? Was she waiting for it to burst of its own accord? The thought of the resultant mess disgusted me. My opinion of MOs, fairly low since the FFI, sank even lower.

Square-bashing took place on the promenade. Expecting to encounter a replica of the elderly sergeant at the induction centre, it was a great relief on our first drill morning to find ourselves facing a friendly corporal, who looked to be in his late twenties. He was just as much a stickler for precision in all our movements as his Innsworth counterpart, but achieved results without bullying. He was even known to make a joke every now and then. His drill sessions were popular, and so was he.

Two or three times a week we had PT, stripped down to our shirts and regulation navy blues, our 'passion killers'. In dry weather we exercised on the promenade. This was fun when the day was mild, not such fun when the late March winds whipped in from the sea to freeze our bones. Earlier recruits must have caused quite a sensation, but by 1942 Morecambe was used to seeing half-dressed young women doing physical jerks in public, and mostly took no notice. Only the old men stayed to watch. Huddled together for warmth on the benches with the best view of the action, they dreamed of their youth and wished they could have it back. In wet weather they were deprived of their entertainment as we retired into the bus garage, a gloomy cavern of a place smelling of oil and old exhaust fumes. I never obeyed the instruction to "Breathe deeply," after choking on my first lungful of damp air behind the buses.

The lectures we attended were held in different halls, wherever there was a stage to speak from. One was held in a concert hall on the pier. This was the one place we did not march to but walked at our own pace. The order 'Break Step' was always given as we moved onto the pier; apparently the rhythm of marching feet could cause the structure to collapse.

The lectures were no doubt all very interesting and informative, but only the one on hygiene has stayed with me, because it made us laugh so much. It was given by an immaculately groomed young WAAF officer with a frightfully posh accent. She requested anyone who was going to be a waitress in the Officers' Mess not to use Lifebuoy toilet soap. She said the smell of it was unpleasant for the diners. Lifebuoy was always advertised as the cure for B.O. (Body Odour). Did the officers prefer the smell of nature in the raw? Our squad started to giggle. Fortunately we were seated at the back of the hall; we slid down out of sight behind the rows in front. The lecturer continued with hints for new Waafs. These included the useful information that saliva was excellent for setting hair if there was nothing else available. She also told us we should have a bath at least once a w eek and be sure to wash in all the nooks and crannies. By now even Judith, who was not normally given to unseemly behaviour, was rocking on her chair. The rest of us were stuffing hankies into our mouths to deaden the sound of our laughter. And from that time on a bath was always known amongst our little group as a 'crook and nanny'.

We heard mention of 'King's Regs' on several occasions. 'King's Regulations' was the Services bible. It had originated with the Army and been adapted for use by the Air Force. I was once told that somewhere among its myriad rules was one that stated: 'No airman shall sleep more than 'x' yards from his horse'. I forget the actual number quoted and have no idea if the story was true or 'duff gen'.

The most useful thing I learned at Morecambe was how to iron a shirt, and that had nothing to do with any lecture. One evening a week was designated 'Domestic Night', when we had to stay in and clean our rooms prior to an Admin inspection the following morning. We also had to do our own washing and ironing. My mother, like her mother before her, did all her ironing on the kitchen table, covering it with an old blanket topped with a sheet. I had never used an ironing board and the rickety contraption brought into the dining room for our use defeated me utterly the first time I used it. I needed three hands: one to hold the iron and two to prevent the shirt from sliding off the board on to the floor. I was taking so long that Betty, who was next in line for the iron, got impatient. "Haven't you ever ironed a shirt before?" she demanded. Shamefaced, I had to answer "No." At home I had ironed flat articles such as hankies and pillowcases, but I had never been entrusted with Father's shirts. Mother had always insisted on doing these herself, or had asked Mrs Blake to do them.

"Give it here," said Betty in exasperation, "and I'll show you." She elbowed me aside and did my ironing for me. "I don't know," she muttered to no one in particular, "Never polished a floor, never ironed a shirt." She turned to me, her pale eyes scornful, "Didn't you have to help at home at all? In our house we all had jobs to do and we couldn't go out on a Saturday until we'd done them."

Mortified, I thanked her for my shirts and escaped to the bedroom, feeling thoroughly inadequate. The following week I waited until everyone else had finished their ironing before doing mine so that I could acquire this new skill at my own pace, without Betty's sharp tongue to goad me.

Training pay was, if I remember rightly, ten shillings (50p) per week. With careful management this was sufficient to cover routine requirements such as writing materials, make-up, and those newly acquired necessities, cigarettes, with something left over for entertainment. Unfortunately careful management was not my strong point. A cup of tea in a canteen with Judith was about the best I could manage in the way of amusement. I was out with her one evening when we saw Jenny and her giggly friend Eileen with two young airmen. A lively foursome, they were heading for the end of the promenade where there were fewer people about. It was getting dark. Judith said, "I'm sure those aren't the same two boys they were with last time I saw them. They're a flighty pair."

"At least they know enough to keep out of trouble," I said. "I felt sorry for that sergeant, having to explain the facts of life to Jenny with ears flapping all round her."

Judith looked amused. "Yes, so did I."

She said it with such feeling that I asked. "Have you ever had to do that job?"

"Once or twice at boarding school. It was Matron's job really, but she was a bit of a battleaxe. Some of the girls were too scared to go to her for anything personal."

That was the second time she had mentioned boarding school. It was strange how little I knew about her background. From something I had overheard her saying to Pauline one day I guessed she had been at University but that was extent of my knowledge. She never mentioned her parents or her family. I was wondering whether to risk a personal question when she said warningly, "Look out, here comes Freda." As if obeying a silent drill command we left-wheeled smartly and crossed over the road to avoid her. Freda was in Pauline's billet next door, sharing a room with an amiable, if rather ineffectual girl called Penny. In civvy street she was in fact a Lady and Freda was making an absolute fool of herself over her, following her about and talking in a loud voice about "My friend Lady Penelope." She had even gone so far as to borrow a book from the poor girl, cover it with wrapping paper and write in large letters across the front, 'This book belongs to Lady Penelope So-and-So'. It went everywhere with her, making her the butt of jeering remarks and unkind comments. Pauline had done her best to make Freda see how embarrassing this had become for the hapless Penny, but she was wasting her breath. Freda had retorted, "You're just jealous," and carried on as before.

"Why on earth does Penny put up with that girl? I wouldn't," said Judith as we walked along, and I believed her. In Penny's shoes Judith would have dealt with such nonsense firmly yet tactfully, leaving Freda in no doubt that her attentions were unwelcome.

As the end of the course drew near, I felt restless and anxious to have done with all this preliminary training and get on with my real job, photography. I was bored with going to lectures and doing nothing but PT and drill. Above all I was bored with the interminable marching. My groans of protest were therefore as loud as anyone else's when it was announced that there was to be a parade through the town and we were to take part in it. There was to be a rigorous inspection beforehand, necessitating extra polishing of buttons, shoes and cap badges. Nothing less than perfection would be tolerated. Perhaps temper and resentment gave added strength to our elbows, for when we turned out on the day our buttons and badges glinted in the spring sunshine as they had never glinted before, and you could almost see your face in our shoes.

We were positioned behind a band, which gave us a good strong beat to march to, and this was exhilarating in itself. With arms swinging to the regulation height, our heads held high, and our eyes fixed firmly on the head of the person in front of us, we marched through the streets with all the splendid pride and assurance of a brigade of guards. All along the route spontaneous clapping broke out as we passed by. I could have marched for miles, basking in the applause.

The course ended with a passing-out parade, about which my memory is a blank, and the postings were announced. I was going to the No 2 School of Photography at Blackpool. Pauline was being sent on a mechanics course before joining a Motor Transport Unit as a driver. Driving was a popular trade and reputed to be very difficult to get into. Pauline had set her heart on it, and was delighted to have been accepted.

"Give her six months and she'll be running the section," I laughed to Judith.

"Give her half a chance and she'll be running the war," she replied. She herself was one of the very few who had been selected for a commission. I was sure she was pleased and proud in her unemotional way, but her only comment was, "It'll seem strange, being saluted." It was noted with interest that the Lady Penelope was not among those selected.

Back in our room at the billet, I got out my writing pad. "I suppose I'd better write home and tell them where I'm going," I said, as much to myself as to Judith.

"So must I," she said, "my aunt will be anxious for news."

"Your – aunt?"

"She's my guardian." Then, unusually for her, she added an explanation. "My parents died when I was young." Her voice was completely matter of fact.

I ventured a question, "What happened?"

"They had 'flu." Her tone of voice told me the conversation was now at an end. As if to confirm it she picked up her writing things and said, "It's freezing up here. I think I'll go down and see if there's a fire in the sitting room."

She didn't ask if I was coming and I had a feeling this was deliberate. She didn't want to be asked any more questions. I was being kept at a distance. Somewhat chastened, I thought over what she had said and suddenly recalled a time when I was six years old and my brother David was two, in 1929. We were standing in the doorway of our parents' bedroom, gazing at them still lying in bed although it was past getting up time. When we had opened the door, Father had lifted his head off the pillow and ordered us to stay outside. His voice sounded croaky, not a bit like his usual voice. Mother lay unmoving beside him and I was frightened. Father said in the same strange voice, "When Mrs Blake comes, tell her we've got 'flu."

Mrs Blake took charge with her usual efficiency, summoning a neighbour to phone for the doctor and send Nannie a telegram asking her to come and look after us. She was a dour woman who had no children of her own and thought other people's should be seen and not heard. Beyond giving us food at the correct times she took little notice of us, and that day was the longest and unhappiest day of my young life. Even the arrival of Nannie after tea did not make it come right. By that time I wanted my mother so badly nobody else would do.

Now, sitting on my bed at Morecambe over a decade later I tried to imagine what life would have been like if she and Father had both died and I never saw them again. Would David and I have gone to live with Nannie and Aunt Evelyn? That would have been bearable, if dull. Nannie was an old woman. But supposing we had been sent to one of Father's sisters, neither of whom we knew very well? And supposing she had sent us away to boarding school to live among strangers, with only an old battleaxe of a Matron to turn to for comfort if we were miserable? I didn't like to think about it. I might be finding my family ties constricting but with sudden insight I knew I didn't want to break free of them entirely. I would never be able to do that, they were too strong. I merely wanted to loosen them enough to let me be myself, not just Daddy's little girl. I had now achieved that freedom, I reflected happily, and I intended to enjoy it

Chapter 8

Welcome to Blackpool

"WHORE! Whore!"

Struggling up from the railway station with my kitbag over my shoulder, I heard shouts and the ugly sound of jeering on the other side of the street. I looked across. Half a dozen middle-aged civilians, men and women, were teetering on the edge of the kerb. They looked drunk. It was the men who were jeering. The women were shouting insults and shaking their fists. With a shock that knotted my stomach, I realised that the object of their abuse was me. One woman stepped off the kerb, the rest followed. They were coming over. I didn't know what to do. I couldn't abandon my kitbag and run. I would have to face them out and hope that some of the passers-by, who were carefully ignoring the situation, would come to my rescue.

Firm footsteps came up behind me. A WAAF corporal with a determined air of authority drew level and halted by my side. The civilians hesitated, the jeering and the insults faltered. The drunken group began to straggle back to the pavement. Disregarding them entirely the corporal asked, "Where to? Admin?" I nodded, my mouth too dry to speak. "I'm going that way," she said, "Come on." She caught hold of the bottom of my kitbag, easing it off my shoulder. I grasped the top end and together we manhandled it to Admin, where she left me. Neither of us had referred to the civilians as we walked along. In fact I can't recall that we spoke at all until I said, "Thank you, Corporal," and she surprised me by smiling and saying, "Good luck."

Having been checked in and told where to find my billet I hoisted up my kitbag once more and set off for Palatine Road, some distance away. The house was not as imposing as the one at Morecambe. It had a small neglected front garden and the usual gap in the front wall where a wrought iron gate had once stood. By this time thousands upon thousands of houses all over the country had lost their wrought iron gates and railings, ripped out and carted away by local councils as scrap metal to be recycled into warplanes.

I dragged my kitbag up the short concrete path to the front door. Here I stopped and listened. The civilians had shaken my confidence and made me nervous of my reception. I was hoping another Waaf would appear from somewhere to give me moral support. However, the house was silent. I would have to go in alone. The front door stood slightly ajar. Gathering my courage I rattled the knocker, pushed open the door and stepped inside. In the dim recesses at the back of the hall a door opened immediately, and a tall lady came out. On seeing me she bustled forward, smiling warmly. My confidence returned and I smiled back. I thought the lady was old, somewhere in her sixties. She had straight grey hair drawn back in a bun and her face was lined. She would have looked careworn but for her lively smile and her lively blue eyes. She said, "That's right, dear, come in. I'm Mrs Gilmore. Everyone calls me Mrs Gillie. I'll show you your room," and, gesturing towards the kitbag, "Can you manage?" I was tired and my arms were aching from lugging the wretched thing about. But I assured her brightly that I could, and followed her up the stairs, dragging the kitbag behind me and bumping it on every step.

"Supper will be ready soon. It's early tonight. We thought you'd all be hungry. My sister does the cooking. Her name's Rawson. Miss Rawson. Here we are." She threw open the door of a room very similar to the one I had shared with Judith in Morecambe.

There was the same heavy furniture and two comfy-looking beds. "That one's yours." She pointed, then stood in the doorway with her hands folded comfortably over her stomach, clearly ready to gossip. I untied the top of my kitbag, pulled out my spare uniform and hung it up in the empty half of the wardrobe. "That's right, dear, let the creases hang out." She gestured again to my kitbag. "Why they make you girls drag those heavy things about on your own, I don't know." She launched into what sounded like an oft-repeated catalogue of all the ills that could befall a woman in later life if she strained her insides in youth. I wished she would go away and leave me in peace to unpack, but she showed no sign of leaving until a voice from downstairs yodelled "Em - leee" on a rising note. Mrs Gillie said, "There now," with a satisfied air - her prediction about supper was being fulfilled. "Nearly ready. I must go and help." With a couple of cheery nods she shut the door and I heard her yodel back, "Com-ing," as she went downstairs.

I threw myself spread-eagled on the bed, exhausted, only to leap up again at the sudden recollection of Pauline and the fleas. Hastily I stripped the bed down to its feather mattress, shaking the bedclothes cautiously as I did so and heaping them on the floor. To my great relief nothing either hopped or jumped. I heard the door open behind me and turned to see a Waaf standing in the open doorway, staring at the chaos I had created in amazement. Like a naughty child caught out in mischief I said lamely, "They had fleas at Morecambe."

The girl made a face of disgust and came in, stepping carefully over my scattered bedclothes to sit on her bed. I could feel her watching me as I put mine together again. Not having found anything untoward I was regretting having panicked myself into pulling it to pieces in the first place. That done, I turned my attention to my new roommate. Conscious that I had ignored her since she came in, I apologised. She looked unconcerned.

She had an interesting face, plain but strong. Her smoky blue eyes exactly matched the colour of our uniform. Her thick fair hair was rolled off her face to make a halo round her head. Briefly I wondered how many hairgrips it took to keep it in place. (Later I discovered that she tied a shoelace round her head and rolled it round that.)

"I'm Yvonne," I volunteered.

"Are you French?"

"One of my grandmothers is." She nodded as if this explained my curious behaviour. "And you?" I asked.

"Gina."

"Italian?" I queried, not to be outdone.

"No. Dad's name is George and he wanted a boy." She left me to work my way from George to Georgina and shorten it to Gina for myself.

A little bell tinkled down in the hall and Mrs Gillie called "Supp - er" in a voice that made the bell superfluous. We stood up and straightened our skirts, ready to go down and meet our fellow inmates. I noted that Gina was not quite as tall as me and even in uniform she had an eye-catching figure. The kind that attracts whistles in the street.

The smell wafting up from the kitchen made my mouth water. As usual I was ravenous.

The dining room was in the front of the house, a pleasant room with a bay window that made it look larger than it was. There were six of us round the square table and I was disconcerted to see that Gina and I were the only new Waafs present. The other four obviously had months of service behind them. Three wore propeller badges on the arms of their jackets, indicating they were LACWs (Leading Aircraftwomen), the fourth girl was a corporal. I had expected to be among other trainees like myself, all of us still learning the ropes, and was conscious of disappointment to find myself with confident Waafs who were presumably based in Blackpool permanently.

Mrs Gillie bustled in from the kitchen bearing a tray laden with dishes of vegetables, followed by Miss Rawson carrying a large shepherd's pie. Mrs Gillie came in talking. "We're very lucky. Brother's got a smallholding. There's always plenty of veg." Miss Rawson gave a shy smile round the table as she helped dish up and said nothing. There was a strong family resemblance between the sisters. Apart from looking alike, they both radiated the same goodwill. Miss Rawson appeared to be the younger of the two; her hair had not yet turned completely grey and her face was not so lined as Mrs Gillie's. She gave the impression of being overshadowed by her loquacious elder sister.

Conversation was slow to start as we all tucked in, but picked up as the meal progressed. It emerged that the other girls were not permanent staff as I had thought, they were trainee photographers too, transferring from other trades. Their talk was all of the previous stations they had been on, and the hardships they had endured living in huts in the winter, especially the metal Nissen huts. "I think ours had been thrown together in a hurry," said one, who had apparently been up on the East Coast somewhere. "There were gaps between the panels you could drive a bus through. The wind whistled in and it was so cold at night we had to put our groundsheets over our beds for warmth."

"We had the same thing," said another girl, "and when it snowed it was nothing to wake up in the morning to find an inch of the stuff on your bed."

The others both had similar tales to tell. In fact I began to suspect they were trying to outdo one another in horror stories. "I must say it's marvellous to be living in a proper house for a change," said the corporal at last, and the others heartily agreed.

Gina and I, sitting next to one another and having no such experiences to relate, ate in silence. It was not until Mrs Gillie interrupted when she came in to clear away the dirty plates that the girl called Beryl, sitting opposite me, asked across the table, "I hope we're not putting you off?" and drew us into the conversation. Beryl was a buxom, untidy-looking girl. She had undone her jacket and discarded her collar and tie for comfort's sake. Her shirt buttons were strained to the limit of their endurance across her chest. Her dark curly hair framed her face in a wild mop. She had a cheerful gap-toothed smile and dark laughing eyes. She looked good-natured and easy going. When I got to know her better I found she also possessed sound common sense.

Miss Rawson brought in a big dish of stewed apple for pudding. Mrs Gillie followed with a large jug of custard. "It's not all milk, I'm afraid. Not like the old days," she apologised. As before, Miss Rawson smiled vaguely round the table and said nothing. Mrs Gillie was evidently the spokeswoman for both of them. She went on, "The sitting room is the next door along. I'm sorry there isn't a fire in there tonight as it's quite warm. We only light one if it's cold. There will be cocoa and something to eat at nine o'clock for anyone who wants it. Just knock on the kitchen door." There was a buzz of appreciation round the table and she beamed with satisfaction, then added, "If you're going out, don't forget you have to be back by half past ten. The SPs patrol the streets after that to make sure nobody's out late."

As soon as Gina had finished eating she excused herself from the table and left the room. Minutes later we heard the front door pulled to and watched her go down the garden path, through the empty gateposts and turn purposefully towards the sea front.

"Where's she off to, I wonder?" said a girl called Edna.

"Perhaps she's got friends here," suggested the corporal. She sounded indifferent. Edna looked put out at her lack of interest. I didn't take to Edna. Her sharp grey eyes were not friendly, the tight line of her mouth made her look ill-tempered and resentful. She also turned out to have a slanderous tongue.

The fourth girl, Irene, pushed back her chair and said, "I'm going out for cigarettes. Anyone want to come with me?" She was a small girl but with her lively manner she was never likely to be overlooked. Her high colour, red hair and sparkling green eyes warned of quick temper as well as high spirits.

Beryl said she'd go, and Edna said she'd got nothing better to do, she might as well join them. I went back to my room. I still had to finish emptying my kitbag, and I wanted to write a letter home. This done, I was at a loose end. Gina had not returned, unless she had come in and gone directly to the sitting room. I went downstairs to have a look.

The sitting room was not large, the comfortable chairs ranged round the unlit fire almost filled it. Only one was occupied, and not by Gina. The corporal sat with an open letter in her hand and I hesitated, feeling I was intruding. If I was, she didn't show it. She laid the letter down in her lap and said, "Come in," with a welcoming smile. I said, "Hello," and hesitated again, not knowing whether to address her as Corporal or not. Reading my thoughts she said, "I'm Sylvia," and indicated the chair next to hers. I had gathered over supper that she and Beryl were roommates and I couldn't imagine a more contrasting pair. Sylvia was as fair as the other was dark, with alert bright blue eyes and a slim figure. Her fair hair was trimmed well above her collar, her buttons shone and so did her shoes. If a snap inspection had been sprung on us she would have been ready for it, her turnout faultless. I noticed she wore an engagement ring, a small diamond solitaire in a plain setting. In time I learned that her fiancé's name was Ian. He was a Petty Officer in the Royal Navy, and as soon as they could organise their leaves to coincide they intended to get married.

At first I was slightly in awe of her stripes, but she proved easy to talk to and I asked her the question that had been puzzling me since supper. "How do you and the others come to be training as photographers when you already have a trade?"

She explained that they all came from trades that were full, or 'closed'. It was now Air Force policy to allow anyone in a closed trade to retrain for one that was still open if they wished to make a change. "It leaves vacancies for new recruits, gives them a wider choice."

"What trade were you in?" I asked.

"I was a driver," said Sylvia, which surprised me.

"I thought that was one of the most popular trades, and people were fighting to get into it?" I said, thinking how pleased Pauline had been to be accepted.

"It is. And while I was driving I enjoyed it. But once I got my stripes I was stuck inside doing paperwork most of the time. I got browned off."

Poor Pauline, I thought. Mad keen to be a driver, but an obvious NCO in the making. Would she end up in a desk job after all?

My opinion of corporals was undergoing a change. During the last six or seven weeks I had tended to regard them as a breed apart, specially selected for their loud voices and ability to shout orders. Now, twice in one day, I had come across corporals who didn't fit the pattern. This one was friendly and seemingly quite unconscious of her rank. The tough-looking girl who had stopped to help me earlier on and wished me luck had also shown a softer side to her character. I described the ugly little incident with the civilians to Sylvia.

"I've come across their attitude before," she said, "but nothing as bad as that. You were unlucky. The trouble is that up until now servicewomen have all been volunteers, and a lot of people saw us as camp followers, no better than we should be. They'll soon change their tune when their own daughters are called up – as they will be once conscription gets under way."

The three cigarette hunters returned and came in to join us until nine o'clock. Time for the promised bedtime snack. Miss Rawson must have been listening out for us, she opened the kitchen door before anyone had time to knock. "The kettle's almost boiling," she said with her shy smile. She handed out a pile of plates, a bowl of sugar and a plate of bread and scrape. "Would you take these through and put them on the table for me? There's enough for two slices each. It's only margarine, of course, but it tastes alright when you sprinkle it with sugar." I hadn't eaten bread and sugar since I was a small girl. In recent times the sugar ration wouldn't run to it, anyway. "My sister and I don't take sugar," explained

Miss Rawson. "You might as well have the benefit." Gina was still out. "Only five for cocoa, is that right? You go in and I'll bring it in a minute."

Mrs Gillie was nowhere to be seen, which probably explained why her sister had been forced to do the talking. While waiting for the cocoa we helped ourselves to our bread and sugar and put a plate over Gina's two slices to keep them fresh. A few minutes later Miss Rawson came in with mugs of cocoa on a tray, smiled vaguely round as she had done at supper, and left without a word. Evidently she only felt able to speak when she was in her own domain, the kitchen.

"Where do you reckon they get all this sugar from? I'll bet it's black market," said Edna, almost before Miss Rawson was out of earshot.

"Didn't you hear her say it was their own ration?" snapped Irene. I didn't envy her, having to share a room with Edna, but thought she looked more than capable of putting her sour-faced roommate in her place.

Gina came in just before Mrs Gillie locked the door for the night. They met in the hall and stood talking for several minutes. I heard Mrs Gillie give a sudden laugh and Gina came into the dining room smiling. Fishing for information, Edna asked, "Have you been down at the front?" Gina said, "No." She said it quite pleasantly but managed to make it clear that she was not going to answer any more questions. Edna looked at her with dislike, aware she had been snubbed. I thought Gina might be more communicative when we got up to our room, but she wasn't and I forbore to ask questions. I did not want to risk being snubbed like Edna.

Our course started next day and lasted about fourteen weeks. It was not only the girls from our billet who had re-mustered from other trades. Rookie trainees like Gina and myself were in the minority. The School was housed in a single storey building further up Palatine Road. The syllabus included lectures on everything from the history of photography and the development of the camera to the practicalities of taking aerial photographs. The building had once been a council school. The lectures took place in the old classrooms and we sat at the original desks. It was like going back to childhood. We even had homework. It had to be given in every morning for marking, and in case anyone was tempted to ignore it, we were warned that the marks would all count towards our eventual pass - or failure - at the end of the course.

As well as theory there was a good deal of practical work. I met again my old friend the camera in the grey metal housing, and learned that it was used for photographic reconnaissance. I found that it did not have to be loaded or unloaded in complete darkness, as I had assumed at West Drayton. The film darkroom was lit by a dim green bulb and it was quite easy to see what you were doing once your eyes became adjusted to the eerie light.

Printing was far more of a challenge. In a second darkroom, this time lit by a red bulb, the negatives had firstly to be assessed for quality then printed on the appropriate grade of paper, hard, normal or soft, whichever would give the clearest prints. This was supremely important, as it was the prints, not the film, that would be sent to Intelligence for interpretation. We therefore practised printing films taken under every sort of condition, from bright sunlight to heavy cloud, at high noon or at twilight, until we could produce a batch of prints on the right paper quickly, without wasting too much time on trial and error. The film we used for practice had mostly been taken over rural areas – fields, woodland and farms. Laid out in sequence the prints made a map of the district and the exercise was a useful test of the pilot's skill. If he did not hold the plane steady at the correct height the prints did not match one another.

We also developed cine film from the cameras attached to the guns. This showed what the gun had been aiming at when it was fired, an enemy plane if the shooting was accurate, empty sky if it wasn't.

I can only remember three of the instructors, all RAF flight sergeants. Flt Sgt Jordan was tall and blond and good looking, with a pleasant if slightly impersonal manner. To avoid raising any false hopes about his availability, he let it be known that he had a permanent girlfriend and was not interested in anybody else. In any case the instructors did not go out with their pupils. Flt Sgt Burdon was a big, hearty man with a huge laugh and he took the mickey out of me unmercifully. It was his habit to begin his lectures by reading out the best of the homework essays from the previous lecture. When he came to mine he would announce, "And now we come to Ethel M. Dell," (a well known romantic novelist of the day). And getting to his feet he declaimed my wordy prose in a melodramatic voice, with all the exaggerated theatrical gestures of the old-time stage actors. It never failed to reduce me to helpless giggles and had the rest of the class nearly falling off their chairs with laughter. The third one, Flt Sgt Chapman, known as 'Chappy', was different again. Not very tall and slightly built, he was older than the others with the settled air of a family man. He had dark wavy hair and two deep lines running down his face, one on either side of his mouth. He was a popular instructor, friendly and always helpful.

Officially, Blackpool was an RAF Station. Many hundreds of airmen and Waafs passed through it each year on courses of one sort or another. There was also a large contingent of the Polish Air Force stationed there. In addition several Government departments had been evacuated to the town and had requisitioned many of its hotels for their staff. It did not seem possible that there would be room to accommodate the yearly influx of holidaymakers as well. Nevertheless, as soon as the mill towns began shutting down for their annual Wakes Week break, the workers flooded the town in huge numbers, almost beyond its capacity to cope. When we first arrived in May all the cafés had notices in their windows saying "Services Welcome". But when the holiday season started the notices were changed to, "No Services".

It was not only the café owners who changed their attitude. We were sitting round the dining room table doing our homework one evening when there was a sudden commotion next door. An angry voice shrieked something incoherent from an upstairs window; something thudded to the ground. Beryl and I, being seated nearest the bay window, were the first to reach it and look out, the others close behind us. Clothes and shoes were raining down into the small front garden. As one we rushed outside. The landlady was pitching the girls' belongings out of the front bedroom window. Personal possessions as well as uniforms were dropping onto a growing heap below. A camera bounced off the pile and crashed onto the concrete path. A picture followed, there was the sound of breaking glass. Several girls came staggering out of the front door laden with armfuls of whatever they had been able to save from the clutches of the harridan upstairs.

We surged out into the street, meaning to go and help. Two SPs, one a Waaf, the other RAF, were standing on the pavement, watching. They barred our way and ordered us back inside. Astounded, nobody moved. "Why don't you stop her?" demanded Sylvia in a voice I had not heard her use before.

"We can't. She's a civilian. Out of our jurisdiction," said the Waaf SP,

"You could at least let us go in and help," protested Sylvia, but they ignored her. Irene stormed, "Standing there like dummies!" The RAF SP squared his shoulders and confronted us. "Inside. NOW," he barked. Reluctantly we backed into our own billet to watch from the doorway in frustrated anger. The landlady continued to throw out whatever she could lay her hands on. The girls, one or two with furious tears coursing down their cheeks, brought out all they could and started sorting out their jumbled belongings in the garden. All of them were too burning with rage to care what they said and gave as good as they got in abuse before the woman finally locked them out. A truck came to collect them and that was the end of the matter as far as we knew. Our neighbours were civilian holidaymakers for the rest of the time we were there.

It was our good fortune that our two warm-hearted landladies continued to treat us like family. We were a happy billet. Which is not to say there was never a cross word spoken. Edna's sour tongue grated on us all at times and Irene, her hot-tempered roommate, was never slow to let her know it. Sylvia was the peacemaker, who intervened to restore calm when they fell out. Beryl just laughed and let them get on with it.

Gina continued to go out immediately after supper every evening and did not return until Mrs Gillie was about to lock the door. She scribbled her homework in the short interval between dismissal and supper, sitting on her bed with her book on her knees. If necessary she finished it before breakfast the following morning. As might be expected, she got the lowest marks in the class for her written work, which did not bother her in the slightest. I asked her one morning, "Aren't you afraid you'll fail the course?"

"No," she said confidently, "they won't fail me."

"How can you be so sure?"

"Listen," she said, "When we get on a section, no one's going to give a damn whether we know how the pilot sets for drift in a wind, or who invented the pinhole camera. All they're going to care about is - can we do the work? And I can." Which was true. She had a good eye for the all-important printing and got high marks for all her practical work. I admired her for having the courage of her convictions and hoped for her sake that her logic didn't let her down.

When she came in at night she often went straight up to our room without speaking to anyone else. Inevitably she became an outsider in the billet. She was also the subject of speculation, especially by Edna. Where did she go? What was she doing? And why was she so secretive about it? Edna was convinced she was a prostitute. The other three girls were dubious. Gina had never been seen hanging about the streets. Indeed she had never been seen anywhere. She left the billet before anyone else had finished supper and virtually disappeared. As we heard the front door close behind her one evening Edna proposed we follow her to find out where she went and what she was up to. It was clear from the look on the faces of the others that they found the idea as distasteful as I did. Sylvia said, "It's really none of our business," and Irene said irritably, "So don't keep going on about it." However, Edna would not let the subject drop. She rounded on me aggressively, "You're her roommate. You must know where she goes." I shook my head, but Edna persisted. "She must have said something."

My temper, which had been rising for some time, finally boiled over. "No, she hasn't. And even if she had I wouldn't tell you. So shut up about her," I snapped.

On domestic nights, when Gina had to stay in like everyone else, and I had a chance to chat to her, she talked quite freely about her home and her life in civvy street. This was so different to my own that I listened spellbound. By day she had been a clerk in the local council offices, but by night she was a singer with a dance band.

"A famous one?" I asked eagerly when she told me.

"Only locally," she laughed. She had been with them since she was sixteen, travelling to gigs all over Yorkshire at the weekends. I learned a great deal about her life on the road with 'the boys'. As a matter of fact I learned a lot about life in general from Gina, far more than I had ever learned at my mother's knee. From some of the things she told me I suspected she was no innocent little virgin. But that did not mean Edna was right, I assured myself. I disliked Edna so much I would have loved to be able to prove her wrong. Once or twice I had been tempted to ask Gina outright where she went each evening, but had never done so. I sensed she had no intention of telling me. So I continued to seethe on my roommate's behalf, knowing even as I did so that I was being silly.

If Gina was prepared to put up with Edna's snide remarks and innuendoes rather than satisfy our curiosity, why should I worry?

Apart from the irritation I felt with Edna, I would have been perfectly happy in the billet but for one thing – shortage of money. Blackpool was the entertainment capital of the north. All the top Variety stars played there, its ballrooms were famous. The legendary illuminations had been switched off for the duration of the war and the Golden Mile was dark, but the Pleasure Beach was still open for business in daylight hours. There was always something to do, somewhere to go as long as you had money.

The girls who had remustered were all being paid according to their rank in their previous trade. They could afford to go out in the evening more often than I could. I was still on a trainee's meagre rate of pay. If they were all out at once, I found myself alone in the house. I didn't mind too much at first. I was behind with my letter-writing and I took the opportunity of catching up.

However, once I had brought my correspondence up to date and had nothing left to write about, I quickly became bored with my own company and thoroughly fed up with feeling like Cinderella. There didn't seem to be anything I could do to improve the situation and I would probably have become resigned to it if it had not been for Sylvia. A top class Variety show had opened at one of the theatres and everyone was mad keen to see it. The four girls from our billet were planning to make up a party with others on the course and all go together one evening. There was much laughter and excited talk over the supper table as they discussed the arrangements. I kept quiet until Irene asked me if I were coming too. I was going through one of my penniless phases at the time and I had to say "No". Nobody asked why, or tried to persuade me to change my mind. In a way I was thankful for that, though it made me feel unwanted. Gina wasn't even asked. She left the table almost before she had finished her last mouthful of pudding and went out as usual. As soon as the meal was over I went up to my room, where I could let my face look as miserable as I felt.

After some minutes there was a tap on the door and Sylvia came in. I was sitting on my bed with my legs curled under me. She sat on the edge of Gina's bed, facing me, and said diffidently. "Look, please don't take offence, but – is it money that's the problem?" I was unprepared for the direct question and unable on the spur of the moment to think of any other reason for not going with them. I nodded. She hesitated, then went on, "Will you come as my guest? Please."

I stared at her, not knowing what to say. I was torn two ways. On the one hand I was not happy about being a charity case, on the other she looked so genuinely concerned it seemed churlish to refuse. Besides, I badly want to see the show.

"Do come," she urged, and abandoning my pride I said, "Thanks. I'd love to."

"Good!" she smiled. "I'll tell the others." She stood up briskly and went out, leaving me feeling like Cinderella again, but this time after the fairy godmother had told her she could go to the ball.

The show was as good as its publicity, we had a marvellous evening. It was not until afterwards that I gave thought to the weeks ahead. Although no one had commented on my change of mind, I was certain they knew what Sylvia had done and were being tactful. Next time I stayed behind when they went out, I thought, everyone would know I was broke again and we would all be embarrassed. Or I would, anyway. Also, having had a taste of the high life, I could not face going back to sitting alone in the evening. I had to get hold of some extra money, but how? Reluctantly I came to the conclusion that the only way I was going to solve my problem was to go cap in hand to my parents.

One of the last things Father had said to me on Paddington Station was, "Don't forget. If you're ever in any trouble, get in touch with me. You've got my office number, haven't you?" I was not sure what sort of trouble he was talking about, but to me my money problem was important enough to warrant a phone call. It was not until I was in the telephone box at dinnertime next day with his number in front of me, ready to dial, that I realised I only had enough money for a local call – and Llandudno was not local. What I ought to have done was go back to the billet and write him a letter. What I actually did was put the call through and reverse the charge. The concern in his voice when he asked me what was wrong vanished when I told him why I was phoning. In frozen tones he said, "I'll put some money in the post this evening," and rang off.

I thought he was annoyed that after all my blather about being independent I had come to him for money. I was taken aback by his cold angry reaction. I felt very uncomfortable and awaited his letter with apprehension. A few days later it was waiting for me at the billet when we came in after dismissal. I scooped it up and ran upstairs to the bedroom to read it in private. Inside were three pound notes tucked into a small folded sheet of notepaper. This was far more than I had hoped for and I was overcome with relief and gratitude for his generosity.

His letter gave me no clue to his feelings when he wrote it, but his letters always sounded like government memos, so this was nothing unusual. Mother was the letter-writer of the family. She sent me all the family news and I replied with all mine, which she passed on to Father. We rarely communicated direct. Now I wrote him an almost effusive letter of thanks and thought no more about it.

Months later Mother told me that Father only expected me to contact him if I was in really serious trouble, not just broke. And even then, it was strictly against civil service rules to accept personal reverse charge calls. Having done so he had received what amounted to an official reprimand. I don't think he ever quite forgave me.

Chapter 9

Stepping Out

THE GIRLS FROM the billet preferred the Tower Ballroom to the Empress when they went dancing, I don't know why. They went as a group, taking over one of the tables under the balcony as a base to come back to between dances. On the first occasion I went with them I sat at the table and gazed around me wide-eyed. Nothing at Miss Murphy's Dancing Academy had prepared me for the Tower. I marveled at the sheer size of the place, the tiered balconies, and the gilt and plush decoration. The rhythm of the band generated an excitement I was not sure Miss Murphy would have approved of. And the dancing! She certainly would not have approved of the jitterbug, a wild new craze sweeping in from America. It was light years away from the measured steps we had taken round the floor in time to Victor Sylvester. It took me a little while to adapt to the freer style of dancing in vogue and I never was much good at the jitterbug. Unlike Irene who was a star performer. I sat lost in wonder and admiration as her partner tossed and twirled her to the beat of the music, her red hair flying. The more acrobatic movements of the jitterbug were not officially allowed, on the grounds of safety. Irene and her partners usually kept to the rules but every now and then, if the floor was not too crowded, they abandoned themselves to the insistent rhythm and gave what turned into an exhibition dance in the middle of the floor. It brought the other dancers to a standstill as they drew back to watch and enjoy the performance before management moved in to put a stop to it.

I was standing by one of the balcony pillars one evening, watching one of these displays and jigging my feet in time to the beat, when a voice beside me said, "Will you dance?" I turned to find a young airman smiling at me. He had a broad smile that lit up his eyes, which were chestnut brown. I couldn't help smiling back. He jerked his head towards Irene and her partner, "I'm afraid I don't do that."

I said, "Oh good, neither do I," and followed him beyond Irene's audience to a clear patch of floor. He was three or four inches taller than me and sturdily built. His hair was a rich brown and straight, with what my mother called a 'cow's lick' over his left temple, a contrary tuft that would not lie down. It made him look very young, although he turned out to be a year older than I was. We danced well together and when the dance ended we remained where we stood, exchanging personal information. His name was Paul. I already knew by the white flash at the front of his forage cap, which he had tucked into the belt of his tunic, that he was training for air crew. I asked him what as, and he replied, "Wop A G" (Wireless Operator/Air Gunner) and he was in Blackpool learning Morse. After the second dance he came back with me to our table. Beryl was lounging back on one of the chairs. The top button of her jacket was undone and she had loosened her tie. At some point she had run a hand through her unruly dark hair, making it look even more like a mop than usual. She was listening with every sign of interest to an earnest young airman who appeared to be telling her his life history. She looked up when Paul and I joined them and studied him coolly before accepting him with a warm smile. Like many large people, Beryl was light on her feet and a good dancer. She had no difficulty getting partners but seemed just as happy to sit and talk to them as dance. I asked her one evening what she found to talk about. "Their girlfriends and their wives, mostly," she replied with a grin. "They treat me like an older sister."

Sylvia came back to the table a few minutes later followed by a young airman who was probably hoping she would forget her engagement ring for the time being and allow him to escort her back to the billet at the end of the evening. Beryl smiled at him vaguely, knowing he hadn't a hope. Sylvia enjoyed dancing, but never made a boyfriend, even a temporary one, of any of her partners. If they wanted to see her again she insisted they meet her inside the ballroom and said goodnight to them there when the dancing ended. Beryl always made sure her roommate was not left to walk back to the billet alone. Few of Sylvia's partners lasted more than a couple of evenings, but there were plenty of boys ready to take their place.

Discounting Gina, who did not feel like one of us at all, Edna was the odd one out in the group. She was tolerated, not popular. I don't think she particularly enjoyed going to the Tower, but it was preferable to being left behind on her own. A feeling I could sympathise with wholeheartedly. She did not attract partners as easily as the other girls, and even when she did she did not keep them long. She had never mastered Beryl's conversational technique with the boys. "They're all only after one thing," she would grumble. "It's not worth trying to talk to them."

I knew the girls were weighing Paul up and felt uncomfortable on his behalf until I realised he was doing the same to them, quite unabashed. When we got up to dance again he whispered, "Did I pass muster?" and his eyes shone with laughter. I said defensively, "We look after one another," and he replied, "Quite right too."

We arranged to meet again the following evening. I had homework to do and could not get away until mid evening. Beryl was in the hall as I went out. She stopped me and said, "Don't do anything I wouldn't do." and I gave her the usual flippant answer, "That should leave me plenty of scope."

"Never mind about plenty of scope. Just you keep out of trouble. Remember, nothing below the waist."

I was shocked. According to my convent upbringing 'below the waist' was an area not to be spoken of out loud. It was best not even to think about it. Paul and I had only met the previous evening. Surely she didn't seriously think we would venture into the forbidden territory on so short an acquaintance? If she did, where on earth did she think we would do it? There was nowhere private enough to do much more than kiss on these light evenings. With double summer time in operation it didn't get dark until quite late. Waafs and airmen were forbidden to enter each other's billets, and landladies saw to it that the rules were strictly adhered to. Quiet walks into the lovely countryside surrounding Blackpool were out of bounds. We were not allowed beyond the outer limits of the 'station', and SPs patrolled to make sure we did not stray. We could walk in Stanley Park, but any couple seen heading in that direction were assumed to be 'at it', especially if one of them carried a groundsheet. The girl immediately lost her reputation. Which only left the sands under the South Pier. The goings on there were notorious and the place was not even private.

It was too late to do anything else than walk along the promenade and talk. "Have you got a boyfriend?" asked Paul after a while.

"No. I wasn't allowed to mix with boys until I left school and by that time they were all disappearing into the Forces. What about you? Have you got a girlfriend?"

We were leaning on the promenade rail watching the tide come in. Paul did not reply at once and I knew the answer was "yes", but he didn't say that. He said, "There's a girl I've known since we were kids. It's sort of understood - " he stopped.

Politely I asked, "Is she in the Forces too?"

"Not yet. But she will be soon," he said dully, obviously not liking the idea. I wondered why, but did not feel I knew him well enough to ask.

The incoming waves were demolishing a sandcastle some child had built earlier. I saw the citadel fall while I waited to see if he would say any more about his girlfriend, but he clearly did not want to talk about her. We left the rail and strolled on. Later, back at the billet, I lay on my bed and stared at the ceiling, thinking. What was a 'sort of' understanding? It hardly sounded like one of the world's great romances. Or were there depths to the affair that he did not wish to reveal to someone he had only just met? Either way, I felt I had been warned not to take him too seriously. Fair enough. At least he had been honest and I liked him the better for it. I had agreed to meet him again.

Paul's course only had a few more weeks to run; we had to make the most of every opportunity to meet. Neither of us had much money as Paul was also on training pay. Father's £3 was a godsend, though I had great difficulty persuading Paul to let me use it, even occasionally. We went to the Tower Circus and like two big kids we gripped each other's hands in suspense during the high wire acts and laughed until it hurt at the clowns. We had a great time at the Pleasure Beach, and once he took me to a place where we could enjoy a bit of snogging – the back row of the stalls at one of the cinemas. Here the seats were double width and the usherette never shone her torch along the row. I had to keep Paul's girlfriend very firmly in mind on that occasion or I might have been tempted to let things go further than they did.

For the rest of the time we walked along the prom, explored the fascinating streets behind it with their beckoning sideshows and exhibitions, and sat in canteens and talked. Over mugs of stewed tea I learned that his family lived in New Brighton. He was the younger of two children, his sister Louise being two years his senior. Their mother had been a widow for many years; he hardly remembered his father. Louise, whom he called Lou, had married very young. Her husband was in the Merchant Navy. She was pregnant when his ship was torpedoed and sank with all hands. Lou had left her rented flat and gone back home to have the baby. Living with her mother had worked out so well for all of them that she had stayed on permanently.

"And the baby?" I asked.

Paul smiled fondly. "A girl. Susie. She's two now. Bright as a button and a right little madam."

The one person he never mentioned was his girlfriend. I took this to mean that our friendship was the equivalent of a peacetime holiday romance and once he was posted the affair would be over.

When I told him about life in Finchley I played down my difficulties with my father. Compared with Louise's problems mine seemed insignificant. Paul was very impressed by David's work with the ARP, acting as a messenger. He said admiringly, "It must take nerve to cycle through shrapnel."

"Yes, but if he's scared he never lets on. His main fear is that the war will be over before he can join in."

"I was just the same," said Paul. "I'd done two years of a three year engineering degree course but I didn't wait to do the third one. I'll have to go back and finish it after the war."

The weeks passed quickly. Paul made no arrangement to meet me on the night his course results were to be announced. The boys were going to celebrate their success – or drown their failure – with a booze-up somewhere, men only. On the following evening I waited for him at our usual place on the prom, and as soon as I saw him coming I knew he had passed: he looked so pleased with himself. As we sauntered along his talk was all about the course results; who had passed, who had failed and, finally, where they were going next. "Yatesbury. More Morse. This was just the basics. Now we have to work up to operational speed."

"When do you go?"

There was a short silence. When he replied it was in an altered tone of voice, knowing I might not like the answer. "Tomorrow morning, first thing."

"Then this is our last date?" I could not help feeling dejected.

Paul said comfortingly, "We can keep in touch. You will write to me, won't you?"

Slightly surprised by the earnestness of his tone I said, "OK," trying to sound bright and positive.

He said with a forced cheerfulness, "How about going for a drink? I know just the place; we were there last night."

He took me to a small pub in a side street, furnished with an odd assortment of chairs and tables. Paul led the way to a high-backed settle standing against the back wall. "Have you ever been in a pub before?" he enquired as I looked about me.

"No. At home this would have been unthinkable."

"You'd better stick to a half of mild, then."

The place was fairly busy; several women who all seemed to know one another were perched on high stools along the front of the bar, their menfolk and friends stood around them in groups, talking loudly and laughing a lot. Holidaymakers presumably. Paul pushed his way between them, bought our drinks and returned to sit beside me. "Cheers," he said, raising his pint in salute. I did the same and we both took a swig of beer. I grimaced and Paul laughed. "You'll get used to it," he promised. Then, "I'll give you my new address. Have you got anything to write on?" When I said "No" he took an envelope from his top pocket and extracted the letter. This he returned to his pocket, taking care not to crimple it. He opened out the envelope and tore it in half. Digging into his side pocket for a stub of pencil, he wrote his number and new station on one half and added his home address "in case we lose touch at any time." I wrote my number and home address on the other half and we swapped. "But I warn you," said Paul, "I'm no great shakes as a letter-writer."

He had returned the letter to his pocket so carefully that I was convinced it was from his girlfriend. He had still not mentioned her since the evening he told me about their 'sort of' understanding' – I did not even know her name. I had managed to ignore her existence for most of the time, but now she came into my mind and I could not get her out. The pub was filling up. The atmosphere was cheerful and noisy, but I was quiet and depressed. For the first time since we met I had nothing to say. I was aware of being very dull company. Paul bought more drinks, but they failed to enliven the evening. We left the pub earlier than we need have done and walked back towards the billet in silence. An invisible curtain had come down between us. We had nothing to share any more.

Suddenly he turned to me and said solemnly, "I want you to promise me something."

"I don't like making promises unless I know what they are," I said cautiously.

"I want you to promise you won't do - it - with anyone," he said.

My hackles rose. I was not his girlfriend. We had no understanding, 'sort of' or any other kind. What I did or did not do was my own affair. I asked sharply, "Why do you want me to promise that?"

"If you could hear the men in the barracks, the way they talk about the girls they've had and pass their names around, you wouldn't ask. I'd hate to think of anyone talking about you like that."

It shook me. I had had no idea what went on behind the scenes. I was also touched by his concern. I had no intention of doing – it – with anybody but to put his mind at rest I gave him my promise with a solemnity that matched his own.

At the door of the billet we stood looking at one another. Paul took my hand and pulled me towards him. He put his arms round me, held me close and kissed me. It was a different sort of kiss to those he had given me before. It was exciting and, having drunk more than the half pint originally recommended, I felt light-headed. I kissed him back with equal fervour. Two soldiers passing by on the other side of the street saw us clinging together and stopped to whistle and catcall. I broke away and Paul said something blasphemous under his breath. He moved to kiss me again, but the spell was broken, I held back and said tartly, "I don't think your girlfriend would like this."

He dropped his arms. He looked first wretched then annoyed.

"Look – "

I interrupted, "We had a lot of fun. Thanks for everything," and turned to go in. He gripped my arm to stop me. The soldiers whistled and shouted explicit advice and encouragement. Paul swore again. I wrenched my arm away angrily, slipped into the billet before he could stop me and slammed the door in his face.

Upstairs I flung myself on my bed and gave way to angry tears. I was furious with Paul. I had enjoyed our time together so much and now it was spoiled.

As he had seemed so anxious that we should keep in touch, I hoped – expected – that he would write to try and restore our light-hearted relationship. But days passed and no letter came. I snapped Gina's head off one night when she asked if I had heard. Then, sorry for what I had done, I told her what had happened, why I was so upset.

"You were a bit hard on him, weren't you? It was only a kiss, after all," she pointed out.

"I know, but it was different. I didn't expect him to turn serious. I was confused."

"If you ask me you weren't the only one," said Gina sagely.

Mindful of her criticism, I took all the blame for our ill-tempered goodbye on myself and wrote to say I was sorry for spoiling his last evening in Blackpool. I told him I blamed the beer, adding with a touch of malice, "You should not have given me the second (or was it the third?) half pint. I don't think I have a good head for drink!"

Days passed again before he replied. As always, I took the letter upstairs to read. He had spoken the truth when he said he was no great shakes as a letter-writer. In stilted phrases he thanked me for my letter and apologised for the delay in getting in touch, though he did not explain it, except to say he had been very busy; the course was very hard work. He hardly mentioned our disastrous last meeting, merely saying that he too blamed the beer. I was painfully disappointed. I had wanted something more, some assurance that he had enjoyed our time together as much as I had. However, he did say that when this course was finished they would be moving on to do a gunnery course. He would let me have his new address and he hoped I would write again. This cheered me a little. At least we were still on speaking terms.

Chapter 10

Moving On

WE WERE NOW near the end of our course, with nothing to worry us but our final marks. Until, that is, an Admin sergeant called at the billet one morning. We were in the middle of breakfast. We heard her go along to the kitchen and exchanged uneasy glances. Minutes later she came through to the dining room to announce, "You are being moved to another billet nearer the school."

"When?" asked Sylvia.

"After supper this evening. I will be back at 1830 to escort you."

The minute she left there was a concerted rush for the kitchen to see Mrs Gillie, but she had no further information for us. All she knew was that there would be six airmen coming in to take our place when we had gone. Looking at our woebegone faces she tried to be consoling. "You'll still be together, after all, and you'll probably be just as happy there as you have been here."

"I doubt it," said Beryl. So did we all. The two sisters had made this billet into a real home for us. Could we possibly be so lucky again?

We packed our kitbags before supper, which was a gloomy meal. Even Mrs Gillie was subdued. Almost before we had finished eating the sergeant was back, hustling us out into the street at the double. Mrs Gillie and Miss Rawson came out to see us off. As always when they were together, Mrs Gillie spoke for both of them, "Goodbye, my dears, and good luck." The sergeant set off up the road, and we straggled along in her wake, weighed down by our heavy kitbags. We hadn't gone far before I realised Gina was not with us. I turned round to see where she was and saw her talking to our erstwhile landladies on the front path. They all had their heads together as if they shared a secret, and they were laughing. Mrs Gillie saw me watching them and waved. She said something to Gina, who drew away and followed the rest of us up the road. Mrs Gillie gave me a last wave and she and Miss Rawson went back into the house to prepare for the lucky airmen who were coming to take our place. I didn't wait for Gina. I had long ago accepted that she never explained her actions and we would only have walked along in constrained silence.

Our new billet was a tall house reminiscent of the one at Morecambe. There were steps up to the front door, which bore a notice, 'Wipe your feet'. The sergeant stood on the top step and waited for her cheesed-off followers to catch up. Little Irene was the one having the hardest struggle. Edna, who was a strapping girl, reached the steps first. She leaned her kitbag against them and went back to give her roommate a helping hand. To me Edna was just a pain, but perhaps there was another side to her that I was unable to appreciate. When we were all assembled the sergeant pushed open the door and led us inside. We were in a rectangular hall with several doors leading off it, each one bearing a notice of its own. "Your rooms are right at the top" said the sergeant, and started up the stairs. Resigned to a hard climb we dragged our kitbags after her. Struggling up through the house we passed more notices: 'Bathroom' with a list of times when hot water would be available, and 'No Smoking' on some of the bedroom doors. The others were marked 'Private'. There were only three rooms on the top floor; the sergeant allocated them at random and went away. They contained the standard furnishings, wardrobe, dressing table and two beds. But instead of the comfy feather beds we had become accustomed to at Morecambe and Mrs Gillie's, we now had thin hard mattresses that reminded me of the biscuits at Innsworth. The beds had yet to be made up. Two blankets, two sheets and a pillowcase lay folded on each one, reminding me again that we were in the services, not on holiday. Gina dumped her kitbag beside her bed. She said, "I'll empty it later," and hurried out as if she were late for an appointment. When I had made up my bed and stowed my kit away I went along to Beryl and Sylvia's room for company. Irene and Edna appeared a few minutes later. Edna felt Beryl's hard bed. "I'll bet she never put holidaymakers on these mattresses," she said. "Mine isn't even clean."

Sylvia wasn't listening. After not having heard from Ian, her fiancé, for weeks, she had that morning received a batch of letters, forwarded to Mrs Gillie's from her home. She had been waiting all day for an opportunity to do more than scan through them to make sure all was well, and had now settled down to read them properly, oblivious of her new surroundings.

Irene said, "I'm dying for a smoke. Let's go down and find the sitting room. She surely can't stop us smoking in there." Beryl, Edna and I went downstairs with her to investigate. The house was absolutely quiet. Evidently everyone else was out.

The door marked Sitting Room was opposite the Dining Room, and next to another one marked Private. Irene grasped the doorknob and tried to turn it. The door was locked. "Bloody hell!" she swore, "That means we can't smoke anywhere."

"And where are we supposed to spend our evenings when we don't go out?" demanded Edna, "In our bedrooms?"

We were sure we had a right to the sitting room. Irene was all for knocking on the Private door and demanding the key. Her green eyes flashed, ready for battle if battle was called for. Beryl said she thought it would be better to wait until we met the landlady before disturbing her evening on our first night there, and I agreed with her.

As we stood debating, the front door opened and two Waafs came in, obviously surprised to see us. "Have you just arrived?"

asked the taller one. We said we had. "We were looking for somewhere to smoke," said Beryl, "but the sitting room door's locked. Is there a key somewhere?"

"The door's always locked," said the tall girl, Joan, "and we're not allowed a key."

Irene swore again. Beryl said, "We haven't met the landlady yet. What's she like?"

Both the girls looked quickly towards the Private door to make sure it was shut before Joan said in lowered tones, "She's a shrew."

"What's the food like?" I asked, keeping my voice low too.

"Rotten – what there is of it. She's a lousy cook," said the second girl, Rita. She looked as if she were going to say more, but Joan was already moving towards the stairs, uneasy in case we were somehow overheard, and Rita followed her. After a gloomy pause Beryl said, "Let's go out." It was decided to leave Sylvia to enjoy her letters and the four of us went out on our own.

We spent what remained of the evening in a canteen, drinking tea and smoking and trying to assure ourselves that the billet probably wasn't as bad as Joan and Rita had made it sound. Edna said morosely that she'd bet it probably was, if not worse.

Unfortunately she was right. During the night I awoke with a start. Something was crawling on my neck. In panic I brushed it off, leapt out of bed and turned on light, which glowed weakly. Gina stirred and mumbled, "What's the matter?"

"My neck. Something was on it. – it's bitten me,"

Gina suddenly kicked back her bedclothes and slapped at her leg. "God! I've got them too, whatever they are." She pushed the clothes further back and a very small brown beetle scuttled across the sheet and disappeared over the side of the mattress. "Ugh. Bedbugs," she exclaimed in disgust.

I sat up in bed for the rest of the night. I couldn't bear the thought of anything crawling over my face. I tried to keep awake, but exhaustion defeated me. I awoke next morning cold and stiff, with a crick in my neck where my head had lolled sideways as I slept. In the queue for the bathroom I met Joan, Rita and several other girls waiting their turn at the washbasins. "We've been bitten," I told Joan accusingly, implying that she should have warned us. "We've got bedbugs."

The girls nearest me drew away as unobtrusively as possible. The shock on their faces made it plain they hadn't known about the bugs. "There hasn't been anyone up on that floor since we've been here," said Rita, apologising for their ignorance.

Sylvia and Beryl joined the queue. Both of them had the telltale red bumps on their arms. "Irene and Edna are the same," said Sylvia.

Our unhappy band went down to the dining room for breakfast together. It was a good-sized room, big enough to hold two large rectangular tables. On each one was a plate piled with slices of cold toast, one piece for each person seated at the table. Joan and Co, eight in all, were ahead of us, seated in their accustomed places at one table. We took our seats at the other one. The landlady bustled in with a tray laden with cups of tea and a stack of saucers. She was a hard-faced peroxide blonde of about forty; her brassy hair permed into stiff waves and tight curls. She doled out the cups of tea without speaking or looking at us and took the tray back to the kitchen. I thought she had gone to fetch the breakfasts, but Joan leaned over to our table and said in a stage whisper, "That's all there is." Irene said "What!" in outrage. I asked, "Are you serious?"

"'Fraid so," said Joan, with a doleful face.

We held a council of war as we walked to the school. First thing after dismissal we'd go to Admin, display our bites and complain.

The mid-day meal had always been a rushed affair when we lived further from the school. Now we had more time, but a lot less to eat. By coincidence, the first meal we were given was the same as the one we had had for supper at Mrs Gillie's, shepherd's pie. But whereas Miss Rawson's had been beautifully cooked, thick with gravy and topped with a rich brown crust of mashed potato, this one was dry and the meat was tough, with a dollop of lumpy mashed potato on the top. The portions were about half the size we had enjoyed at Mrs Gillie's, even the vegetables looked pitiful on the plate.

"Is it always as bad as this?" Sylvia asked Joan in the hall afterwards.

"Usually."

"Hasn't anyone complained?"

"We did when we first arrived," said Joan. "Admin came along and had words, and you should have heard her! She's frightening when she gets going. The meals improved at first, but not for long. Now they're as bad as they were before."

"How long have you been here?" I asked.

"Three weeks, but it feels longer," said Joan.

"You must be starving," I said.

"We would be if we didn't stoke up in the canteens in the evening," she agreed.

"Is that where everybody was last night?"

"Yes."

The £3 Father had sent me was all but gone and I could not afford to eat in canteens every night. The thought of asking my family for more money entered my mind but was instantly dismissed. Pride forbade it. I had a doleful vision of myself fainting for lack of food in the middle of a lecture or maybe in one of the darkrooms, and was seriously worried.

As planned, we went to Admin after school. Sylvia, being a corporal, was our spokeswoman. The duty sergeant, a brisk, matter of fact lady in her thirties, examined our red marks. "Looks like bed bugs," she agreed, "but I can't do anything without evidence."

"Evidence? We've seen them, and you've seen the bites. Isn't that evidence enough?" asked Sylvia, with an edge to her voice. "What more do we need?"

"Bugs," said the sergeant shortly.

Feeling thoroughly dejected after a meagre and unappetising supper we went out again to a canteen. We had only been in our new billet for one day, but I was already starving and needed more than a cup of tea to go with my cigarette.

We went to bed armed with matchboxes that night. They were not ideal for catching bedbugs, but they were all we had. The plan was simple. At the first suspicion of a bite both girls would jump out of bed. The one who had not been bitten would rush to the light switch, the other would grab her matchbox ready to slam it down over the bug when the light came on. The only trouble with the plan was that it didn't work. In the dim light of the 40-watt bulb hanging from the middle of the ceiling we couldn't spot the little beasts quickly enough. They knew their way back into the mattress by instinct and moved with surprising speed. Not one of us caught a single bug.

The result was the same on the following two nights and desperation set in. Flt Sgt Chapman caught sight of our miserable faces as we entered the school on the third morning and asked if anything was wrong. He listened attentively as we all talked at once, pouring out our tale of woe. Then he smiled and said, "Don't worry. Leave it with me for a couple of days and I'll see what I can do."

"What does he think he can do," said Edna bitterly. "The mattresses need taking out and burning, and he can't do that, can he?."

"Oh, shut up," Irene was hungry for a decent meal, itchy from the bug bites and tired from the nights of broken sleep, as were we all, and her patience with Edna was running out.

"He seemed very confident," said Beryl. "Perhaps he can get some special insect killer, extra powerful."

Beyond hunting bugs with me at night, Gina had kept pretty quiet about our situation. She continued to go out after supper and reappear at locking up time. She did not join us in the canteen but she did not seem to be hungry. Wherever she was spending her evenings they must have been feeding her.

Two wretched days later a miracle happened. Flt Sgt Chapman met us as we entered school in the morning. With a knowing smile he handed Sylvia a matchbox sealed with sticky tape. "Be very careful with it," he said. "There are four of them and they're alive. For God's sake don't let them escape." For one speechless moment of joy we stared at him, then Irene gave a yell of delight and I burst into uncontrollable laughter. Even Edna had a smile on her face for once.

"Where did you get them?" asked Sylvia when she could speak.

Chappy tapped the side of his nose with his forefinger. "Ask no questions and you'll hear no lies."

At Admin Sylvia placed the matchbox carefully on the sergeant's desk. "There are four bugs in there," she informed her.

"Alive?" asked the startled sergeant.

"They were when they went in," Sylvia assured her.

"How did you catch them?"

"It was difficult," said Sylvia, straight-faced, and went on quickly, "There's something else. I don't know what our landlady is spending her billeting allowance on, but it's not on food for us." She described the meals we had been given so far. "We're having to go out and buy food in the evening," she concluded.

"Right," said the sergeant, "She's had one warning already. I'll see the MO as soon as possible." The knowledge that the landlady was misappropriating Air Force money carried as much weight as the knowledge that we had bedbugs.

"How soon is 'as soon as possible', do you reckon?" wondered Irene when we were outside.

"I doubt if she'll want to keep live bugs any longer than she can help," said Sylvia.

"What do you think will happen? Will we be moved?" I asked eagerly.

"With luck. Of course, they'll have to inspect the billet first," said Sylvia.

"It's a pity they didn't inspect it properly before they moved us in," said Edna sourly, and for once she spoke for us all.

We returned to the billet exhilarated but anxious. What if someone turned up with a can of insect powder, antagonised the landlady still further and left us to face the consequences? Sylvia said we ought to warn Joan and Co. Beryl waylaid her in the hall on her way in to supper and told her what we had done. She didn't mention the help we had been given in catching the bugs. We took all the glory for ourselves. The word went round in a buzz of suppressed excitement. If the landlady had taken the trouble to notice us, she would have realised the atmosphere was highly charged, but she didn't. Whatever was going to happen was gong to hit her without warning.

'As soon as possible' turned out to be sooner than we had dared to hope. As we sat down to supper the following evening, a WAAF MO attended by the sergeant and a corporal, walked into the billet and came straight into the dining room. The MO inspected our plates without comment and went along to the kitchen. There was a quiet pause while she explained her mission, followed by a scream of rage from the landlady. We had all stopped eating. Nobody spoke. I suddenly realised I was holding my breath and let it out as quietly as I could. Footsteps passed through the hall and ascended the stairs. The landlady was still screaming, but now we could hear the words. "Sluts! Dirty bitches! If there are bugs in my beds they brought them in themselves." Her voice trailed up through the house as she followed the MO and the NCOs into our bedrooms. Still nobody spoke in the dining room as we strained our ears to follow the action. Rita got up quietly and opened the door a crack to make it easier to hear. Several minutes passed and still the landlady was yelling insults both at us and the MO, the sergeant and the corporal. As far as we could make out, none of them replied, which inflamed the landlady even more.

The footsteps were descending. The MO left the house and walked swiftly away. The sergeant came to the dining room door. Her face was white with anger. She announced in a tightly controlled voice, "We are closing the billet. You have fifteen minutes to get your kit packed before the transport comes to collect you. Get going." To add 'at the double' would have been ridiculous. She had to stand back smartly to avoid being knocked off her feet in the stampede as the dining room emptied.

As Gina and I snatched clothes from the wardrobe and emptied the dressing table drawers, cramming everything into our kitbags at speed, I said. "It's funny really. I'd have thought she would be glad to see the back of us, to take in civilians."

"It's getting near the end of the season," said Gina knowledgeably. "They don't get many bookings in the winter."

I tied off the top of my kitbag, slung my gas mask over my shoulder and picked up my greatcoat. There were bumping noises and the sound of nervous chatter coming from the stairs. Gina and I gave the room one last glance to make sure we hadn't left anything behind in our rush and went out to join the procession lugging their kitbags down to the hall. Here the sergeant and the corporal stood with feet firmly planted and slightly apart, poised to take immediate action if there was any trouble from the hysterical landlady. The lorry was already outside. The RAF driver stood in the back and hauled up our kitbags one by one then hauled us up after them. An interested audience of neighbours had gathered at their gates to watch, accompanied by the Waafs billeted on them, some of whom were on our course at the school. The landlady's voice could still be heard inside the house. The two NCOs waited until the last girl was safely off the premises then left their posts to come down the steps and make sure everyone was aboard and the lorry ready to move off. As they turned to march away, their task complete, the landlady emerged on to the top step. "I'll get even with you for this, you see if I don't" she yelled. A ragged cheer answered her as the lorry pulled away. In the back relief and glee mingled in excited laughter.

I can't recall where we went or what our next billet was like. After the nightmare of the one we had just left I can only remember that it felt like heaven. Flt Sgt Chapman, our hero of the hour, was delighted for us.

The course was coming to an end and I had very mixed feelings about moving on. I had had my fill of training. I felt as well prepared as I would ever be to cope with life on a working section and was eager to get started. At last I would be a part of what I thought of as 'the real Air Force'. On the other hand, we had become a very close-knit little group at the billet and I hated the idea of leaving them, especially Sylvia. I had done my best not to rely too much on her for company, but I knew I was going to miss her if we were not posted to the same station.

The day came when the last lecture had been given and the last exam taken. The course was over. The results were announced and I was proud to be able to write and tell my parents I had come top of the class. There were no failures. Gina had been quite right when she predicted they would pass her on the strength of her practical work.

During our final days at the school Chappy managed to have a private word with each member of the course in turn. When he came to me he enquired if I had enjoyed it and I assured him I had. He then wanted to know who my roommate had been at the billet? I could not think what he wanted to know that for, but gave him Gina's name. His next question was: how well had we got on together? I had to think before I answered. Within the confines of the WAAF Gina was leading a life of her own that excluded everyone else, including me. She and I had nothing in common and would never be close friends. But she intrigued me and I admired her independence of spirit. I said we got on OK. His last question was also unexpected, "Where would you like to be posted?" I had gained the impression that lowly rankers went where they were sent and, like Tennyson's Light Brigade in their historic Charge,

'Theirs not to reason why; theirs but to do or die ', though I hoped it wouldn't come to that. I said, "Anywhere with planes and flying. Not a depot."

I don't know how Gina answered these questions when her turn came, but when the postings went up on the board I found we were both being sent to No 13 OTU (Operational Training Unit) at Bicester in Oxfordshire. Sylvia was one of several girls who were bound for Medmenham, near Marlow on the Thames in Buckinghamshire. I wished very much that I were going to be with her instead of Gina. Later I discovered that the girls at Medmenham did nothing but printing, working shifts round the clock and thanked my stars I had not been posted there.

I wrote to Paul to tell him of my success and let him know my next address. My letter was so short I filled up the page with an account of the bed bug saga, glad of having something to write about.

Chapter 11

The real Air Force

THE TRAIN SLOWED, then pulled into Bicester North station and came to a halt. I climbed down onto the platform and dragged my kitbag after me. Not many other passengers had alighted and I was the only one in uniform. There was a slamming of doors, the guard blew his whistle and the carriages began to slide away behind me as the train moved off. A middle-aged lady paused beside me on her way to the ticket barrier and smiled. "Where are you going to?"

I told her, "Bicester House".

She nodded, "Ah yes. It's quite a way." She eyed my kitbag dubiously. "Will you be able to manage?"

I said airily, "Sure, I'll be fine".

She watched me make two abortive attempts to hoist it over my shoulder, then helped me hump it into position, and we left the station together.

The station is situated where the railway line crosses over the Buckingham Road by way of a bridge. My new friend accompanied me down the incline to the road and here she stopped. "It's on the other side of the town," she said, "but wait a minute." A market cart drawn by a drooping piebald horse was approaching us at a leisurely pace, heading into the town. A little old man stood in the cart, the reins slack in his hand. My companion stepped to the roadside and smiled. The driver called "whoa" to the horse, which stopped immediately, dropped its head still further and started cropping the grass verge. "Good morning, Fred," said the lady. The old man's lined and weatherbeaten face did not alter its expression, neither did he speak, but he touched his cap to return her greeting and waited to be told what she wanted. She asked, "Are you going near the House?" He surveyed me solemnly. With my gas mask over my shoulder, my greatcoat over one arm and my kitbag weighing me down, I looked as much a drooping beast of burden as the horse.

He said at last, "I could be," and swung his legs over the side of the cart. He jumped down in surprisingly agile fashion for one who looked to me like Methuselah, and went round to drop the tailboard of the cart. I had let the kitbag slide to the ground. He picked it up as if it were a weekend case and swung it up into the cart among several bulging muddy sacks. Then he hitched the tailboard into the horizontal position and motioned me to sit on it. Having seen me settled, with my legs dangling down from the tailboard, my kind lady wished me luck with a friendly nod, then beamed approval at Fred before going on her way. Still solemn-faced, he touched his cap again, more I thought as a goodbye salute than a gesture of deference, and climbed nimbly back into the cart. I heard him click his tongue to the horse and with a jerk that nearly unseated me the cart moved forward. In this way I entered this latest phase of my life backwards, hanging on to the chain that held the tailboard in place and bouncing precariously with every bump in the road. When we left the School of Photography we had been given a short home leave before reporting to our new stations and had been obliged to take all our kit with us. Travelling with a kitbag had proved to be much easier than I had anticipated. Unlike the day I arrived at Blackpool, civilians as well as servicemen had gone out of their way to be helpful, but this novel ride into Bicester was the best yet. It was a lovely day, sunny but not too hot. We clip-clopped into town at the same leisurely pace, giving me plenty of time to take in the departing view of the main street as it unrolled behind us. It was lined with small, old-fashioned shops on either side. But for the presence of a modern cinema I would have guessed that nothing had changed here since well before the demise of Queen Victoria. The horse suddenly stopped of its own accord. Fred turned round and pushed one of the sacks onto the tailboard beside me, jumped to the ground and hoisted it on his back. I could now see that it was full of potatoes. He disappeared down an alleyway beside a hotel, presumably to deliver them to the kitchen. The horse stood patiently waiting until it heard its master's footsteps returning, then moved forward, to stop again some minutes later. I realised Fred was doing a delivery round and, like our milkman's horse at home, the piebald knew exactly where to halt and when to walk on. I sat swinging my legs and smiling at the passing shoppers, most of whom smiled back. I was remembering the day I made up my mind to volunteer for the WAAF. Sitting in the bus on my way home from work I had dreamed of being billeted in a little country town and here it was, small and quiet and friendly. A dream come true.

At the end of the main street Fred made another delivery, after which we turned right and picked up speed. The piebald trotted along one side of a market square and down an ancient narrow road with tall terraced houses on either side. Their front doors opened directly onto the almost non-existent pavement. I could have put out my hand and touched them if I had not been clinging on to the tailboard for dear life, determined not to be jerked off the cart. The road widened past a large church and further along on the right stood my new billet. With relief I slid to the ground, beating dried earth off my skirt with my hands. Through a gateway in a high wall I could see Bicester House, a large square attractive mansion standing in extensive grounds. This time I was to be billeted in style! Before I could collect my kitbag Fred hoisted it over his shoulder. "I'll see you in, girl," he said, and marched up the drive with an old soldier's gait, leaving me to follow. They were the first words he had spoken to me throughout the drive.

Yet he had not made me feel I was a nuisance, merely an extra delivery to be made and all in a day's work. When we reached the portico he put my kitbag down on the step and waited. A Waaf opened the door almost immediately. Fred touched his cap in the same polite gesture he had used before, and walked smartly away, ignoring my attempt to thank him for the lift.

The Waaf and I exchanged greetings. She looked me over, decided I was hardly out of the rookie stage, and enquired, "Is this your first posting?" I confirmed that it was. She stood back to let me drag my kitbag into the large hall. "The first thing to do is go up to camp and report to Admin," she said. "You can leave your kitbag here." I was glad to hear it. I pulled it over to a corner, flung my greatcoat over the back of a nearby chair and was ready to go. "Have you got your irons?" asked the Waaf. "You'll need them to get a meal in the mess. We don't eat here." I had forgotten the RAF's obsession with knives, forks and spoons. I fished them out of my kitbag and put them in my pocket. "Go back to the road, under the railway bridge and keep going. It's about a mile. You can't go wrong," said the Waaf.

Beyond the railway bridge the houses petered out and the road, bordered by high hedges, ran between fields. I strode along happily in the afternoon sunshine, pausing to look over a gate and survey the peaceful countryside. From somewhere unseen came the whirr of a tractor. It was hard to believe there was a war on and harder still to believe that at long last I was going to be a part of it. My only regret was that I was going to a Training Unit not an operational squadron. I wished I had been more specific when Flt Sgt Chapman asked where I wanted to be posted. "Anywhere with planes" had not been enough.

In the distant sky I could see planes flying backwards and forwards, seemingly at random. Proud of my newly acquired knowledge, I could tell they were photographing the ground to make maps like the ones we had put together at the School.

As I drew nearer the airfield my happy mood began to fade.

'HAVE YOU GOT YOUR IRONS?'

Trepidation took its place. No longer was I one of a squad or a class at school, with moral support all round me to rely on; I was on my own. What would I find ahead of me? I wished most fervently that Gina was with me and we could arrive on our first station together. I quickened my pace, anxious to get the initial daunting moments over as soon as possible. Also I was ravenously hungry and wanted to catch up on a belated dinner without delay.

As the Waaf had said, I couldn't go wrong. Not only did the road go straight to the camp, it went straight through it. To the right I could see assorted brick buildings set higgledy-piggledy among trees. Behind them rose huge aircraft hangars, and beyond them lay the airfield stretching away into the distance. Planes were taking off or landing every few minutes. The roar of their engines deafened and excited me, despite my apprehension. There was a barrier across the road at the entrance to the camp. I showed the guard my papers and he directed me to WAAF Admin on the left hand side of the road, the 'domestic' side, as against the technical and engineering sections on the right.

"Go and get a meal," said the Admin sergeant when she had checked me in. "Have you got your irons?" She nodded approval when I said I had. "Report back here when you've eaten," she ordered and delegated one of her minions to escort me to the Waaf mess. I thought the girl might come in with me but she left me outside the door. Squaring my shoulders, I pushed it open and went in. It was not as large as I had expected. The mid-day meal being over long ago, there was no one about. A long counter ran down one side of the hall. Behind it the door to the kitchens stood open. I stood at the counter, opposite the door, hoping someone would see me and come out. After a few moments a girl dressed in the cook's uniform white overall and mop cap glanced out and turned away to call to someone out of sight, "Rosie! You've got a customer." A few more moments and another cook emerged unsmiling to serve me. Rosie was short and plump. Her hair was completely hidden under her mop cap, which protruded in angular bumps all over her head. I guessed that underneath it she was wearing curlers. Feeling like a thorough-going nuisance, I explained apologetically that I had only just arrived and had been sent by Admin to get something to eat. I added plaintively that I was starving. The girl looked me up and down, taking in the newness of my uniform and my brassy buttons. "This your first posting?" she enquired. When I nodded, she said heavily, "OK, I'll try and find you something," as if the WAAF larder was nearly bare. She disappeared back into the kitchen and I sat down at the nearest table to wait. She was gone so long I began to fear she had forgotten me. But eventually she reappeared, and I was dumbfounded. What she had 'found' for me filled a large plate with bacon, egg, baked beans, fried potato, and plenty of it. "You can have some of the sponge left over from dinner for afters, if you like," she offered, and brought it to me with a mug of tea. "I can remember what I felt like on my first day on camp," she said, explaining this largesse and I looked at her face more closely. It showed signs of strain and her dark eyes had shadows under them. It came to me that if she had been less than welcoming when I came in it was because she was bone-tired. I gave her my broadest smile in gratitude and she smiled back. Her face was transformed and I saw she was really a very pretty girl. I liked her – and not just because of the food.

When I reported back to Admin the corporal asked, "Can you ride a bike?" I had never owned a bicycle. I hadn't even ridden one since the day I fell off a friend's fairy cycle when I was about seven years old. (I still had the scars on one knee to show for it!) However, I said "Yes", realising that the alternative to cycling backwards and forwards to the billet was to walk. As the corporal handed me a chitty for the cycle stores I gave her Gina's name and asked if she had arrived yet. She had, but was in another billet. I would not see her until we went on duty the following morning.

They say that one of the things you never forget is how to ride a bicycle. They lie! Or perhaps I had never really mastered the art in the first place. I think it took me longer to ride back to Bicester House than it had taken me to walk from there to the camp. The bike refused to co-operate. I managed to keep it upright most of the way, but I could not control the brakes. When I applied the back one nothing much happened; when I pulled the front one I nearly went over the handlebars. I put this down to my lack of expertise and with airy optimism assured myself that by the time I had cycled to camp next morning I would have got the feel of the thing.

At the house I leaned it up against the portico. A corporal materialised from somewhere and asked me to take it round the back, where I would find a row of cycle racks. When I got back she said, "Your room's upstairs" and helped me manhandle my kitbag up to the second floor. Our footsteps sounded loud and hollow on the bare wooden floorboards as she led the way into a very large room with a beamed ceiling. It held a dozen or so standard issue iron beds, each with its regulation stack of three biscuits, two blankets and two sheets precisely folded, topped off with a bolster. The corporal indicated a bed at the far end. "That one's free. But come with me first and I'll show you where the ablutions are." They were some way from our sleeping quarters, down an echoing passage. I hoped I would not get lost if I had to get out in the night.

She left me to sort myself out and I made up my bed and stowed my kit away in my locker. It was now late afternoon. I wished I had asked the corporal what time the other girls would be back. I stretched out on my bed and stared up at the beams above me, thinking over my few days at home. Mother had welcomed me so proudly but I thought there was a certain reserve in David's manner. I had been puzzled and a little hurt by this at first. I thought I must have done something to upset him. It transpired that it was my uniform, not me personally that was the trouble. "You are lucky, Sis," he said in a quiet moment when we

'HAVE YOU GOT YOUR IRONS?'

Mollie (right) and me during our schooldays

Me pictured at home in about 1937 or 1938

A

'HAVE YOU GOT YOUR IRONS?'

Me and my brother David when he was still at school

Mollie and Ted on their wedding day

B

'HAVE YOU GOT YOUR IRONS?'

My father in pensive mood

My father and mother in the mid-1930s

C

'HAVE YOU GOT YOUR IRONS?'

This page and facing page: photographs of me at varying stages during my WAAF service

'HAVE YOU GOT YOUR IRONS?'

Left: my favourite picture of me, grabbing something to eat!

Above: a more serious pose
Below: busy at work

E

'HAVE YOU GOT YOUR IRONS?'

My brother David in a photograph taken at Skegness

David and me in Trafalgar Square with the pigeons - I liked this picture so much that I had lots of copies made! It became a family joke and was known for years as "the pigeon picture".

F

'HAVE YOU GOT YOUR IRONS?'

My discharge papers from the WAAF during the period of my father's illness

'HAVE YOU GOT YOUR IRONS?'

Above: Bristol Blenheim Mk 4 (Photograph Chris Burkett)
Below: My identity card

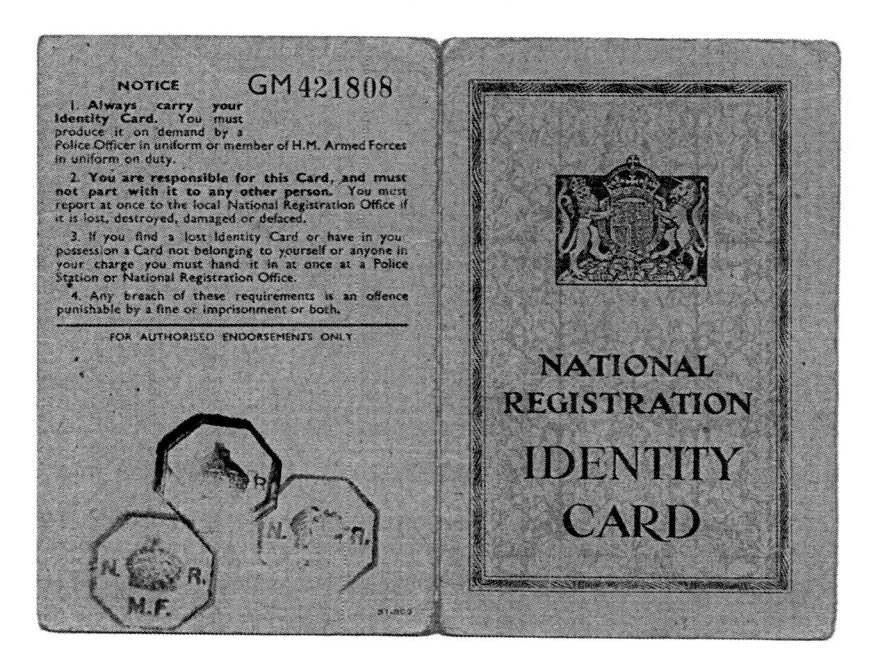

H

were alone, "It'll probably all be over by the time I'm old enough to go." I knew how deeply he was involved with the ARP. I said something about his having seen more of the war than I was ever likely to in the WAAF, but even as I spoke I knew this was beside the point. He had already been half a head taller than me before I left home. He had grown even taller in the six months I had been away. At fifteen he was no longer a boy, he was a young man. "There's not much doing with the ARP these days," he said. "and I've had enough of the Scouts. I want to do a proper war job."

The following morning after he had left for school Mother said, "I hope and pray that it will all be over before David has to go. He'll be disappointed of course if it is, but at least he'll be able to feel he did his bit."

She still sees him as her little boy and she doesn't understand, I thought. He won't just be disappointed, he'll be heartbroken. As I would have been had the war ended while I was waiting to come into the WAAF. I sighed and reached for one of the books I had brought back with me from home to read off duty.

I heard voices echoing along the passage, the other occupants of the room were returning. I looked at my watch and was astonished to see that nearly two hours had gone by. I had been so engrossed in my book I had not noticed the time passing. The girls came in talking and laughing together. I felt very much the new girl and wished for the second time that Gina were with me. She might not be much company generally, but at least she was a face I knew. However, the girl who plumped herself down on the unmade bed next to mine said, "Hello, just arrived? I'm Elaine," and, eyeing my new uniform, "Is this your first posting?" I said it was and she went on cheerfully, "Don't worry, you'll soon get used to it. What trade are you in?" I told her my name and trade. "I don't think we've got any photographers in this billet. Has anyone shown you round yet?"

"Apart from the ablutions, no."

"There's a place downstairs where we can make cocoa. I'll show you later on." Elaine was a lively girl with merry brown eyes and a bubbling laugh. That first evening she did her best to include me in the general chatter and I felt I had found a friend.

The day shift for most trades started at 0800 hours. From before 0700 the following morning, groups of girls left the billet in increasing numbers to cycle to the mess for breakfast. "Come with us," said Elaine. I wobbled along precariously amongst her group, hoping to improve my skill en route. We went a different way back to the main road, one that cut out the market square. The girls accelerated to a good speed and so perforce did I. Although not fully in control of my bike I was doing well until we approached the camp. Just before the entrance a road came in from the right. A small convoy of lorries was about to emerge and turn right, heading into camp. The SP on traffic duty gave it priority. Putting out his arm to bring us to a halt, he beckoned the lorries on. The other girls braked. I pulled my back brake hard. Nothing happened. Too scared to put on the front one, knowing I would crash and bring down everyone around me, I shot past the girls in front. The first lorry had pulled out of the side road and was right in front of me. The bike headed straight towards it. I heard shouts of alarm from the girls. Instinctively I aimed for the SP's outstretched arm, grabbed it wildly and clung on. He all but lost his balance and swore viciously. Appalled, I gasped, "It wouldn't stop." He gave me a look to kill and snarled, "Stay there," Obediently I waited beside him, stranded in the middle of the road until the convoy had gone by. He beckoned the girls on. Their cries of alarm had turned to shrieks of nervous laughter when I grabbed the SP's arm. They were still laughing as they streamed into camp. "WALK!" roared the SP as I made to remount and join them, "And get those brakes checked. NOW!"

Having to walk to the mess left me little time for breakfast, but I hadn't eaten since the previous afternoon and I was too hungry to wait until the mid-day break. I queued at the counter and prayed the service would be quick. Across the hall I saw Gina and waved to attract her attention. She had finished eating and came over to join me for a moment. "You're cutting it a bit fine," she greeted me. As briefly as possible I explained what had happened. "Tell them on the section. With luck I won't be long."

I gobbled my breakfast and set out to find the photographic section, not daring to ride my bike in case I met the angry SP again. The time was now close on 0800. I stopped an airman and asked him the way. "Over the road," he said, "above the armoury." On the technical side I got lost. "Where's the armoury?" I called in desperation to a Waaf scurrying by. She waved vaguely along a path. "Down there somewhere," and disappeared into a doorway like the white rabbit bolting into his tunnel. Pure luck brought me to the right door in the end. I leaned my bike up against the wall with numerous others, dashed inside and climbed the stairs immediately in front of me.

A wide corridor ran across the top of the stairs. I halted, not knowing whether to turn left or right. A tall RAF corporal with a lordly air appeared at the end of the corridor on the left and waited for me. I hurried towards him, all set to make my apologies. But he gave me no chance. Before I reached him he announced, "Flight wants to see you in his office." He was standing where the wide main corridor ended at a 'T' junction with a second, narrower one. He pointed down the right hand arm of the 'T'. "Down there. The last door on the left. And look sharp about it."

The flight sergeant's office was quite small. He was sitting behind a large desk, facing the door. Probably in his fifties, he was a heavily built man with grey hair, cold grey eyes, and a grey moustache. He regarded me without enthusiasm. Flustered, I started to apologise. He interrupted me with. "You're fifteen minutes late. I'm putting you on night duty for a week, starting tonight. Report back at 1800 hours. Dismiss." I gaped at him, not sure if I had heard aright. The correct procedure was to about turn and leave the office, but I was too stunned to move. He stood up and turned away from me towards a tall filing cabinet. The movement brought me to my senses. I said, "Yes, Flight," to his back and left the office.

Walking back down the narrow corridor I could see through an open door at the other end of the "T". Several airmen and Waafs were standing around, seemingly doing nothing. Those nearest the door looked out to watch me and one or two smiled as I drew nearer. I walked slowly, hoping Gina would appear but I was unlucky. Behind me I heard the flight sergeant leave his office and follow me. I walked faster, turned into the wide corridor when I came to it and went back to the stairs.

I had the whole day in front of me and had to decide what to do with it. My first priority was to find the cycle store and get my brakes adjusted - something I should have done the day before if I'd had any sense. That done, I spent the rest of the morning cycling round camp, partly because it seemed wise to stay within easy reach of the cycle mechanic in case my brakes gave trouble again, partly because I wanted to get my bearings. I learned later that the station had been built towards the end of the 1914-18 war. Some of the buildings – like the Waafs' mess - were original, others had been added as the need arose. These included the airmen's mess which was far larger than ours. There was a hall that evidently did duty as the camp theatre and was also used for dances. Tacked to the door were several posters and I stopped to read them. A well-known actor and film star, Emlyn Williams, was bringing his West End play, *Night Must Fall*, to the camp theatre at some date in the future. I hoped I would not be on night duty when he came. There was to be a station dance – and here my attention was caught on Gina's behalf – the station band would be providing the music. Tucked away on the outer edge of the 'domestic' side I found two tennis courts, remnants I supposed, of more leisurely pre-war days on the station.

I was enjoying my morning on my own, gaining confidence on my bike and free of authority, when I got shouted at again. I was cycling across the top of the parade ground, taking a short cut. At the far end the SWO (Station Warrant Officer) was drilling a squad of 'erks' (aircraftmen). I was about half way across when he spotted me. "YOU!" he bellowed. I dismounted and waited while he stomped towards me.

"Name?" he demanded. I drew myself up to attention, or as near to attention as I could get while holding a bicycle, and gave him my surname and the last three digits of my number as we had been taught. I also remembered not to salute. Only commissioned officers were entitled to that courtesy.

He eyed my brand new battledress, which still showed the original storeroom creases, and growled, "How long have you been on camp?"

I said brightly, "Since yesterday, Sir". So far as I could recall no one at Morecambe had told us it was a hanging matter to set foot - let alone wheels - on a parade ground while the SWO was using it. He remedied this omission in a voice that must have carried as far as the camp boundary in all directions. It certainly reached the ears of the squad he had been drilling; they were all grinning like idiots at my discomfiture. When he finally ran out of steam and dismissed me, I left at the double, as much to get away from the grinning squad as from the SWO.

The incident reminded me strongly of my schooldays at the Convent. The black and white tiled floor of the entrance hall was forbidden territory. We were only allowed to walk on the coconut matting strip that ran round the edge. If we were ever caught walking across the tiles we incurred a reprimand from the headmistress on exactly the same lines as the one I had just received from the SWO. Sister Patricia did not make as much noise as he did, but I thought that on the whole she was the more formidable of the two. Or was it just that I had been younger then and more easily overawed? I took myself off to the mess for a meal then cycled back to the billet before I could get into any more trouble.

Chapter 12

Nights and Days

IT WAS GOING to be a very long day indeed. The sensible thing to do was to spend the afternoon resting. I laid out the three biscuits on my bed, threw a blanket over them and stretched out on top of it, prepared to lose myself in my book for a couple of hours. My only worry was that if I became too engrossed I might not notice the time passing. If I was late on duty again I dreaded to think what might happen: the flight sergeant did not strike me as a tolerant man. I cursed myself for not bringing my little pink alarm clock back with me from home. I would have to keep one eye on my watch as I read. Not an easy thing to do, as I quickly discovered. It disturbed my concentration and kept me on edge. After reading the same page twice without being able to remember a word of it, I closed the book and stowed it away in my locker. I knew my mother would be expecting a letter assuring her I had arrived safely and describing the billet, but I didn't feel like writing just then. I wanted to wait until I could write in a lighthearted manner about the day's events and at this moment they did not seem in the least amusing. Somewhere footsteps echoed along a passage, an eerie sound in the silent house. A beam above my head suddenly creaked and made me jump. It was useless to try to rest; I got up, restacked my bed and went out.

It was far too early to return to camp so, having nothing better to do, I went for a ride of exploration round the little town and into the surrounding countryside. I did not dare go very far in case I got lost. All signposts had been removed at the beginning of the war in order to confuse the Germans if they ever dared set foot on our land. Only the locals could possibly find their way around the winding lanes that might or might not take you where you wanted to go. They were just as likely to peter out in a deserted farmyard. It was safer to stay within the vicinity of the airfield. The aircraft taking off and coming in to land told me exactly where I was even if the airfield was out of sight.

At five o'clock I went back to the mess for something to eat and shortly before six I climbed the stairs to the section for the second time, keyed up and nervous about my reception. To my relief the first person I saw in the main corridor was Gina. "I was waiting for you," she said quietly. Before I could speak she put her finger to her lips and beckoned me to follow her. Round the corner to the left we slipped like two conspirators into a large room where the day shift were putting on their caps ready to go off duty. "The general room," said Gina. "We're OK in here." To my puzzled look she explained, "He always leaves his door open and he can hear every word you say in the corridors. They echo." I didn't have to ask who 'he' was. "How did your day go?" I asked. "Lousy," she said crossly. She had spent most of it cleaning the darkrooms and polishing the floor on which we now stood. From a polisher's viewpoint this was vast, a daunting task even with a bumper. I was impressed by the shine she had produced. To cheer her up I asked, "Did you know there's a station band here?" Her face changed from gloom to lively interest. "Who's running it, do you know?" I had not noticed, but I could tell her where to find the notice and I bet myself a pound to a penny that she went straight round there before doing anything else. I was conscious of the others eyeing me with curiosity as they started to leave. Several of them smiled and my nervous tension eased a little. "They look a nice crowd," I murmured to Gina, who nodded. As she followed them out she said in a loud voice, making sure the flight sergeant would hear her and know I was on time, "Bye

Yvonne. See you in the morning."

Left on my own I wondered if I should go down to the office and report in or wait for the rest of the shift to turn up. Where were they anyway? It was past six o'clock. I decided to wait for a few more minutes to see what happened. While I waited I looked about me. There were windows down one side and across the end of the room, all of them criss-crossed with the ubiquitous strips of brown paper. Beneath the windows and along the second side wall ran a wide workbench. Ten or so familiar grey cameras and a stack of cine film cans were lined up under the end windows. Were they awaiting attention by the night shift? I heard footsteps coming along the corridor from the stairs. At last! Someone to tell me what to do. A tall, lanky, dark-haired LAC (Leading Aircraftman) appeared in the doorway; incongruously he carried a cardboard box with a large loaf of bread protruding from the top. He was surprised to see me and looked round as if expecting someone else to be there. The flight sergeant had left his office and was coming down the corridor, advancing with military tread. He greeted the airman by his surname and informed him, "Cpl Jenkins will not be your shift partner this week. I have altered the rota." He did not explain why or introduce us or acknowledge my presence in any way, but turned on his heel and left. Should I have gone down to report? I did not know and my shaky confidence began to ebb away. It left me completely when I realised with growing dismay that this young man and I were the entire shift.

We introduced ourselves. His name was Bill. As the SWO had done, he eyed my new battledress and asked, "Is this your first posting?" I said it was. "When did you arrive?"

"On the section? This morning."

"And he put you straight on nights?" He looked incredulous.

"Yes." I explained how this had come about.

Bill asked, "Do you know your way around, yet?"

"I wasn't here long enough for anyone to show me." I said dryly.

He swore softly, and looking at the situation from his point of view I could sympathise. He was saddled with a rookie who had never done the job except as an exercise in school, knew nothing of the section routine, did not know where anything was kept and was altogether an unknown quantity. With the resigned air of one who knows he has been dealt a poor hand with no option but to make the best of it, Bill said, "Come on then. I'll show you round. We'll start with the chemical room."

Still carrying the cardboard box he led the way to the room I had been facing when I left the flight's office that morning. A tall metal cupboard standing in one corner dominated the room, which was quite small. The cupboard contained jars of chemicals, including hydrochloric acid, an array of thick white china mugs, a stack of plates and a frying pan. Beneath the window stood a lead-lined sink with a draining board on which stood a Primus stove. Two stools completed the furnishings. Bill placed the box on the draining board beside the stove. "Supper," he explained, "We cook our own." He indicated the Primus, "Can you work one of these?"

"Sorry," I said, feeling inadequate, "I was useless at Guide camp and we didn't do Primus stoves at Blackpool."

He snorted with sudden laughter. I looked at his face, not handsome but pleasant, and saw that he was genuinely amused. If he was feeling hard done by he was not going to take it out on me, for which I was grateful.

"You'd better come and see the darkrooms before we turn the lights out," said Bill. He took me to a door halfway along the corridor to flight's office. It opened into a light trap, a small space with two doors leading off it, one to the film room the other to the printing room. Apart from the layout being slightly different, they looked much the same as those at Blackpool. The equipment was familiar and I felt at home. All I had to do was remember what I had been taught and everything would be all right.

"OK," said Bill, "Let's get started." We returned to the general room and Bill pointed to the line of cameras. "Can you log this lot in?" I assured him I could. He stood over me until he was satisfied I knew what I was doing, then took the first camera off to the darkroom to start the developing. I finished the paperwork, lifted another camera off the bench and went along to join him. There was now a red warning light showing above the door in the corridor, indicating the darkrooms were in use.

Between us we had developed all the aerial and cine films and looped them over the racks in the drying room before Bill said anything about supper. This consisted of cheese dreams (fried cheese sandwiches), which I gathered were his favourite snack. Watching him trying to get the temperamental Primus to light, I felt more worried about doing the cooking when my turn came than I did about the work.

We ate perched on the two stools in the chemical room. Bill was relaxed and friendly, which I took to be a sign the work was going well, given our slow start. "How long is the night shift?" I asked him. He looked taken aback for a moment, forgetting I knew nothing about the work routine except what he himself had told me. "Officially we're here all night, but actually we can go off duty as soon as we've finished whatever there is to be done. It depends how much aerial photography the pilots have done that day, and that depends to a large extent on the weather. On a good day they might all be up and we'll have a busy night. If it's been low cloud and pouring rain there won't be much for us to do and we can get a good night's kip."

"It's been beautiful today," I said, surprised there were not more cameras to do.

Bill grinned, "So think yourself lucky they weren't all doing photography. We should be finished by two or three."

"And then we go back to the billet?"

"No. There's a couple of bunks in the storeroom for the girls. I go back to barracks."

I was relieved to hear it. For an uncomfortable moment I had wondered exactly how far this night shift partnership was supposed to go. Later I discovered that there were usually either two men or two girls on nights together and they both slept in the bunks.

I had held my own when we were dealing with the films but I could not match Bill's speed at printing. He had been a photographer before joining up and had two years experience in the RAF to fall back on. After watching me set up the enlarger and produce the first few prints he suggested that he did all the printing while I dried, glazed and sorted the prints. I was ready to agree to anything that would speed up the work. I collected batches of wet prints from the darkroom, fed them onto the conveyor belt that went round a big heated glazing drum and sorted them when they were dry. It was important that the prints from each film should be kept separate and attributed to the correct pilot. As they all flew over roughly the same area when they were mapping, it followed that all the films were much alike and produced similar prints. If they got mixed up it would be time-consuming – if not impossible - to sort them out again.

The system worked well at first, but in the small hours of the morning I found myself getting slower and slower and was too tired to speed up. My legs ached from the unaccustomed cycling I had done that day, and the ache was spreading up my back. To ease the pain I fetched a stool from the chemical room and did the job sitting down. It was a monotonous, repetitive operation and the room was very warm. Once or twice I started to doze and jerked awake as I lost my balance on the stool. I leaned against the conveyor belt support frame - and fell fast asleep. Some time later Bill came through to see why I had not come to collect another batch of prints for some time and found the last lot dried to a crisp and scattered all over the floor, where they had fallen off the unattended drum. He woke me up and suggested somewhat curtly that I go and crash out on one of the bunks. What the flight sergeant would have said had he known of such consideration - even if it was prompted by concern for the prints' welfare not mine - I didn't know, and at that moment I didn't care. In a daze of sleep I flung myself on the lower bunk and spent what remained of the night unconscious among the drums of chemicals, boxes of printing paper, cleaning materials and spare odds and ends in the storeroom. Poor Bill had to try and sort out the fallen prints and finish the shift on his own.

Gina woke me with a mug of tea when the day shift was brewing up next morning at elevenses time. "How did it go?" she enquired. At first I couldn't think where I was or what she was talking about. Then as I came fully awake I remembered and felt a stab of guilt. I had let myself down as well as Bill. I said cautiously, "It was tiring."

"It must have been," Gina sounded genuinely sympathetic. "Charlie says Bill woke up the whole barracks clattering in at four o'clock this morning. That was a hell of a long day you had yesterday. I must go," she finished hastily, "or I'll be polishing floors again."

I drank my tea and worried. Bill had been well and truly lumbered last night. I couldn't blame him if he had complained about it as he crawled into bed at dawn. Yet Gina clearly didn't know I had fallen asleep on the job although Charlie, whoever he was, had lost no time broadcasting his moans about being woken up. Was Bill covering up for me? He would probably be asked by the flight sergeant to report on the new girl's work. What would he say?

To try to make amends I turned up early that evening. The day shift looked mildly surprised when I started the logging-in but no one said anything. One of them was a corporal, a beetle-browed stocky man of about thirty. I heard someone address him as 'Jenks', which identified him as the Cpl Jenkins whose place I had taken on the night shift at such short notice. He gave me a keen look, weighing me up, but did not interrupt what I was doing. By the time Bill arrived with the rations I had finished the bookwork and was ready to start the developing. My embarrassed apology for not finishing the shift the previous night was accepted with a forgiving grin, and I don't think he ever told anyone about my lapse. Not officially, anyway. I thought Jenks had a knowing look about him once or twice when I spoke to him later. I was very lucky to have been teamed with Bill for my punishment week. He was even tolerant of my indifferent cooking when after several unsuccessful attempts I mastered the Primus stove. My cheese dreams were very inferior to his.

We had one really heavy night that week. About three o'clock in the morning, when we had stopped for a second break, I asked him, "Why does all the printing have to be done at night? Why can't the day shift do some?"

"Because the prints are needed first thing next morning. They have to be assessed before the crews go up again," he replied.

During other supper breaks he told me about the work of the section and the station in general. I learned that an OTU was the final stage in the air crews' training. The planes in use at that time were Blenheims. They carried a crew of three: pilot, navigator and gunner, and up until this point they had been on separate courses. Here they mingled for the first time to crew up and practise flying together before being posted to operational squadrons.

"You mean they choose who they want to fly with for themselves?" I asked.

"As far as possible. If they're flying with men they're at ease with it can make all the difference in a tight spot. We've got one pilot who's been here for months," said Bill, "he's so bad tempered nobody will fly with him."

I had only two contacts with the daytime world that week: Rosie the cook and Gina. Rosie spotted me coming to the mess by myself at odd hours and on my third morning she asked, "You're surely not on nights already?" I must have sounded forlorn when I said that indeed I was, for she came out from behind her counter to keep me company for a few minutes. I was delighted to have someone to talk to before returning to the empty House to spend the rest of the day alone. I think she felt sorry for me, because she always came over for a chat, whatever time I went to the mess.

Gina kept me in touch with the gossip on the section when she brought in my mid-morning mug of tea. Our conversations were necessarily brief, she was sure Flight clocked her in and out. "They're closing the billets. We're all being moved into Nissen huts," she announced one morning. I could never really relax in Bicester House in the afternoons and usually gave up the attempt and went out. Cycling along the road that led to Launton I had seen Nissen huts being erected in fields not far from the camp and wondered who they were for. Now, remembering how glad the girls at Blackpool had been to escape from them into a 'proper house', I was dismayed. Bicester House was giving me the creeps with its unseen echoing footsteps, but at least it was weather-proof, its walls were not running with condensation making everything damp, and we did not have to run through the rain to get to the ablutions.

On the day after my last night shift I went back to the House and relaxed for the first time for a week. I had managed to settle down to letter-writing in the afternoons, but not to reading. Now I could lose myself in my book knowing that time was of no importance. At a convenient stage in the plot I cycled up to the mess for my evening meal and dawdled over it deliberately, savouring my freedom.

"We thought you'd deserted when you didn't come back that night. Or ended up in hospital with that bike," said Elaine when I saw her that evening. She was sympathetic when I told her how I had fallen foul of the flight sergeant, but couldn't help laughing. And suddenly I found myself laughing with her. It was so good to have company in the billet after my lonely afternoons. The house felt totally different; footsteps along the passages no longer sounded hollow and faintly alarming, they were signs of life. My feeling of isolation left me as Elaine chattered on. In a way it was a pity, I thought, that we would be split up when the Nissen huts were ready for occupation, but I consoled myself with the hope that I would be with the other girls on the section when we moved. No matter how well I got on with Elaine and the rest of them, I would always be odd one out, being the only photographer there.

The following morning I was due to start on the day shift. I was so determined not to be late that I cycled into camp early for breakfast. I had nearly finished when Gina came in. She spotted me and brought her breakfast over to my table. We had had no real opportunity to talk since arriving at Bicester and we had a lot of catching up to do. "Did you see the band when you were on leave?" I enquired.

She shook her head. "That broke up ages ago. It was only a small band. The young ones got called up."

I was surprised she had never mentioned this before. I asked, "And the others?"

"They got other jobs." She inspected a piece of sausage on the end of her fork, then looked at me with an awkward smile. "One of them works in a club in Blackpool."

I stared at her in astonishment for several seconds before finding my voice. "So that's where .... ! You were working?" I felt hurt. "You might have told me."

"Sorry," Gina sounded contrite. "Mrs Gillie said the fewer people who knew the better, in case I got caught."

"Mrs Gillie? You told her?"

"I had to. I didn't want her getting the wrong idea, like Edna. Poisonous cow." She said it dismissively, without venom.

"I still think you could have told me," I said huffily.

"Sorry," she said again, "I couldn't. You got so upset over Edna I was afraid you'd have a row and let it slip. And God knows what she'd have done with the information."

My feathers were still ruffled, partly because I knew that what she said was true, but I didn't like to admit it. I said, "I should have thought the uniform was more likely to get you into trouble."

"Oh, I didn't wear uniform. Mum sent some of my civvy togs and I changed at the club. Just as well I did. The SP's came in one evening, looking for someone they'd lost. I thought I'd had it for a moment."

The hurt suddenly left me and I crowed with laughter. For sheer brass nerve Gina would be hard to beat.

We carried on chatting until I looked at my watch and scrambled to my feet. "Come on, I daren't be late again."

While we were cycling over to the technical side of the camp we overtook a young airman walking in the same direction. "See you tonight," he called after Gina and she waved a casual acknowledgement. "Band practice. We've got a gig on Saturday night," she explained. I noted that it was already 'we', not 'they' who had the gig.

We reached the section a split second before 0800 hours. In a rerun of my arrival the week before, the same lordly corporal was in the corridor. He tapped his watch significantly and said, "I see you only just managed to get here on time."

I said, "Yes, Corporal," in neutral tones and stood more or less to attention in front of him. He looked as if he were about to say something more, changed his mind and strode down to the flight sergeant's office. Gina and I went in the opposite direction. From behind the closed door of the chemical room came the muffled sound of voices and the clink of mugs; someone was making the first brew of the day. Gina turned in at the general room door and I followed. When it was safe to speak I asked, "Is he always like that?"

Gina nodded. "Pompous ass. He's not very popular. Too full of his own importance."

"What's his name?"

"Small."

The name was so inapt I giggled. "I suppose everyone calls him

'Lofty'?"

"Not to his face, they don't. It has to be 'Corporal' every time. And don't forget to touch your forelock or you'll be in trouble."

"What's Cpl Jenkins like? He looks nice," I said, still laughing.

"He is. You have to watch your step until after the mid-morning brew up if he's been out on the booze the night before. Otherwise he's OK."

A dozen or so airmen and Waafs were standing around doing nothing, chatting in desultory fashion. I knew their faces from passing them going out as I went on duty each evening the week before, but did not yet know their names. I whispered to Gina, "Which one's Charlie?"

"The grouser? He's not here. He's gone on nights with a new bod called Lennie. Lennie's the cheeky sort, insists on being cheerful non-stop. They'll drive each other barmy," she chuckled.

I looked automatically towards the long line of cameras laid out on the bench under the windows. "I shouldn't think they had much time to fall out last night by the look of that lot," I remarked.

I had expected everything to be hustle and bustle and was puzzled by the continuing inactivity around us. "What are we waiting for?" I wanted to know.

"We're waiting for Training to tell Flight how many cameras they want fitted today," she replied. Moments later the telephone rang in his office. The tea-drinkers came along from the chemical room, including Bill. He grinned at me and I smiled back almost shyly. I felt we were meeting out of context and I would have to get to know him all over again. As footsteps came down the corridor, there was a general air of straightening up in readiness to receive orders. I watched the door and braced myself, expecting to see the flight sergeant. Whatever his orders were for anybody else, I was afraid my job for the day would be polishing floors, like Gina. However, it was not Flight who appeared, it was the sergeant, and I took heart.

"Right, let's be having you," he said, "they want the lot today.

So we'd better get cracking." He detailed ten people to fit cameras and to my joy I was one of them. We worked in pairs. As each pair was named they grabbed a camera apiece and made for the stairs. I was teamed with an unsmiling girl called Ruth. She said, "Follow the others," and hauled a camera off the bench. I did the same. Waiting for us outside stood a large van with its engine running. The whole section, even the lofty Corporal Small, helped to carry down cameras and film cans, heaving them into the back of the van. We climbed aboard. The driver put his foot down hard on the accelerator and we spurted away. This was the moment I had been dreaming about all through our training. I felt as excited as if I were going flying myself, though I tried not to show it. I was still a rookie in the eyes of my partner and the other teams; I wanted to impress them as a responsible member of the working party, not look like a child going on an outing.

The van raced across the airfield to the dispersal pans (aircraft parking spaces) round the perimeter. It stopped at the first plane, dropped off a team with their camera and film can and sped on to the next one. Ruth and I were dropped off last. She clambered on to the wing of the plane and I handed her up the camera and went up after her with the film can. She climbed on top of the fuselage and dropped down through the hatch into the body of the plane. I handed down the camera and followed. It only took her a couple of minutes to clamp the camera into its frame by the pilot's seat. The lens pointed downwards through an aperture in the floor. There was very little room to move around; I manoeuvred my way to the gun turret at the rear, slotted the film can into position on the gun and checked the fitting. I assumed Ruth would come and check it too, as Bill had done when I loaded my first spool of film into the developing tank, but when I looked round she was already hauling herself out through the hatch. She jumped to the ground and I scrambled out after her. Together we walked away from the plane to sit on the grass and wait for our transport to return. We could see the van in the distance, dashing to and fro across the airfield, picking up the teams who had been dropped off ahead of us and depositing them beside the next planes to be fitted. Ruth took off her cap and shook out her hair. It was light brown and curly, with golden lights glinting in the sunshine. Her face looked cold and aloof and I was not sure I liked her. Suddenly she screwed up her eyes and peered towards the distant hangars. She said urgently, "The crews are coming out." and scrambled to her feet. Alerted, I did the same. Our transport was speeding towards us. "Come on," cried Ruth and started running to meet it, jamming her cap back on as she ran. I followed close behind. The van screeched to a halt in front of us, stopped just long enough for us to throw ourselves into the back and raced off again. There was one camera and can left to fit. Across the airfield came the roar of the first engine to be started up, followed by another and another. We tumbled out beside the last plane as the crew wagon headed in our direction. This time everything had to be done at the double. We completed the job in half the time it had taken us to do the first one. The crew wagon had already stopped and the crew were lumbering towards us as we emerged from the hatch. Each man was strapped into a parachute harness and wore a helmet. They started to climb aboard almost before we were off the wing. All three of them ignored us, brushing past as if we did not exist. "They're always like that before a flight," said Ruth when I complained. "Don't take it to heart, it's nothing personal." She had a soft Scottish accent that was very soothing.

Thinking about it, I could see their attitude was understandable. Up until then they had only flown with instructors. Navigators and gunners now had to entrust their lives to novice pilots with no more experience than themselves. And the pilots were for the first time solely responsible for the lives of their crew. They had more to think about than camera fitters who should have been out of their way before they arrived.

Our transport had gone to pick up the other teams, Ruth and I settled ourselves on the grass again. Behind us the plane's engines thundered into life. Conversation was impossible. I was drowning in noise and blissfully happy.

The van returned in due course, having picked up everyone else first. It dropped us at the end of a queue for the Naafi wagon parked on the apron in front of one of the hangars. Now I came to think about it, I was famished. 'Char and a wad' was just what I needed. I stood with the others, clutching my hot mug of tea and munching my slab of cake and felt I was on my way to becoming a veteran and proud of it.

"Do the same people go out to collect the cameras later?" I asked Ruth. My voice was eager and I saw two of the men exchange amused glances. Ruth said "Uh-huh," and smiled for the first time. It made her look friendly and reassured me that I had been a satisfactory team-mate.

Up in the section I found Gina making a map. She was struggling to fit together prints that did not match because the pilot had not maintained a level height. Roads and hedges were disjointed. "The prune who took this lot needs a bit more practice," she said irritably. Waiting to be told what to do next, I leaned against the bench and watched her. After a few minutes the sergeant, whose name was Finch, came over to speak to me. Presumably he wanted to make his own assessment of the rookie Waaf who had made such a shaky start on the section. I straightened up and answered his questions smartly, determined to make a good impression. I had been too bound up with my own feelings when he gave us our orders in the morning to notice much about him. Now I observed him more closely and saw that his surname suited him. He was a small man with a sprightly manner. He had bright black eyes and a way of turning his head sharply, like an alert bird watching out for the neighbourhood cat. As the days passed and I settled down to the routine, I found him to be a strict disciplinarian but approachable, easy to get on with as long as the work was done well. He had his office in one of the hangars, where the cameras were stored when not in use, and divided his time between there and the section. He was a popular NCO and I often wished that he were the one in full-time charge of the section and Flight was the one who disappeared into the hangar at frequent intervals.

Chapter 13

Winter

IN THE LATE AUTUMN Bicester House closed as expected and the inmates were transferred to the new Nissen huts. None of the girls wanted to go, especially with winter coming on. "They'll be freezing cold," said Elaine, "and then in summer they'll be stifling hot." Other girls took up the theme with stories similar to those I had heard at Blackpool – rain driving in through gaps between the curved metal panels that formed the walls and roof, snow drifting in over the beds, frozen pipes in the ablutions. Gina said the girls in her billet were saying exactly the same sort of thing. I faced the move with apprehension.

I don't know how it happened but in the scramble for beds in a hut near the ablutions Gina, Ruth and I became separated from the other photographers. For this I was secretly thankful, although I had originally hoped we would all be together. It was not that I disliked any of the girls, but there were two, Cynthia and Dorothy, with whom I was not at ease. They were great friends and did everything together. They were also extremely efficient. I found them rather daunting and was somewhat in awe of them.

To look at they were a contrasting pair. Cynthia was tall for a woman and slim, Dorothy was short, bordering on stocky. Cynthia had very dark hair drawn straight back off her face into a bun at the nape of her neck, ignoring any old nonsense about hair having to be kept off her collar. She also had very dark brown eyes. Fine eyes my father would have called them. Her mouth was wide and she wore brilliant red lipstick. She looked exotic and the way she moved reminded me of Grace, the ballroom dancing champion at the tax office. Dorothy was of medium height, brisk and business-like. I guessed she was about ten years older than Cynthia, somewhere in her mid thirties (getting on a bit in my eyes). She wore her light brown hair in a conventional style, parted at the side and held off her face with a hairgrip. Her make-up was unobtrusive. Cynthia wore a sizeable diamond solitaire on her engagement finger. Her fiancé was a flying instructor, currently out in Canada where a lot of our aircrews were trained. I do not think she had worked in photography before the war; Dorothy had had her own portrait studio and had photographed several well-known film stars, including Margaret Lockwood.

It was a mystery to me why some people seemed to be posted from place to place for no apparent reason while others were left on the same station for months – years in some cases. Cynthia and Dorothy belonged in the latter category. They had been on the section longer than anyone else, which gave them an unassailable advantage over later arrivals. They were the leading lights on the section socially, although they were only LACWs. Whenever they considered life was growing dull they would round up all available members of the day shift and we would cycle in a body to the Crown Hotel in Sheep Street to liven ourselves up in the lounge bar. They also organised 'welcome back' parties in the same way. Anyone returning from leave on an evening train would be met at the station, sometimes by the whole party, and carried off to drown their sorrows in beer. Any excuse was good enough for a party. Jenks was always well to the fore on these occasions. Sgt Finch and his wife had a house in the town (known, of course, as 'The Nest') and he often dropped in to join us for a beer. Off duty he was a natural comic, always good for a laugh and always welcome. Flight and Cpl Small never came. Whether this was because they were never asked or because they did not care to come, I don't know.

I enjoyed these gatherings enormously. They made up for the social life I had missed out on at home. I never became much of a drinker. Half a pint of mild, as advocated by Paul, lasted me well into the evening. I did not really like the taste but, as he had promised, I got used to it. I had to; beer was all we drank in the ordinary way. Shorts were too expensive.

The only person on the section to decline the party summons was Gina. As she had done at Blackpool, she disappeared about her own affairs every evening except on domestic night. I was very glad of Ruth's company when we moved into the hut. On the morning I first met her I had thought she looked formidable, but I had quickly discovered that her looks belied her nature. True, she did not laugh easily, but she was always friendly and helpful in her quiet way and we had become good friends.

I think there were about twenty beds in the hut. The corporal in charge occupied one of those tucked in a corner beside the little entrance lobby that acted as a light trap during the hours of blackout. Gina, Ruth and I chose beds at the opposite end of the hut, as far away from authority as possible and out of the draughts that whistled under the door. When the nights turned cold we rather wished we had chosen beds nearer the iron stove that stood in the middle of the hut. However, being in the end beds gave us an illusion of privacy and you can't have everything. You could always put your groundsheet over the blankets to keep the warmth in at night, as the more experienced girls did.

On the day we moved in I prowled around, squinting to see if any daylight showed between the metal panels where they overlapped. Gina, who remembered the day she had caught me checking my bedding for fleas at Blackpool, asked, "What on earth are you looking for now?"

"Gaps, of course," I said briefly.

"I shouldn't bother," she said in her dismissive way, "You'll soon know if we've got gaps when it rains. And there's nothing you can do about it, anyway."

For the record, there were no gaps and the rain and snow did not drift in, but we did suffer from condensation running down the walls. Apart from that our worst problem was one I had never heard mentioned - how to deal with the earwigs that took up residence with us. They used to crawl up the walls until they reached the point where the panels curved inwards to become the roof, and there the little pests lost their grip and fell onto our beds, just about level with our heads. One girl was so frightened they would live up to their name and crawl into her ears that she always wore a pixie hat in bed. I never went that far but I pulled my bed away from the wall, hoping to be out of range. This also helped to keep the bedclothes away from the condensation. Occasionally an earwig would fall into someone's hair as she slept. In the early days her shriek of panic as it struggled to free itself would disturb the hut, but after a while we got used to them and nobody took any notice. I lost track of Elaine after we moved, for which I was sorry. She had been lively company at Bicester House where she was happy, I hoped she had settled down in her new billet despite her foreboding. It probably depended on how strongly she detested earwigs.

To compensate for our unforeseen problem we had an unexpected luxury – a toilet, reached by a door in the end wall of the hut. To have a wash or a bath we still had to go out to the ablutions, but at least we could nip into the loo without having to brave the weather outside. It was a very noisy loo, the cistern clanked and gurgled and at first it woke up half the hut when anyone pulled the chain during the night, but we got used to it in time and learned to ignore it, as we did the earwigs.

We had girls from a variety of trades in the hut: at least one ambulance driver, two Admin clerks and several cooks, one of whom was Rosie. This was a real stroke of luck. Rosie was a born carer, as I already knew, and she took everyone's welfare to heart. She kept us supplied with the wherewithal to make cocoa in the evenings, producing a tin kettle to boil the water on the top of the stove. She brought in ready-sliced bread, which we toasted by holding it up against the sides of the stove with our forks, and tins of margarine and bright red unidentifiable jam. An absolute feast on a cold winter's night! The corporal in charge of the hut at that time, Phyllis, was easy-going and the atmosphere was a relaxed and happy one.

In November I heard from Paul. Apologies for the delay in answering my letter. Belated congratulations on passing my course so well. The saga of the bed bugs had made him laugh. He was now on the gunnery course. He hoped to be on the last stage of his training by Christmas. He would send me his new address as soon as he knew it.

There was nothing of himself in the letter apart from his enjoyment of the bed bug story and again I was disappointed. I could not think of anything interesting to write about and decided to wait until he reached his next station, presumably an OTU, before I replied.

I also heard from my mother, who wrote to say that Father would be coming home from Llandudno for three days at Christmas. Was there any chance I could get home, if only for a day? Sgt Finch said there would be no flying on Christmas Day and therefore no night shift on Christmas night. Although several of the others had already been granted leave over the holiday he saw no reason why I could not be spared for forty-eight hours. With my hopes high I went along to see Flight. He eyed me coldly. I put my request to him, explaining why it was important to me. He said, "You're not entitled to any leave, you've hardly been here three months," and dismissed me.

I was choked with disappointment, which turned to fury when Gina asked for Christmas leave a few days later and her request was granted. Two or three members of her old band were going to be home over the holiday and she wanted to see them again. To my mind her reason for wanting leave was no more important than mine and I stormed at Jenks, "All I asked for was a lousy forty-eight. Gina hasn't been here any longer than I have and she's got three days. What's he got against me?"

Jenks was a diplomat. He avoided giving me a direct answer. He said, "Flight's a career man, see. Been in since he was a boy. He doesn't hold with women in the Forces. He says they've got no sense of discipline." Here he paused to give me a very hard look from under his beetling eyebrows. I refused to acknowledge that this could apply to me and he went on, "He's afraid they will lose us the war."

With only eight months service behind me, most of which had been taken up with training, I had the sense not to comment, but privately I thought the man was an idiot.

As there would be no work to do on Christmas Day, I asked Jenks why the section had to be manned all the time. There had to be a skeleton staff on duty, he said, in case there was an emergency of some sort. I asked sarcastically, "If the Germans land here, what are we supposed to do – take their pictures?" He ignored this, rightly attributing it to spleen because I could not have my own way. In the end everyone was allowed to go home except Charlie the grouser, Lennie (who was also told he did not qualify), Ruth and me. Being Scottish, Ruth did not give Christmas the importance we Sassenachs did. She had been granted leave to go home for New Year and was looking forward to celebrating Hogmanay in traditional style with her family.

On Christmas morning I awoke at the usual time, momentarily puzzled by the unaccustomed quiet in the hut. Then I remembered; only a handful of girls were left. Everyone else had gone home. I closed my eyes again to delay getting up as long as possible. My mind went back to the past. I remembered Mother and Father sitting up in their big bed enjoying an early - often extremely early - cup of tea and watching David and me delve excitedly into pillowcases bulging with brightly wrapped packages. Realistically I knew that although Mother and Father might be having an early cup of tea this morning it was doubtful if David had bothered to hang up a pillowcase. He was now nearly sixteen and would have thought it childish. Apart from which, I knew from one of Mother's letters that there would be few presents to unwrap this year; everything was either rationed, unobtainable or too expensive to afford. Prices had rocketed since the beginning of the war. Nevertheless, whatever the family's Christmas was like I yearned to be with them.

Flight having granted himself leave, Sgt Finch was nominally in charge of the section. However, after paying us a brief visit when we reported for duty he disappeared back to The Nest, leaving us lumbered with Cpl Small. RCs were allowed time off to go to Mass on this special day. I had obtained permission from Sgt Finch to leave the section to go to church; the lofty corporal made it plain that he was only letting me go because he had no choice.

There was an RC church on the camp, but I wanted to get away from uniforms. Thinking there would be a more homely atmosphere in a civilian church, I cycled to Mass at the parish church in Bicester. This turned out to be a mistake. I was a stranger there among people who all knew one another. Families bunched together in the crowded pews, excited children fidgeted and whispered to their friends in front or behind them. There was a good sprinkling of fathers present, mostly in uniform, but it was the mothers who hissed threats of dire punishment later if their offspring did not sit still and behave themselves. It was all very like I remembered it at home, but I was not part of it. I found it hard to concentrate or pray. Outside afterwards, as friends gathered in little knots to greet each other, I was only too glad to mount my bicycle and pedal back into my own world for company.

On the section I found the others kicking their heels in the general room. Charlie was grousing about having been refused leave, Lennie was looking bored, and Ruth was living in a little world of her own. Physically she might be here on the section at Bicester but her spirit was obviously somewhere over Aberdeen, floating on a little pink cloud as she dreamed of first-footing and whisky and pieces of coal. Cpl Small was nowhere to be seen. I went along to the chemical room, poured myself a mug of stewed tea and went to kick my heels with the others.

At midday Cpl Small emerged from Flight's office and came down to inform us we had to report back to the section after dinner as our officer, Pilot Officer Roland, would be coming in to see us. Almost before he had finished speaking and before he had pronounced the important word "Dismiss" I grabbed Ruth by the wrist and all but ran her off the section. At all costs I wanted to escape being joined by Charlie. I had no intention of having to listen to him moaning all through the meal. Halfway down the stairs we were passed by Lennie, making an even quicker getaway than ours.

The airmen's mess, vast in comparison to the Waafs', was filling up fast and the babble of voices was deafening. It was a tradition throughout the Services that on Christmas Day the officers waited on the Other Ranks at dinner. Ruth and I found seats together at one of the crowded tables and watched our high-class waiters and waitresses move quickly down the long counter collecting laden plates to set before the hungry hordes. Being new to the tradition, it made me feel slightly uncomfortable. I would have been perfectly happy to collect my dinner for myself in the usual way. The cooks had done a magnificent job, producing roast turkey or some other fowl with all the trimmings, Christmas pudding that could have passed for pre-war, with mince pies to follow. The officers patrolled up and down between the tables making sure everyone had their fair share of whatever was going. The whole operation was a masterpiece of organisation, though I don't think I appreciated this at the time.

Towards the end of the meal the officers, though still dutiful, began to look bored, and it was noticeable that although no one was neglected some people were receiving more attention than others. One girl sitting opposite us seemed to be surrounded by RAF officers the whole time. She was not a particularly good-looking girl, but obviously had some attraction I could not recognise. I whispered to Ruth, "What's she got that the rest of us haven't?"

"I think you've got that the wrong way round," she whispered back. "It should be 'what have we still got that she hasn't?' They call her the officers' ground sheet." I was amazed: it was the sort of remark I associated with Gina, not our solemn and staid Ruth. I put it down to the spirit of Hogmanay exerting its influence early.

The noisy, cheerful atmosphere in the mess had banished my earlier depression and I came out in buoyant mood. Back in the general room, hanging about waiting for our officer to visit us before we could be dismissed, the mood was difficult to sustain. Cpl Small was tetchy with Ruth and me for leaving the section without waiting for official permission and addressed us at some length on the importance of discipline. Our blank, unimpressed stares annoyed him still further (as they were meant to do). Charlie was complaining that his sprouts had been cold. Only Lennie, who had lost some of his chirpy manner in the morning, now managed to stay cheerful. Ruth and I thought we knew why. We had spotted him leaving the mess with a very pretty Waaf. Doubtless his mood reflected his hopes for the evening ahead. Idly I speculated. Was she someone special, or was he merely hoping this was going to be his lucky night? And if he did persuade the girl to do it, would he pass her name round the barracks, as Paul had said they all did? Studying his cheeky face I was prepared to bet that he would.

Paul had written in mid December sending me his latest address as promised, the OTU at Moreton-in-Marsh. He said he was with a good crowd. I did not mind the dearth of information. I realised it was as difficult for him to write more fully as it was for me. We were not supposed to write about our work, the station in general or anything else that might be of use to the enemy should the letter fall into the wrong hands. What upset me was the lack of any warmth or personal feeling in his letters. Not that there was much of either in mine. We were not the same people who had laughed and talked so much at Blackpool. I had made up my mind to let the correspondence peter out. I sent him a Christmas card with a message wishing him all the best, but did not write a letter.

The arrival of our officer was welcomed with relief. Pilot Officer Roland, who doubled as the Entertainments Officer, was a genial man, somewhere in his middle forties. His nickname 'Roly' was predictable, inspired as much by his well-padded figure as by his surname. He did not appear amongst us very often, preferring to leave the running of the section to his senior NCOs, both of whom were perfectly capable of managing without him. Now he came bustling in with a beaming smile, his eyes twinkling behind horn-rimmed spectacles, expecting to find his skeleton staff in festive mood. In his role of Entertainments Officer he was responsible for all the arrangements made to celebrate Christmas on camp. He had not been in evidence in the mess hall, but had presumably been busy behind the scenes. He was now looking for confirmation that the day had been a success so far and we were enjoying ourselves. The air of bored irritation that met him in the general room caused his smile to falter; he looked deflated. "Did you enjoy the dinner?" he enquired anxiously. Before Charlie had time to tell him about the sprouts, Ruth, Lennie and I assured him firmly that we had.

"Good, good!" Roly's smile returned to full beam. "Are you coming to the dance tonight?" He looked round with resolute good humour. Lennie's enthusiastic "Yes, Sir," was enough to convince him that his arrangements were going well.

"Splendid, splendid! Well, if you've finished for the day we might as well close the section. Carry on, Corporal!" Pleased with our genuinely warm response to his suggestion, he hurried away.

Ruth was not interested in going to the dance; I wanted to go, but not by myself. Diane, one of the Admin girls, therefore suggested that I go with her. She had a date, but at least she would be someone to walk in with. The dance was being held in the all-purpose hall that adapted to every type of entertainment. Diane's date was waiting for her in the entrance lobby and she introduced us. Reg was a pleasant-looking boy, too polite to let his face show what I was sure he was thinking – "I hope we're not going to be saddled with her for the evening." We all stood chatting for a few minutes until the band struck up a lively number and the other two went through into the hall. I was looking round to see if there was anyone else I knew when a tall, dark, good-looking young sergeant navigator came up to me. Obviously imbued with the party spirit (acquired in the sergeants' mess bar earlier, I subsequently realised) he invited me to come and have a drink. I thanked him. He took my elbow and propelled me towards a room off the lobby, set out as a bar. Warning bells sounded in my mind when he spotted another sergeant who had just arrived and called out, "Hey, Pete! Grab yourself a woman and join us. I'll get the first round in." To me he said, "Go and grab a table," then thrust his way through the crush at the bar counter ordering "Four pints" at the top of his voice as he went. I made my way across the room and laid claim to four chairs round a small table, already sure that my warning bells had rung true, accepting his invitation had been a mistake. Moments later he emerged from the scrum carrying four pint mugs of beer and slammed them down so hard on the table they slopped over to form spreading puddles. "Where the hell's Pete?" he demanded impatiently, flopping down beside me. The table was not level. The puddles formed themselves into a stream and began to flow in my direction. I moved my chair sideways to avoid getting beer in my lap when the stream reached the edge of the table and spilled over. This had the unintended benefit of putting more space between myself and the sergeant.

I thought it was time we exchanged names, and was about to ask for his when Pete appeared at the door with a Waaf in tow. My escort leapt to his feet and waved his arms, shouting, "Over here," and the opportunity was lost. Pete came down the room, unsteady on his feet. He took the chair on the other side of me to my sergeant and reached for his pint, raising it in a wobbly salute. His words were slurred, "Thanksh, Malc". As the Waaf took her seat between the two men she looked at Malc, cast a cool eye over me to assess the opposition, and switched on the charm. Turning her chair slightly so that she could look more directly at Malc she gazed at him over the rim of her beer mug with obvious favour. He caught her look and responded with a broad wink, the prelude to an exchange of flirtatious remarks that left Pete and me firmly out in the cold. If we were about to change partners – assuming we had not already done so - he and I would be left together. I glanced round at him to see how he was taking it, but he had his face buried in his beer mug, seemingly unaware of what was happening. He was a bulky individual, thick-necked and ginger-haired, with pale blue eyes. I thought he looked the type who could turn nasty if he was upset. I did not take to him and I certainly did not want to be his woman, even for one evening. Malc leaned towards the Waaf and whispered something that made her splutter with laughter. I decided to leave. I stood up saying, "Back in a minute." Pete, who had finished his pint, said, "OK," assuming I was going to the Ladies. Malc did not appear to have heard me, nor did he notice me walking away. When I reached the door out to the lobby I turned to look back. Pete was lurching towards the bar clutching his empty mug, intent on getting a refill. Malc was pulling his chair closer to the Waaf's. I saw her lean up against him and reach out to finger the top button of his tunic. He was on to a good thing there, and judging by the look on his face he knew it. I wondered how long it would take Pete to realise I had abandoned him and he would have to go and grab himself a replacement.

I did not feel like hanging around waiting to be picked up again. I collected my greatcoat and cap and left. Outside it was a lovely clear, crisp night. I rode slowly down the lane towards the huts, thinking back over the day, my first Christmas away from home. The lively atmosphere over dinner had been fun, but the rest of the day was a dead loss. I tried to imagine what my family were doing at this moment. Were they playing the childish card games that were a tradition at home on Christmas night? 'Snap', 'Old Maid' and 'Newmarket', gambling with buttons? A wave of homesickness hit me so hard I could hardly breathe. I dismounted, leaned against a five-bar gate and took in great gulps of the cold air until I felt better. The screech of an owl nearby made me jump. Across the dark fields a second owl answered. It sounded eerie and I shivered. At the same moment something rustled loudly in the hedge beside me. Without waiting to find out what it was I jumped on my bike and pedalled for the hut.

On my birthday in February I was astounded to receive a note from Paul wishing me a happy day. I recalled sitting in a canteen in Blackpool one evening talking about birthdays and exchanging dates. Guiltily I realised I had forgotten his. And I had certainly never expected him to remember mine. My resolution to let the correspondence lapse went out of the window. I wrote back at once, delighted to have something personal to respond to at last. At the end of my letter I had to own up to having forgotten his birthday and asked him to remind me of the date. I did not receive a reply.

Chapter 14

Springtime 1943

WHEN WE HAD BEEN been on the section for six months, Gina and I sat our exams to become LACWs, Leading Aircraftwomen. Being happily confident that I could remember all I had learned at Blackpool I did not bother with revision and got a nasty shock when I read the exam questions. I had forgotten more than I would have believed possible. I struggled through the paper somehow and was greatly relieved when Flight told me later that I had passed, but only just. After the way I had topped the class at Blackpool, I felt I had let myself down and said as much to Gina. She had done no better than I had but, being Gina, her view of the results was totally different to mine. "A pass is a pass, and the money's the same, so why worry?" I had no answer to that. Gina's self-esteem did not depend on anything connected with the Air Force. She genuinely could not understand why my low mark troubled me. We would now be earning £1.8s.0d. (£1.40p) a week. Not a fortune, but we were being housed, fed and clothed at His Majesty's expense and I looked forward with relish to having the extra cash to play with.

I applied immediately for seven days leave and this time it was granted. In high spirits I wrote to my mother telling her to kill the fatted calf – or at least open a tin of corned beef – as I was coming home to show off my new props. I also wrote direct to my father telling him of my success. I did not mention to either of them that I had only passed the exam by the skin of my teeth. Father replied by return of post. He said he was very pleased with my news, adding that he was looking forward to the day when he could address me as 'Corporal'. Poor Father. I knew he was going to be disappointed in me again, because I was never likely to get my stripes. I was the youngest on the section and probably the least experienced in more ways than one. As well as having been in the Air Force longer than I had, most of them had had their props up for months. The idea of my being given authority over such as Cynthia and Dorothy was ludicrous. I might stand a better chance of promotion on some other photographic section but that was debatable. At this stage of the war most sections would already have their full complement of NCOs. I would stand no better chance of promotion than I had on my present one. Apart from which I was too happy at Bicester to even think of applying for a posting anywhere else.

I arrived home on David's sixteenth birthday at the end of March. I gave him his present when he came in from school, sixty cigarettes hoarded from my Naafi ration over previous weeks. Mother was disapproving, but he was thrilled. Cigarettes were scarce in civvy street - under-the-counter merchandise reserved for regular customers only. And David did not have enough spending money to become a regular. After supper and the ritual cutting of a very small birthday cake, he said rather tentatively, "I'm going out to meet a couple of pals for a drink. You wouldn't like to come too, would you?"

"A drink?" I said, surprised. "Are you allowed in at sixteen?" The official age was eighteen.

"I look older," he pointed out. This was true. He was now six feet tall and he had gained enough self-assurance to be accepted by any landlord who did not ask awkward questions. Mother appeared to accept David's drinking but was not happy about my joining him. "Your father won't like you going into a pub," she warned.

David kissed her on the cheek. "Then don't tell him." He ushered me out of the house before she could reply. It seemed my young brother was growing into a force to be reckoned with in the family.

Outside, his manner became tentative again as we walked to the pub, picking our way carefully by the light of our little torches. "I hope you won't be bored. Everyone's a bit young by your standards."

"Everyone? How many are we going to meet?"

"Well," he said, "it depends how many turn up. There's usually about ten of us."

This was not a couple of pals, this was a gang! I asked, "How often do you go out with them?"

"Not that often. I've got my Schools Leaving exams coming up. If I want to go to university I need more than just a pass, I need Matric Exemption, so I've got to keep my head down. And there's still the Scouts and the ARP, though I don't go to either of them as often as I used to."

As soon as David pushed aside the blackout curtain over the door and we entered the bar I knew by the noise that the gang was out in full strength and several pints ahead of us. For a split second I thought it was David's birthday they had been drinking to, but one of them shouted, "I've got my call-up. Get yourself a beer. The first one's on me." He saw me hovering and added – reluctantly I thought – "and one for..." he stopped, uncertain of my status.

While David ordered a pint for himself and a half for me, I surveyed the group and saw with surprise that it included several attractive young girls. Beers in hand we went over to join the party. Room was made for us in silence and we sat down. From the atmosphere I gathered it was not the done thing to bring in an unknown female. David said, "Meet my sister, Yvonne." He pulled out one of the packets of twenty I had given him and passed it round. "Courtesy of the Naafi," he said, gesturing vaguely at me. Everyone took a cigarette and made appreciative noises as they lit up. Any chill there may have been in the air vanished. I was in.

The laughter and horseplay we had interrupted picked up again. I looked at the girls, all perfectly at ease and joining in the banter with gusto. Like the boys, they couldn't have been more than seventeen years of age or they would have been conscripted. Unless they were all in reserved occupations, which seemed unlikely. I thought back to myself at that age, to the restricted life I had led then, and marvelled. Life had certainly changed in the last year. They made me feel old and out of place.

The older boys, those who were working, could afford to put away an impressive amount of beer. They became more rowdy and the horseplay grew rougher. The landlord strode over with a tough air to collect the empties and cautioned, "Steady on there, you lot," but did not threaten to throw us out as I expected. Perhaps the fact that we were officially celebrating the departure of one of the gang into the Army stayed his hand. No one mentioned David's birthday. "Best keep quiet about that," he murmured when I pointed this out in a whisper. "Someone might ask which one." As the whole lot of them were patently under–age drinkers, I thought he was being over-cautious, but kept quiet as advised.

A few days prior to coming on leave I had received a joyful note from Mollie saying, "I'm home!!!!" I had not replied; it would be fun to visit her without warning and surprise her. It certainly surprised her mother when she answered the door. "Yvonne! Come in." She took my greatcoat and hung it on the hallstand. "You're Mollie's first visitor. I'm afraid it will have to be only a short visit. She mustn't get over-tired." Although she was cured of TB, she was apparently still low on stamina. Her mother opened the sitting room door saying brightly, "Look who's here!"

Mollie was curled up in an armchair in front of the fire, watching the door eagerly. "I thought it was you," she beamed, adding as I walked towards her, "I like the uniform. It suits you."

SPRINGTIME 1943

"Thanks." I tapped one of the new props on my sleeves and preened, "Leading Aircraftwoman, no less,"

"Good for you."

I sat down in the other armchair, facing her across the hearthrug. She looked fit, relaxed and happy. Her mother said, "I'll go and put the kettle on," and left us alone to talk. Mollie was full of plans for the future. She and Ted wanted to get married on his next leave, but her father was against it. He still thought they should wait until Ted was established in a career. Luckily her mother was on their side. Mollie was relying on her to talk her father round. She held up crossed fingers for luck and I did the same.

I asked, "Where will you live?"

"Here."

"Here?" Given her father's attitude, I had expected her to be anxious to get away. She saw my surprise and guessed what I was thinking. "Father likes Ted. He wouldn't object to him living here. It's just that he and Mum had a bad time in the Depression after the last war and he wants our future to be secure before we get married." She stopped speaking as her mother came in carrying a tray, which she placed on a small tale between us. It held two cups of tea and a plate of plain biscuits, two each. Luxury fare. "There you are." She smiled and went out again. We helped ourselves before Mollie turned her attention to me. "Have you got anyone special yet? Or are you still playing the field?"

"I don't know about playing the field, but no, there's no one special. Not really."

"What does 'not really' mean?"

"Remember I wrote to you from Blackpool about a boy called Paul?"

"I remember. You fell out over his girlfriend."

"Sort of. Well – I do like him, but I don't know where I stand. He asks me to keep writing, then doesn't answer for weeks. And when he does he sends me a few scrappy lines with nothing personal in them. I don't really feel in touch with him at all."

"Perhaps he can't write about personal feelings. Not everyone has the gift of the gab writing letters that you have."

"Then there's this 'sort of' fiancée in the background," I said, ignoring her back-handed compliment.

Mollie thought about it. "If he's known her for a long time," she said at last, "perhaps she's become a habit. And now he's attracted to you and he's confused. He doesn't know what to do about it."

Gina had once said something similar. "I do wish he'd sort himself out," I grumbled. "I'd just decided to stop writing when he remembered my birthday. So I had to write back. Since then I haven't heard a word."

When her mother came back she did not sit down and join us, but remained standing by the door. I took this to be the signal for me to go. "Take care of yourself," said Mollie, as if I were the delicate one.

"You can bet on it!" I assured her.

The rest of my leave was pleasant, if uneventful. Mother and I went to see Nannie one day. After my uniform had been admired and I had been congratulated on my props, the talk was all about shortages, rationing, rising prices and the impossibility of getting anyone in to come in and do the 'rough' housework. Mother insisted on our leaving in time to be home before blackout. I had been hoping we could stay until Aunt Evelyn came home from work to liven up the conversation, and was disappointed.

Having touched base, as it were, and assured myself that my family was still there for me, I was happy to go back to camp. A cluster of shaded bicycle lamps at the bottom of the incline at Bicester North told me Cynthia and Dorothy had rounded up a welcome committee as usual. Bill had wheeled my bike down, riding his own one-handed and wheeling mine alongside. As I took it from him with thanks he asked the standard question, "Good leave?" and I gave the expected answer, "Great."

In The Crown I sank happily down on a settee in the lounge bar, tucked in between Ruth on one side and Bill on the other. Someone handed me a beer and I took a swig and asked, "What's new on the section since I went home?"

"Don's coming back," said Cynthia.

"Who's Don, and where's he been?" I enquired.

"Sorry, I forgot. He went before you came. He was sent out to one of the satellites and now he's coming back."

"More broken hearts," said Dorothy and everybody laughed.

"Do you remember that girl in the met. section?" Cynthia's question caused more laughter. "Pined for weeks when he was posted, silly little thing."

"Serves her right for going out with a married man. We did warn her." The influence of Ruth's Presbyterian upbringing showed itself.

No one appeared to have any sympathy for the girl, I noticed, neither did they attach any blame to the man, which puzzled me. If he was married, what was he doing taking her out in the first place?

"I heard his next one was a civilian, a barmaid somewhere," said Cynthia.

"Does he always have a girl in tow?" I asked.

"He does," answered Jenks. "Noted for it. Comes of being a photographer on a cruise liner before the war. A girl in every port, that's our Don." He sounded admiring and Bill chuckled, "Not to mention the girls on board."

I wasn't too sure I liked the sound of this Don. He sounded like a menace.

He arrived on the section a day or two later, a man of medium height, solidly built, who – to my surprise - looked nearly old enough to be my father and not at all menacing. (He turned out to be thirty-five.) He wasn't particularly handsome. He sported a small black moustache of the type much favoured by the screen heartthrobs of the day. His hair was dark brown and smarmed back with hair cream, but sprang into waves as the day wore on. It reminded me of my father's, which did exactly the same if he didn't keep it tamed. His eyes were dark and they always looked as if he were laughing at some secret joke. It was noticeable that all the girls were aware of him in a way they never were of, say, Bill or Jenks. Even Gina seemed to notice him, which was remarkable given that he was not a musician.

After my first night shift with Bill I was usually teamed with Gina. We worked well together and I felt quite close to her on the section. Far more than I did any other time. Everyone disliked working nights. Developing and printing almost identical films time after time was monotonous and boring. The arrival of visitors from the day shift was usually a welcome interruption. Except if it was Flight, who sometimes came up to check that all was as it should be. Sgt Finch never came. Once he had returned to his 'Nest' at the end of the day he stayed there. The men sometimes came up to kill time after the pubs closed before going back to barracks. If there was not much work to do, after a poor day for aerial photography, we could stop and talk and make tea for our visitors. If we were busy we had no time to stop and they made tea for us.

By chance, Gina and I were on nights the week after Don returned. He came up to the section on more than one evening, making himself useful on each occasion. He cooked supper for us and once, when we were really up to our eyes, he helped out in the darkrooms. After he had gone I said to Gina, "You know, Don's not a bit like I expected. All that talk about his broken-hearted girlfriends. I thought he'd be a menace, but he's not. He's not even a flirt, is he?"

Gina said thoughtfully, "I think he's a man who likes women. Not just in bed – though I don't suppose he'd turn down a good offer if he got one – I mean, he likes them as people, enjoys their company. He's probably quite harmless if you don't get too involved."

Perhaps, I thought, the old hands all know this, and that's why they don't blame him when the girls get hurt.

It was around this time that Gina started talking about someone called Raymond. He was not in the band; he was an actor who was hoping to organise a concert, using whatever talent he could find on camp. Auditions were to be held in the hall and Gina was first in the queue when the doors opened. She was chosen to sing two popular songs, accompanied by the station band. Rehearsals began and immediately absorbed all her interest. Which could have landed her in serious trouble on one occasion.

We were on nights the week before the concert was due to take place. We always went over to the mess for a meal before going on duty, and one evening, as we were parking our bikes outside, Gina was waylaid by one of the other girls in the concert party. "I've been looking for you," she said. "Ray wants everyone at rehearsal tonight. He's not happy with the running order. It's at half past seven." Gina thanked her and she rode away.

I said, "That's a bind. Doesn't he know you're on nights?"

Gina said, "Mmm," absent-mindedly.

We collected our meals and sat down to eat. A few minutes later Gina said, "Yvonne," in a tone of voice that put me on instant alert. I looked at her sharply, half knowing what was coming. "You couldn't manage on your own for an hour or so, could you?"

"You're mad," I said. "What am I supposed to tell Flight if he comes up? That you're in the loo?"

"You'll think of something," she said with greater confidence in my ability to keep her out of trouble than I had.

"You're mad," I said again, more firmly this time. "You'll be on a charge if you're found out." But she wasn't listening. In her mind her problem was solved. I knew it would be useless to argue.

It had been a beautiful day. A long line of cameras was waiting for us on the section. I said, "Oh, my God! How long do you reckon you'll be away?"

"My numbers are near the beginning. I'll tell Ray I can't stop long. With luck I'll be back in an hour."

"You'd better be or we shan't be finished by morning," I warned.

We made a good start and the work went well until just before seven thirty when Gina said, "I've got to go now," and put on her cap. "See you later."

"One hour," I shouted to her retreating back.

One hour passed, then two. I resented being taken advantage of so flagrantly and my temper was beginning to fray. Damn Gina and her bloody concert!

I was in the chemical room making myself a much needed mug of tea when I heard footsteps coming from the stairs. "Please don't let it be Flight," I prayed, and held my breath. There were two sets of footsteps. I heard Bill's voice and he and Don emerged from the main corridor. I breathed again.

"Where's Gina?" asked Don when he realised I was on my own.

"At rehearsals," I said sourly.

Bill whistled. "Taking a chance, isn't she? What time will she be back?"

"I've no idea. She was supposed to be back an hour ago."

Without being asked he went along to the darkroom and took over the printing. Don took over the cine films. I took them both a mug of tea, gulped down my own and started drying and glazing the prints.

Gina came dashing in at half past ten, full of apologies. I cut her short. My temper had improved with the tea but my mood was still far from sweet. "One hour, you said," I snapped.

"I'm really sorry." She sounded contrite. "I couldn't leave. Roly was there. He stayed all evening. I couldn't say I was supposed to be on duty with him there, could I?"

I was forced to agree. As Entertainments Officer it was only to be expected that he would be there. I wondered if Gina had known this all along, but there was no good having a row about it. Gina was Gina and she would never change.

Bill came out of the darkrooms carrying the next batch of wet prints for glazing. Gina said, "Have you been helping? Wizzo! We shouldn't be too late finishing then."

"Of all the bloody cheek!" said Don, who had followed Bill into the drying room. But I noticed his eyes looked even more amused than usual. As she had done at Blackpool, Gina had chanced her arm and got away with it.

The concert was a great success and so was Gina. In the past I had sometimes heard her singing in the billet or in the ablutions and knew she had a good voice. Even so, I was unprepared for her stage performance. Standing alone in the spotlight in a white dress that accentuated her figure, with her hair curling about her shoulders, she looked both sexy and vulnerable. Gina vulnerable! At first I thought she must be as good an actress as she was a singer. Then it dawned on me that she wasn't acting. The WAAF had been imposed on her by the war; she gave it lip-service and conformed to its regulations when she could, but basically she was indifferent to it. Her world was with the band on stage and here she cared deeply about what she was doing. Her numbers received enough noisy applause to earn her two encores. I think she could have taken a third one if Raymond had not insisted on moving on to the next item on the programme.

Our mail was not delivered to us: someone had to go over to the postal section every day to fetch it. One morning when it happened to be my turn I collected the letters and stood outside on the path riffling through them. There was a bulky one for me, addressed in an unknown hand, postmarked New Brighton, Paul's hometown. Instantly uneasy, I ripped it open. Inside were my letters to him with a covering note from his mother. As I read it I went cold with shock. Paul's plane had been shot down over France. The crew had been posted 'missing'. She had had a letter from an officer at Moreton-in-Marsh to say the crew had all been seen to bale out and there was every hope Paul was alive. My hands began to shake so violently I dropped the other letters on the path, where they scattered. Trying to gather them up forced me to take myself in hand. I continued to read. "Your letters were enclosed. I will write again when I have any more news."

I could not take in what had happened. Moreton was not an operational station, it was a Training Unit, like Bicester. What were they doing over France? At the first opportunity I slipped away from the section, regardless of what Flight might say or do when I returned, and went over to the hangar to see Sgt Finch. "They hadn't been posted on ops yet. How could they have been shot down?" I demanded.

"If there's a big raid on and Command are short of planes they do sometimes use OTU crews. They don't like doing it, but it happens," he said.

Fury made me forget where I was. I almost shouted at him, "But they hadn't finished their training. They weren't ready to go."

"I expect they were near the end of it. In another week or so they'd have been on ops anyway. It's a bad show," he agreed sympathetically, "but at least he was last seen alive. Don't give up hope."

Chapter 15

High Summer

EACH DAY WHEN the post was collected I looked impatiently for the promised letter from Paul's mother, but none came. I began to worry that she had forgotten about me. One morning when I was gazing gloomily out of the chemical room window, trying to reassure myself that she would write as soon as she heard from the Air Ministry, Don came and stood beside me. He said, "Cheer up! Would you like to go to the pictures tonight?" I was surprised and rather flattered. I knew he and Bill sometimes made up a foursome with Cynthia and Dorothy to go out for the evening, but had not heard of anyone going out with him alone. I accepted and we arranged the time and place to meet. Within minutes of his leaving the room I was buttonholed by Dorothy, who had overheard the invitation. She said without preamble, "You do know he's a married man, don't you?"

I must have looked blank before I said, "Yes." How could I not know? Everybody knew. Why did she think she had to remind me? I had only made a casual arrangement with Don, not what I regarded as a proper date. As she knew, the men of the section did not make serious dates with the girls they worked with. Their dishonourable intentions, if any, were reserved for outsiders.

The film was a musical, a colourful, frivolous affair starring Betty Grable and her lovely legs. It was the perfect antidote to the blues. I felt quite light-hearted when we left the cinema.

There was a house near the railway bridge where it was possible to get a cheap cup of tea and a sandwich. The place was extremely popular, although all the owners had to put in the sandwiches was what they could grow in their garden. A favourite filling was beetroot, either with or without onion. The choice was often significant, indicating the level of intimacy between couples. There was just time for us to call in there before I had to be back in the hut. Don ordered 'beetroot without' to be on the safe side. We had to sit on the stairs with our plates balanced on our knees, the rooms were so crowded, but at least we could talk there. Don was good company and also proved to be a very good listener. I found myself telling him all about Paul and how I was on tenterhooks waiting for news. "I doubt if you'll hear yet," he said, "wheels in the Air Ministry turn slowly. It may take weeks before his mother hears anything definite. You'll just have to possess your soul in patience"

As we said goodnight outside the huts he asked, "If there's another good film on next week, would you like to go?" and I said, "Yes, please," without hesitation.

We went out together several times, either to the pictures or a pub. Occasionally he riled me by referring to my lack of years, or calling me 'idiot child', otherwise I continued to enjoy his company. I regarded him as a friend, nothing more, and saw no harm in kissing him goodnight at the end of the evening.

Dorothy disapproved of the friendship. She made this clear without putting her feelings into words. Her attitude irritated me; I could not see that what I did was any of her business.

Ruth did not have to tell me that she also disapproved. Her opinion of girls who went out with married men was well known. It made for a certain constraint between us, for which I was sorry.

I don't know how long it really was before I heard from Paul's mother again but it felt like a long time. She said she had been officially notified that Paul was a prisoner of war in Germany. I felt as if a weight had been lifted off my shoulders. I would have liked to share my relief with her. It would have helped me feel closer to Paul and maybe provided something for me to write about in future letters to him. But her second letter, like the first, was completely impersonal. I surmised that until she saw my name as sender on the backs of my letters to her son she had not known of my existence. When I replied I told her I was "one of Paul's friends from Blackpool" to explain my connection with him. I also told her I was a photographer. I hoped this information might break the ice a little but the ploy failed. Her third letter merely said she had heard from the Red Cross with the name of the camp where Paul was being held. She gave me the address to write to but warned that all correspondence would be censored. I reflected that if it had been hard to find things to write about before, it was going to be even harder from now on. I made one more attempt at a personal approach when I replied. I said what a relief it was to be able to contact Paul at last. This fell on stony ground. It was a year before I heard from her again.

However, I did hear from Paul himself. His letter was so brief it was little more than a note, but I found it comforting. He said he was well and with a good crowd. I hoped this meant the crew were all together in the camp and had not been split up. He said he looked forward to my letters. It struck me that Mother and son had very similar writing styles, not easy to respond to.

I replied as best I could, after which there was a long interval of silence on both sides. Presumably Paul could not find anything to say. For my part, life took an unexpected turn that drove everything and everybody from my mind.

Gina, Ruth and I were cycling along the path to the mess one day when we met a group of aircrew walking towards us. We slowed as we cycled through them and one called out in surprise, "Yvonne!" as we passed. I braked, looked round - and gaped. It was Michael! For a second I was speechless with disbelief and embarrassment, instantly recalling my pathetic attempts to hold his attention outside the church at home. Then I dismissed the memory and smiled. "Hello, Michael! I'd heard it was a small world."

The rest of the group had carried on down the path. One of them turned and shouted, "Come on, Mike. Never mind chatting up the bird." Michael said hurriedly, "I shan't be free till late, but can we meet for a drink?"

Coolly, although my heart was dancing, I said, "OK." We made hasty arrangements for him to pick me up outside the huts and he dashed off to catch up with the others. I rode after Gina and Ruth, hardly able to believe I wasn't having a daydream. Gina said, "Your long lost cousin?"

"Nearly right. A friend from home."

"And?" asked Gina.

"And we're going out for a drink tonight. OK?" I saw her grin at Ruth, who smiled back, and felt my face go pink.

Michael was waiting when I left the hut. He asked, "Where would you like to go?" I suggested the Crown Hotel, that being the only place I knew.

The lounge was crowded, all the settees and comfortable armchairs were occupied and people were standing round the bar. I thought my hopes of an intimate tête-à-tête were lost but a couple got up to leave and I nipped in to stake our claim to their settee before anyone else could reach it. Michael went to get our drinks at the bar. Watching him as he waited to be served, I thought he looked even more attractive than when I had seen him last. He had outgrown the spindly look of adolescence and was more self-assured. His nearly black curly hair and blue eyes were the same, so was his smile, only now it was the smile of a man not a boy. Several female heads turned to watch him as he made his way over to me with our beers and placed them on a low table in front of us. We lit cigarettes and settled down to talk.

Michael asked, "How long have you been in?"

"Over a year now."

"What do you do?" I told him my trade. "Are you one of the girls who fit the cameras?"

"I am." I gestured to the brevet above his breast pocket, the single wing attached to an encircled 'N' for navigator. "And you're one of the men who ignore our existence if you bump into us."

"Sorry," he grinned, "I'll look out for you in future." He took a pull at his beer and enquired, "Are you enjoying the life?"

I took a swig of my own beer. "Loving it. Though some of the discipline rather reminds me of school." I launched into a highly-coloured version of my cycle ride across the SWO's drill parade. "As big a sin as crossing the black and white tiles in the Convent entrance hall, apparently."

He roared with laughter. Before we left the subject of home, I had a question of my own to ask; I approached it indirectly. "Have you managed to get home much since you left?"

"I haven't been home for ages," said Michael. "And you?"

"I was home in April. It was very quiet. Everyone's away in the Forces or evacuated or something. I did see some of the old familiar faces in church, but I was quite glad to get back here in the end."

"Did you see Anna's family?" asked Michael, unconsciously playing into my hands.

"No, but maybe I went to a different Mass." Careful to show no more than polite interest, I asked my question, "Are you still in touch with Anna?"

"Not now. She joined the WRNS. Last time I heard she'd just got her commission." (She would! I thought. And I'll bet she ditched him because he's only a sergeant.) "That was months ago." There was no note of regret in his voice. A lovely warm feeling of happiness spread right down to my toes. I hoped it wasn't too obvious how I felt. But Michael had gone off on a tack of his own. He said, almost to himself, "I loved those parties." I didn't comment, and he went on, "The people, the gramophone playing out on the lawn and the noise. I loved the noise."

"The noise?" I was baffled. That was the last thing I would have expected him to remember.

'HAVE YOU GOT YOUR IRONS?'

Staring into his beer glass, he explained. "I was an only child, and a late arrival at that. My parents were middle-aged by the time I came along. They were very set in their ways, especially my father. They liked quiet; no loud music, no noise. We rarely had friends in, not my friends, anyway. Sunday at Anna's place was..." he paused, trying to find the right words. "It was like stepping into another life, becoming another person." He looked up, embarrassed at having said so much, hoping I understood. I nodded reassuringly. I did understand. Hadn't I joined the WAAF because life was so restricted and dull at home? I said, "I feel a bit like that, being in the Air Force."

Shaking off the past, Michael picked up our empty glasses and enquired, "Another half?" and went to fetch refills. I sat metaphorically hugging myself, still bathed in my happy glow. I had his attention at last!

We did not return to the subject of home. When he sat down again the talk was all about the Air Force, where we had been and the people we had met. I asked, "Where were you before you came to Bicester?"

"In the north of Scotland. A desolate place, nothing but sheep and gales. And cold!"

"Sounds grim," I said.

"It was. But we were lucky. There was a farm a couple of miles away. Marvellous people. They used to keep open house in the evenings. We went down there a lot. Their daughter Laura - " he hesitated just long enough for me to be forewarned. "She's my fiancée." There was pride in his voice and something else. Sadness? My happiness died. I concentrated hard on keeping the smile on my face. I said, "Congratulations," and hoped I sounded more sincere than I felt. He said, "Thanks," and a silence followed. If he was waiting for me to ask what she was like and encourage him to talk about her, he was disappointed. At that moment I didn't give a damn what she was like. The silence lengthened. Michael asked, "Would you like another drink?"

I looked at my watch. "I've got to go or I'll be late in. Our corporal is not the understanding type." It was a lie, we still had our easy-going Phyllis at that time, but I had to get out of there before my face cracked.

We cycled back through the dark saying little. When we reached the huts Michael said, "I'm not too sure what time we'll be finishing, but ..."

I cut in, "Never mind. Thanks for this evening, anyway. It was great," and set off down the path to our hut before he could finish his sentence. I reflected bitterly that I had played this scene before, with Paul. It had hurt then; it was even more painful now.

Ruth asked, "Did you have a good evening?"

I said, "Yes, thanks," and left it at that. Being Ruth, she asked no more questions. She had gone to the ablutions when Gina came in. She looked at my face and asked, "Not the evening you hoped for?"

"He's engaged," I said briefly.

"So what? At least he's not married. He might change his mind. People do. Are you seeing him again?"

"No." I told her something of my vigils outside the church. "I'm not hanging about for him again," I said firmly.

"Suit yourself," shrugged Gina, losing interest.

Some days later I was out fitting cameras with a new girl to the section. She had been working at Medmenham, the photographic printing depot, and had no experience of life on an airfield. I was showing her the ropes. We had fitted our last camera and were lounging on the grass in the sunshine some little way from the plane, waiting for our transport to pick us up. The crews were coming out and she watched with interest as the crew wagon headed towards us. "Don't get your hopes up," I warned her, "They don't know we exist before a flight."

The lorry passed us and decanted the crew near the plane. I heard my name called and knew the navigator was Michael. I got to my feet and went over. "Will you come for a drink tonight?" he asked, wasting no time.

I had intended to refuse, or at least to hesitate and need persuading if he asked me out again, but there was no time now to play games. It had to be yes or no immediately, so I said yes.

"I'll come down to the huts about eight thirty."

The sun seemed to have got warmer in the last few minutes and the day seemed brighter. I returned to my trainee, trying not to look like the Cheshire cat.

"What was that you were saying about the crews ignoring us?" she enquired.

I said offhandedly , "I knew that one at home."

"Lucky you," she said appreciatively.

I was in two minds over my coming date that evening. One half of me could hardly wait for eight thirty, the other half said warningly, "You're going to get hurt again. What on earth made you say yes?" Lamely I admitted to myself, "Because I couldn't say no."

"Where shall we go this time?" asked Michael when we met. "The Crown again?"

I had been thinking about that. I wanted somewhere more private. It was a beautiful evening. "Let's ride out and see where we get to," I suggested. "There must be dozens of country pubs round here if we can find them." Don had introduced me to several but I have a poor sense of direction and had no idea where they were. We cycled along winding lanes that appeared to go nowhere until we found ourselves on the outskirts of a little village of thatched cottages with a small pub in the only street. Ivy smothered its walls, and was beginning to take over the roof. The door was so low that even I had to mind my head when we went in. Michael was in danger of knocking himself out on the lintel if he wasn't careful. It was dark inside and the bar was empty except for the landlord. He gave us a pleasant "Good evening" and asked if we would prefer to sit in the parlour or go "out the back". The parlour looked dismal and shabby, we settled for "out the back".

He indicated a door and we stepped out into an old apple orchard surrounded by a stone wall covered in lichen. The evening sun flickered through the leaves of trees twenty feet or more in height. Rustic seats and tables stood in the lank grass between them. Where it had not been trodden down it was thick with dandelions, tall daises, buttercups and wild plants I could not identify. I settled myself at a table and while Michael was getting the drinks, I looked about me.

We were not alone in our hideaway. Sitting at the table nearest the pub - and the bar - a gathering of old men were playing a serious and cutthroat game of dominoes. A pair of white doves fluttered and cooed on the pub roof and a blackbird sang his evensong in a nearby tree.

"Isn't this lovely?" I said when Michael came back. He grunted in reply. I decided to take the bull by the horns. "Better than the north of Scotland, I imagine?"

"My God, yes! I've never known cold like it."

To make amends for my lack of response to his announcement that he was engaged, I gave him the lead I was sure he wanted. "You were lucky to have somewhere comfortable to go in the evenings."

"We were indeed! A log fire in the living room, hot baths,"

"And Laura," I made myself say her name.

"And Laura," he agreed. But his smile was wry and for a fleeting moment a look of pain crossed his face.

In for a penny, in for a pound, I asked, "Have you got a picture of her?"

He was reaching for his pocket book before I had completed the question. He abstracted a photograph and handed it to me. It was only a snapshot of a girl in trousers doing something vague with a pitchfork, but it was clear enough for me to know with dull certainty that I was never likely to replace Laura in Michael's affections. I was not his type. For with her flowing blonde hair, her wide confident smile and her general air of self-assurance, the girl in the picture could have been Anna. Or at least her sister. "She looks nice," I said, handing it back.

"Oh, she is! I'm sure you'd like her if you met her."

I was damn sure I wouldn't. I did not take to these golden girl types at the best of times. (Envy, perhaps?) "Does she work on the farm?" I enquired. Farm work was a reserved occupation.

"Yes. She'd like to join up but her parents wouldn't be able to cope without her. At least she's safe up there," he added.

I decided I had done my duty by Laura and changed the subject. "How much longer do you think you'll be here?"

"It's hard to say. Some few weeks yet. But let's not talk about that."

So what else could we talk about? Home? Camp gossip? I tried them both, but found that one way or another we always came back to Laura and her family. I began to feel I knew the farm quite well.

I went out with Michael regularly in the following weeks. He was never free early enough to go to the cinema so all we could do was go for a drink. Michael's sense of direction being far superior to mine, we found the little pub again without much trouble. It became 'our pub' and the landlord welcomed us as regulars. It was now high summer. The blackbird had ended his song for the season; the grass in the orchard grew higher and bees hummed over the wild flowers entangled in it; boughs on the apple trees began to droop under the weight of the ripening apples. The old men still played their interminable games of dominoes. At the end of the evening they were joined by younger men, who called in on their way home from the fields, but we were the only people in uniform who ever came there. If it rained the locals moved into the bar and dominoes gave way to equally fierce games of shove ha'penny, bar skittles and darts. Michael and I were ushered into the parlour on our own.

Even though the room itself was dreary without a blazing fire in the grate to give it life, the chairs and sofas offered unexpected comfort. In fact, inside or outside, the setting was all I could have desired for a romantic change of heart on Michael's part. But wherever we were, under the trees in the evening sunlight or at ease in the gloomy parlour, the atmosphere remained disappointingly platonic. I had been cast firmly in the role of 'the friend from home', someone who could talk about mutual acquaintances there, or who would listen, albeit unwillingly, when he talked about "my fiancée". I was never given any encouragement to act out of character. The kiss he gave me when we said goodnight was affectionate, nothing more. If I was very lucky I also got a brotherly hug. Why did I continue to go out with him when I knew he was always thinking of someone else? One reason was that despite his compulsion to drag Laura into the conversation on every possible occasion and his obvious pride in her, I could not get away from the feeling that he was unhappy. This kept alive the forlorn hope that one day he would break with Laura and turn to me, if only on the rebound. Another reason I continued to go out with him was simply because he asked me to.

The irony of the situation was that whereas Dorothy had disapproved of my going out for a drink with Don, I knew by her changed attitude that she considered my relationship with Michael entirely suitable. I wondered what she would say if she discovered he was officially engaged and I was once more going out with somebody else's man. Worse still, I was hoping the engagement would break up. I think Ruth sensed that something was wrong. However, she did not ask any questions - she would have regarded that as prying - and I did not enlighten her. I knew she would disapprove again. Only Gina knew the full story and I trusted her discretion completely. Gina was not an idle gossip.

At the end of Michael's course we went out on our last date. He was not in a good mood and greeted me absent-mindedly outside the huts. He said, "The usual place?" and set off before I had time to answer. It started to rain as we reached the pub. I went straight into the parlour and Michael went to the bar for drinks. He looked distinctly off colour, which I put down to the aftermath of celebrations the night before. It must have been some booze-up if the effects had lasted this long. I settled myself on one of the comfortable sofas; Michael joined me a few minutes later. He had the standard half-pint for me, a pint for himself and, unusually, a double whisky to go with it. I said, "Hair of the dog?" and he gave me an unconvincing smile, but did not reply.

To get the conversation going I enquired, "Are the postings through?"

"Some of them. I haven't got mine yet. Probably tomorrow."

"And then?"

"Seven days leave and straight on ops."

He downed the whisky and turned glumly to his beer. I wondered if, now that training was over and he was faced with the real thing, he was scared. If so, who could blame him?

Michael seemed disinclined to talk. I finished my half-pint; he gulped down the last of his beer and went out for refills. He swayed slightly and I guessed he had already been drinking in the sergeants' mess before we met. He returned with two more beers and another double whisky, which he downed the moment he was settled beside me again. I felt a small niggle of worry. If he kept this up he'd be in no state to ride a bike by the end of the evening. How would I get him back to camp? Determined to get a conversation going and hopefully slow down the drinking, I tried another question, one I was sure would engage his attention. "Will you be seeing Laura while you're on leave?"

"No. The journey takes too long. There's not enough time, and she can't leave the farm to come down here." The misery in his face tugged at my heart. I was sorry I'd asked the question. He took a long swig of beer and said in a dull voice, "I spent my last leave with Laura. I haven't been home for a year. I ought to go and see my mother." The words 'in case I don't come back' hung in the air unspoken. I said optimistically, "Perhaps next time."

He shook his head slowly. "There won't be a next time for me."

It took me a second or so to take in what he meant. Then I said briskly, "You don't know that."

"Yes, I do. I shall never see Laura again."

I thought it was the drink talking and was tempted to tell him firmly that he had had enough. What deterred me was the sudden insight that this certainty of approaching death was what had been making him unhappy all along. I said again, but this time more gently, "You don't know that. You've got the same chance as anybody else."

"You're wrong, " he said, and to my horror I saw his eyes fill with tears. He was going to cry. Desperately I grasped his hand, not knowing what else to do. His answering grip was so tight I gasped with pain and he loosened his hold slightly without releasing my hand. He made no sound but the tears slid down his cheeks until he pulled a handkerchief from his pocket with his other hand and wiped them away. I longed to put my arms round him and comfort him as if he were a child but could not do so; the way he was clutching my hand made it impossible. Perhaps that was why he did it. He was afraid that sympathy would break him up completely and he did not want that.

We sat there until my hand was numb. I prised it from his grip and flexed my fingers to restore the circulation. Michael drew a deep breath. He blew his nose hard and stood up, not looking at me. He said, "I'm sorry. Shall we go?" I scrambled to my feet and followed him out of the parlour.

Outside the pub it was raining steadily. We unrolled our rain capes and pulled them round us swiftly before we got soaked, then mounted our bikes and set off back to camp. There was no communication between us as we rode, heads down, into the rain. It was growing dusk. Beside me Michael weaved erratically from side to side. He had withdrawn into himself and was unaware that he had nearly crashed into me more than once.

Arriving back at the huts I dismounted, holding on to my bike to keep it upright. Michael stayed on his, putting one foot to the ground, poised for flight as soon as the farewells had been said. I was as anxious as he was for this dreadful evening to be over, but could not bring myself to end it. We stood side by side with the rain dripping off our caps and our all-enveloping capes until Michael said huskily, "Good bye, Yvonne, and - thanks." With my throat constricted by emotion I said in a strangled voice, "Good luck, Michael." He leaned over to give me a perfunctory kiss, all but lost his balance and drew back. Our leave-taking descended into farce as I reached up to kiss him on the cheek at the precise moment he bent forward and pushed hard on the pedal to get the bike moving. I missed my target and kissed the air. As he rode off I found my voice and called after him, "Write to me, Michael. Please!" but he gave no sign of having heard. I stood and watched the dim rear light of his bicycle flicker into the darkening rain. Then he disappeared.

Chapter 16

Autumn

AFTER MICHAEL had gone all the old painful feelings of rejection that had haunted me when he left Finchley returned to plague me. On the section it was assumed that my depression was reaction to Michael's departure. Which in a way it was. Only Gina suspected there was more to it than that. We chanced to find ourselves alone in the ablutions on domestic night. Wasting no words, in case someone else came in, she asked, "What's wrong? What happened the other night?" I was reluctant to expose what I saw as Michael's weakness to any sort of scorn or ridicule, and I knew Gina's caustic tongue of old. But I badly needed to confide in someone and there was no one else I could turn to. Ruth was a friend, but not a close one. Briefly I described our last date. Gina was not scornful; she said quietly, "Poor old Michael!"

"And I was useless, I didn't know how to help him," I wailed wretchedly.

"I don't see what you could have done, or anyone else either. If he's so certain he's going to die," she shrugged, "he's only going to be convinced he's wrong if he lives, if you see what I mean."

I felt a little better, but was still not happy with myself. The ablutions door swung open and several girls came in together, chatting and laughing. Gina and I finished washing, gathered up our toilet things and left. Walking down the path to the hut she asked, "Is he going to write to you?"

"I forgot to give him my number." My feeling of inadequacy

returned.

"And he hasn't got your home address?"

"No. I meant to organise addresses that evening, but it went right out of my head," I confessed unhappily.

Gina's response was bracing. "Hardly surprising under the circumstances. Stop blaming yourself for everything. Snap out of it!"

It occurred to me that although I was unlikely to hear news of Michael direct, it was possible that my mother might hear something on what I called the 'shopping grapevine'. With luck she might run into his mother and stop to gossip. After my first meeting with Michael I had written in ultra casual fashion, "I was surprised to bump into Michael C. the other day. He is now a navigator." I had not mentioned him again and had no way of knowing whether or not she knew or guessed what this had meant to me. Now, in my anxiety to make sure she passed on any scrap of news that came her way, I wrote, "I saw Michael C. a few days ago. He has finished here and was waiting to be posted on ops."

I was sure she would try to read between the lines and would probably suspect there was more to our meetings than I was letting on. She would pass on anything she heard, if only to try and draw me out. It was a few weeks before she heard anything, and when she did it was the worst news possible. She wrote, "I am very sorry to have to send you tragic news. Michael's plane was shot down on his second mission. They were apparently on their way back after a raid and were caught by anti-aircraft fire over the French coast. Their plane blew up over the sea and no one survived." There was more, but I didn't read it. I stared at the letter unseeing. My brain stopped working. My senses went numb. I stood by the bench in the general room oblivious to everyone around me. From a long way off I heard Gina's voice say, "Yvonne?" and again, with more insistence, "Yvonne!" Making a great effort I said, "It's Michael."

"Gone?" she asked, shocked. I gave a slight nod. She said vehementally, "What rotten luck. What rotten bloody luck."

AUTUMN

I got through the day somehow. At the end of the shift Gina and I cycled over to the mess together and ate in silence. When we were leaving she asked, "Are you all right?" I said mechanically, "Yes," and we separated. Gina disappeared as usual, I cycled back to the hut.

Ruth was on day off and would not be back until late. There happened to be only three or four other girls in that evening, none of whom I knew well. It was so quiet that I could hear a tiny click as an earwig dropped off the curved roof onto the top of the metal locker beside my bed. I lay flat on my back and stared blankly at the bolts holding the hut together above me. In my head I could hear Michael's toneless voice, "I'll never see Laura again," and my robust reply, "You don't know that." Had he known it? Was it premonition? Or were his fears no different from any other new flyer's and his death just rotten bloody luck, as Gina had said? I was filled with a great sadness. Inside myself I was crying but no tears came to my eyes.

Barbara, the ambulance driver, passed my bed on her way to the loo. Normally I would have acknowledged her but this evening I ignored her. On her way back a few minutes later she came and stood beside my bed. She was about five years older than me, a tall muscular girl with a pleasant rather than good-looking face and a forthright manner. Reluctantly I lowered my gaze from the roof and looked at her. "Are you all right?" she asked quietly. I tried to answer, but my unshed tears had gathered into a frozen lump in my throat and no sound came out. I swallowed hard and tried again. My voice croaked, "Michael," and stopped. Barbara did not ask, "Who's Michael?" She had seen us meet outside the huts on several occasions and knew who I meant. She asked, "What happened?"

I didn't want to talk. I wished she would go away, but she waited for an answer. I swallowed hard for the second time and said, "They blew up over the sea."

Barbara said harshly, "At least it was quick. Not like the poor sods who come down in flames."

Her words and her tone shook me. Subconsciously I had been expecting comfort. Then I remembered. Some months previously one of our planes, out on a test flight, had crashed in flames not far from the airfield. Barbara had been on duty that evening and had gone out to the site with one of the ambulances. The fire wagons were there within minutes but were unable to get the crew out alive. Barbara had known the pilot. She returned to the hut in a state of terrible distress, lying on her bed and sobbing, near to hysteria. Her neighbours did all they could to soothe her; she hardly knew they were there. She was too caught up in the horrors she had witnessed.

She had fallen at last into a restless sleep of nightmares that haunted her every night for weeks. Official counselling had not been invented then. We were expected to pick ourselves up and get on with it. On the surface she appeared to have put the awful scene out of her mind. I was very sorry to be the one to bring it all back to her. I tried to put this into words, struggling to sit up and look in command of myself.

Barbara brushed my inept apology aside. "It's better to face these things – better for both of us," she said firmly.

We had a Primus stove in the hut, thanks to Rosie. It allowed us to make late night drinks throughout the summer when the iron stove in the middle of the hut was not in use. The bubbling rumble of the kettle boiling and the clink of mugs now told us someone was making cocoa. Barbara said, "Come over and get a hot drink. It'll do you good." She waited while I swung my feet to the floor and stood up and together we went to join the little group round the Primus.

As soon as I had drunk my cocoa I excused myself and went to bed. In spite of Barbara's advice to face up to things I tried to go straight to sleep; to blot out what had happened, or at least put off thinking about it until another day. But against my will my brain refused to switch off. It went over and over the little I knew about the last minutes of Michael's life, asking questions to which I would probably never know the answers. They must have been briefed on the position of the French coastal defences. Why hadn't they climbed out of range of the guns? Had their young and inexperienced pilot made a wrong decision? Who had seen the plane explode? At least, as Barbara had said, death must have been instantaneous. They had not had time to suffer. For this I thanked God in one of the few prayers I had said for a long time.

I began to speculate about Laura. How had she heard the news? If she had been his wife instead of only his fiancée she would have been notified officially. Did his mother have the heartrending task of writing to tell her Michael was dead? I wondered if he had ever told Laura of his premonition, if that's what it was. If so, had she taken it seriously? Had she been able to comfort him? I pictured her cradling him in her arms, as I had longed to do. And for that moment I hated her. Yet I grieved for her too. She had lost so much more than I had. As his fiancée (and how he had loved that word), she had linked her future with his, and now it was gone. My future was unaffected. I had only been the friend from home. I mulled over that word 'only' - a mournful, second-best sort of word. Only a friend, only his fiancée. Had Laura been content with her status? In her shoes I would have wanted to be Michael's wife before he went away. How ironic if neither of us had been satisfied with our relationship with him! My tears felt hard in my throat again. I tucked my head well down under my blankets so that no one would hear me and tried to cry. But nothing happened. My throat remained hard and my eyes stayed obstinately dry. Eventually I fell asleep and woke next morning unrefreshed.

I wrote Mother a note saying I was very sorry to hear her news, and asked her to give my condolences to Mrs C. if she happened to run into her. One day, perhaps, I would feel like talking to her about Michael, but not yet. I wanted to put the whole unhappy episode behind me until it had become less painful to remember.

It must have been at least a week later when Dorothy collected the post one morning and handed me a small package firmly tied up with string. "You're damned lucky to get this," she said, "they didn't want to part with it in the postal section. It hasn't got your number on it." It was addressed to me at 'The Photographic Section' in writing I didn't recognise. The postmark was too blurred to read. There was no name and address of sender on the back, nothing to give me a clue who had sent it. Too impatient to untie the string I cut it with the paper shears and pulled open the brown paper. Inside were a pair of nylons, a pearl necklace wrapped in crumpled tissue paper, and a letter. Not stopping to read it, although it was quite short, I went eagerly to the signature. The letter was from Michael.

The general room swayed. My stomach heaved and contracted. I was going to be sick. Abandoning the package on the bench I crumpled the letter into my battledress pocket and fled to the toilets. I only just got there in time. When there was no more breakfast to come up I locked the cubicle door and sat on the loo seat feeling empty and dizzy. After a while I heard someone come into the toilets and Ruth's soft voice asked, "Are you all right?" Carefully I stood up. The dizziness seemed to have passed. I unlocked the door and came out. "I'm OK now", I told her, and went over to the washbasins to splash my face with cold water. Ruth said, "Flight's looking for you." He would be! It was uncanny how he always knew if someone was off the section for more than the minimum necessary time. I dried my face on the roller towel and followed her back to the general room, where Flight was waiting for me. Under his impassive gaze I stuffed the package into my trouser pocket and got on with whatever it was he wanted me to do. It did not enter my head to explain to anyone what had upset me so badly. My only concern was to act as normally as possible, despite shock clouding my mind. At six o'clock I left the section without waiting for Ruth or Gina and went over to the mess by myself. Amidst the babble of voices and the clatter of irons and crockery, I sat alone to eat, but found I had no appetite. After swallowing a few mouthfuls, I took my plate back to the counter and stacked it with the dirty dishes, not bothering to scrape the remains of my meal into the enormous swill bin nearby. The cooks would curse me later when they came to deal with the congealed food sticking to it, but in my anxiety to get away I did not think of that, or care.

I was aching to be alone to read Michael's letter, but trying to find somewhere completely private on a camp is not easy. Mounting my bike I set off into the countryside. I came to a duck pond somewhere, nearly hidden by overgrown bushes. I pushed my way through them to find a rickety old seat tucked away out of sight of the lane. Throwing my bike to the ground I sat down. Everything was peaceful round me. I pulled the letter from my pocket and smoothed it out. It read: "I hope this reaches you OK. I should have asked for your number, but at the last minute I forgot. I can't tell you how much it meant to me to have someone to talk to in these last weeks. I don't know when your 21st birthday is, but I would like you to have the enclosed as a present. I hope you like them. With sincere thanks and best wishes, Michael."

Pearls and nylons. I ought to have been delighted with my presents, and in a way I was. Except that I would never be able to wear the pearls without being reminded of a time I would rather forget. A time when I had allowed myself to dream that one day Michael would wake up to the realisation that it was me he had really wanted all along. A pathetic, foolish dream. I had only been 'someone to talk to', as the letter made plain. I tore it into little bits and threw them into the pond. Two ducks swam over busily, hoping they were edible, only to swim slowly away in disgust. Their wake made the paper swirl. I watched until the pieces began to sink, and then at last I started to weep.

Later the thought occurred to me: nylons were scarce and difficult to find. Having taken the trouble to look for them, and bought the pearls, why hadn't he sent them to me immediately? Where had they been since his death? And who had posted them without a word of explanation?

Dusk was falling when I left the pond and I had no idea where I was or how to get to the huts. I cycled back the way I thought I had come without meeting a soul to ask for directions. It was not until a plane took off from the airfield that I got my bearings, by which time I was getting worried that I might be out all night. I entered the hut with my head down to hide my blotched and swollen face. To my relief, Ruth was out as well as Gina. I grabbed my washing kit and went off to the ablutions to bathe away the evidence of my tears. Both girls were still out when I returned. I knew I owed them an explanation of my behaviour, but I felt empty and exhausted and only wanted to sleep. I made up my bed, undressed quickly and slid down under the blankets. Within minutes I had slipped into oblivion.

My eyes were gritty and my head full of thick fog next morning. I washed, dressed and stacked my bed like a zombie. Gina and Ruth were ready to leave for the mess when I put my hand up to my locker shelf to collect my irons and found they were not there. An increasingly frantic search among my belongings brought Gina and Ruth to my side. "I can't find my irons," I said, beginning to panic. "Shall I have a look?" said Gina, "They must be there somewhere." By chance the first thing she touched on the shelf was the brown paper loosely folded round Michael's presents. She said, "You'd better keep this little lot well out of sight at the back of your locker – and don't forget to lock it."

I nodded obediently and blurted out, "They're from Michael."

Gina's eyebrows lifted and Ruth drew in a noisy breath. For a moment none of us moved. Then Ruth said gently, "We'll have to go. It's getting late." I pushed the package to the back of the shelf, closed the door and locked it, as Gina had suggested. "I'll have to go without them," I said, referring to my irons.

"Think!" urged Gina as we cycled to the mess, "Where did you have them last?" I searched my memory and found them. They had been lying on my plate when I dumped it on the counter the previous evening. If only I had stopped to scrape my leftovers into the swill bin the irons would have been safely in my hand. It was my own fault I had lost them. "I've just remembered. I left them in the mess," I said unhappily.

"Oh, God," said Gina, "You've had it if you left them there."

I queued impatiently at the counter. While I was being served I asked the cook if my irons had been handed in. She looked at me with a mixture of scorn and pity for my naivety, and went on serving the waiting line without answering. In desperation I persisted, "Is Rosie there?" She yelled over her shoulder and Rosie appeared from the kitchen, wiping her hands on a cloth. I told her what I had done and asked, "Have you got any spares you could lend me?"

She shook her head, "but I'll lend you mine. Only bring them back immediately you've finished, or we'll both be on a charge."

"On a charge?" I was taken aback.

"Of course. Losing your irons is a chargeable offence. Surely you knew?"

"I hadn't thought."

She hurried back into the kitchen, fetched her irons and handed them over. It was nearly ten minutes to eight. Ruth and Gina had all but finished eating. I gobbled as much of my breakfast as I could cram into my mouth in five minutes and rushed back to the counter shouting for Rosie as I went. I almost threw her irons at her when she appeared. "Thanks, Rosie. I owe you a favour," I called over my shoulder as I ran out of the mess.

"Yes, you do," her voice followed me.

We reported for duty with half a minute to spare.

I had to wait until dinnertime to report my lost Irons to Admin. The sergeant was curt. She issued me with another knife, fork and spoon as if it hurt her to part with them, and confirmed that losing the first set was indeed a chargeable offence. "Report back at 1500 hours. And be prompt." she ordered. Flight was not going to be happy, but there was nothing I could do about that. I did not

'HAVE YOU GOT YOUR IRONS?'

even care. Which probably showed in my attitude when I told him. He gave me a look that clearly said I confirmed his worst fears about women in uniform and told me to report to him as soon as I retuned.

The Queen Bee (WAAF Officer in Command of Admin) was a grey-haired motherly lady, known amongst ourselves as 'Ma Bee'. She had a reputation for being fair-minded, understanding and approachable. This last attribute was not in evidence that afternoon. I was marched into her office by an Admin corporal, to stand to attention in front of her desk. Her eyes, usually friendly, were a cold grey. I had expected a quick reprimand, something along the lines of, "Be more careful in future." What else was there to say? Quite a lot, apparently. Ma Bee treated me to a good five minutes lecture on the significant role played by metal in the war. It included statistics on the amount needed to keep up with the demand for planes, warships and tanks and how many tons had to be diverted to make knives, forks and spoons for all our Forces, not just the Air Force. Looked at in that light I could appreciate the importance of hanging on to our irons through thick and thin, fire and sword. However, I thought the sergeant could have delivered the same homily equally well; the rigmarole of putting me on a charge was a stupid waste of Ma Bee's time. From the ice in her voice, I deduced that Ma Bee thought so too. The difference was that while I blamed the system for this waste, she was blaming me. I thought for a moment I was going to get the dreaded 'jankers' (a task or tasks performed in off duty time while being confined to barracks. Peeling spuds in the cookhouse for seven days, for example). But I didn't. The cost of the second set of implements would be deducted from my pay, and the charge of losing Air Force property together with the verdict 'Guilty' would be entered on my service record, where it would remain for the rest of my service life. She dismissed me curtly.

The blot on my clean sheet was regrettable, something I would not mention at home, but I could not see that it was going to make much difference to me. It might have spoiled my chances of promotion if I had had any, but I was never going to be up for my stripes anyway, so that did not matter.

I reported to Flight as ordered and he regarded me stony-faced, "Well?"

I answered in a voice as expressionless as I could make it, "A reprimand, Flight." His eyebrows twitched and he frowned in disapproval before doling out his own punishment: "Go and polish the corridor."

A year and a half of weekly domestic nights had accustomed me to floor polishing, but they had never taught me to like it. I fetched the polish and buffer from the storeroom and got down on my knees outside Flight's office in a mood of utter dejection. All the frustrations of the summer months and the more acute miseries of the last few weeks suddenly threatened to overwhelm me. I felt as if I literally had a weight on my shoulders and my arms were heavy and difficult to move. Flight had not shut his door. As I shuffled backwards past it on my way down the corridor I could feel him watching me and I felt a spurt of anger. It was so unfair. If Ma Bee had thought a reprimand sufficient punishment for losing the damned irons, who the hell did Flight think he was to punish me again? Admin matters were none of his concern. He had always had it in for me, ever since my first day on the section when he put me on night duty for arriving late. I remembered too how he had refused my application for Christmas leave and granted Gina's. My anger grew. I thumped the polish onto the floor and rubbed it furiously into the lino, hardly noticing that I was already half way along the corridor. Behind me I heard the teams leave the section and go clattering down the stairs. They were going out to collect the cameras for the night shift. I should have been out there with them, waiting on the transport for the first planes to land, instead of being cooped up inside with only my burning anger for company. I fetched the heavy buffer and pushed it up the corridor until I was once more outside Flight's office. This time I found his door shut. Just as well. I objected most strongly to slogging my guts out while he sat there watching me, and I was in the right mood to storm in and tell him so if he did it again. I pushed the buffer up and down the corridor until I ran out of energy, then slammed it back into the storeroom.

I was in such a flaming temper that I did not at first realise my depression had lifted. Despite being dog-tired and hot and sweaty from my exertions, I felt better in myself than I had done for weeks.

Chapter 17

The End of the Year

"WHY DON'T YOU go and ask him?" murmured Don. We had to keep our voices low because we were in the chemical room and at the other end of the echoing corridor Flight's office door was open.

"He'll only say no," I hissed back. "He always says no to me. He's asked everyone else if they want to go up except me." I was about to add, like a petulant child, "It's not fair!" when Don put his hands on my shoulders, turned me round to face the door and gave me a push muttering, "Go and ask him, idiot!" Thus forcibly encouraged, I arranged my face into what I hoped was a suitably humble expression and went to beard Flight in his den.

"Some of the men are going flying," I told him (as if he didn't already know!). "May I go with them? I haven't been up yet." I made sure my voice sounded hopeful, not plaintive.

He regarded me thoughtfully, as if unable to make up his mind. I held my hopeful look, aware that he was deliberately keeping me in suspense. After several seconds he said, "Yes."

My "Thank you, Flight," was so heartfelt he must have known how unsure I'd been of getting his permission. I left his office on the run to rejoin Don, who grinned when he saw my face. "Come on, idiot! The others have already left." I noted – not for the first time - that he no longer called me 'idiot child'. Since my 'affair' with Michael I had apparently matured into a full-grown idiot. I would have protested but he strode off towards the stairs and I had a job to keep up.

Bill and Lennie were already strapped into their parachute harnesses when we reached the stores. The clerk dragged two more off the shelf and helped us buckle them on. His mate handed out our helmets. I felt like a trussed chicken and the helmet was a ton weight on my head. How anyone could concentrate on flying a plane with all this clobber impeding their movements, I couldn't imagine.

I don't know how it came about that we were being allowed to go flying. I think it must have begun with the Albermarles. Two of these wooden planes had been at Bicester all summer. Officially, I believe, they were there on test. Unofficially it seemed that most of the officers on the station had been taken up in them, including our Roly. Which doesn't really explain how we of the lower orders came to be given permission to go for 'instructional photographic flights' in one of the training planes, but here we were, all togged up and ready to go.

Our plane was parked next to an Albermarle outside one of the hangars. I think it was an Anson. I know it had seats in it. We clambered aboard. Bill and Don, who had both been up before, promptly took the seats nearest the cockpit. Lennie and I were directed to sit behind them. Our pilot was one of the flying instructors, very experienced and dependable. He gave me and Lennie, also a first-timer, instructions how to plug in and operate the intercom incorporated in our helmets, and did a sound check to make sure we could all hear both him and each other clearly. "Are you OK, Yvonne?" Don's voice in my ear made me jump; I answered, "sure" and the pilot's voice said, "good" as he completed his pre-flight checks. The plane juddered as the engines roared into life. I shivered with excitement and anticipation as we trundled out across the airfield to the runway, turned into the wind and waited. As soon as the control tower gave us the green light for take-off the plane began to move forward. The pilot opened up the throttle and the engine noise swelled to thunder as we gathered speed. Suddenly the nose lifted, the noise level dropped. We were airborne.

We banked, turned and began to climb. I was entranced to see the control tower growing smaller and smaller. The buildings shrank to the size of toys, even the massive hangars looked no larger than garden sheds. Once we were out over the open countryside the pilot's voice told us we were gong to simulate a mapping exercise, but without activating the camera.

Mapping was a highly skilled operation. The pilot flew the aircraft in straight lines to and fro across a given area of several square miles, each line parallel to the one before. It was imperative that the plane should be kept level, its height should be accurately maintained and the flight lines should be straight throughout the exercise. In this way each picture taken by the camera, which operated automatically once it had been set running, would match the print before and after it and those on either side. The exercise was presumably important as training for reconnaissance work and also as practice for lining up on targets in a bombing raid. I was fascinated to recognise some of the landmarks I had so often seen on prints: a distinctive clump of trees, an abrupt bend in a country road or an odd shaped field. Features I would not have been able to identify on the ground looked quite familiar from the air.

However, after half and hour or so the novelty of seeing the same landscape pass below us again and again, albeit from opposite angles, had worn off. I wondered what the gunner did while the pilot and navigator were occupied with the technicalities of flying the aircraft. Which made me think about Paul. How was he coping, caged up with the same people day in day out, with no hope of release until the war ended? He could be there for years. What a waste of all his training. What a waste of time. But at least he still had his life. I tried to remember when I had last written to him, but failed. Guiltily I resolved to write that evening.

A village was passing below us, a small village with what

looked like thatched cottages lining a single street. Was it 'our' village, mine and Michael's? It was difficult to tell from that height. Suddenly I was engulfed by a wave of sadness. For one dreadful moment I thought I was going to cry. I fought the tears and the moment passed, but my pleasure in the flight had gone.

As well as feeling low I was beginning to feel hungry. We had not left the section until late morning and it was now past dinnertime. It was therefore a relief when the pilot finally banked and turned and headed back to base. The farmhouses below us grew larger as we lost height; the airfield buildings resumed their normal size; we were down. "JESUS WEPT!" the pilot's voice exploded in my ears followed by something I didn't catch. Bill and Don left their seats to look over his shoulder. A torrent of hard swearing came over the intercom. The pilot ordered, "GET BACK!" The swearing stopped. The plane checked, swerved violently and lurched across the airfield, veering towards the hangar we had started out from. The massive building loomed closer until it filled our vision. Just before we hit it the plane slewed round. There was a deafening crash, a long rending sound, and we shuddered to a halt. The pilot threw open the door and jumped to the ground. I could hear the urgent bell of the fire wagon speeding towards us. After a stunned moment the men scrambled after the pilot, leaving me alone in the empty plane. Somewhat shaken, I lumbered after them, reached the open door and stood transfixed. We had halted side on to the hangar. Behind us stood the shattered remains of the Albermarle. When we slewed round our port wing had demolished its tail fin and sliced into its wooden fuselage for nearly half its length. Our pilot and the three men from the section stood in a little group surveying the wreckage and swearing again, this time in awe. I jumped down and the movement caught the pilot's eye. He turned towards me in amazement, having clearly forgotten my existence. "Oh, my God! Are you all right?"

I suppose I was in shock because I said the first thing that came into my head - "I'm hungry".

He gave a grunt of laughter and relief, "Well, cut along to the mess and get something to eat." The fire wagon had pulled up with an emergency stop; the firemen came dashing over, ready for any emergency. Our pilot went to meet their officer in charge, dismissing me from his mind.

Hearing my voice, Don turned and came over. "What happened?" I asked.

"The port brake failed as we landed. Good job our pilot knew his stuff."

I stared at the wreckage, mesmerised. Don said, "You heard the officer – go and get something to eat." When I didn't move immediately, he shook my arm, "Go on! We'll tell Flight where you are."

A small crowd had already gathered, fitters and mechanics from the hangar and anyone who could slip away from the nearby sections had come running, anxious to see what was going on. They moved to let me through and I trudged off to the stores to return my parachute and helmet.

"What's all the excitement?" asked the clerk.

Freeing myself from my harness, I quoted Don, "The port brake went as we landed. We hit one of the Albermarles"

"Do much damage?" he enquired.

"It's u/s."

"Strewth!" He gave a short laugh, "There'll be hell to pay over this." He turned to summon his oppo from among the racks. "Hey, Stan!" I dumped my discarded gear on the counter and made my escape. I did not want to stay and answer questions. Reaction was setting in and I wanted to get to the mess as quickly as possible.

The bush telegraph had worked fast. The cooks and most of the girls finishing their dinner already knew what had happened when I walked into the hall. I intended going straight to the counter but, instead, I sat down abruptly on the nearest bench.

My legs were threatening to let me down. Someone brought me a drink of water and I gulped it down. One of the cooks left her post behind the counter and came over to ask, "Are you OK?"

"A bit shaky," I admitted.

"You'll feel better with your dinner inside you. Stay there and I'll bring it over."

I took my time over the meal, safe in the knowledge that I could rely on Don to keep Flight at bay. I had come to rely on Don more than I realised. When Michael came to Bicester I had had no time to go out with Don, but it had made no difference to our friendship. Gossip said his latest ladyfriend was a civilian woman living in Bicester, but he had still turned up when Gina and I were on night shift, still cooked our supper when we were busy – which was most nights following the long light days of summer.

When I had been feeling low after Michael left Bicester, Don had said one day, "How about coming out for a drink this evening?" I refused; I did not feel sociable. Don said, "You can't just sit in the hut every night doing nothing. It's not good for you. At least come out for an hour." I gave in. I was poor company, but he did not seem to mind. He went on asking me out and we had slipped into something like our old relationship. He had been comforting after Michael died, and again when I received the unexpected pearls. Oddly enough, Dorothy did not seem to worry about our evenings out this time, I never understood why. Ruth still disapproved, more, I think, because she was afraid I was heading for more heartache than for any moral reason.

As the stores clerk had foreseen, there was indeed hell to pay for the loss of the Albermarle. The story going the rounds was that it should have been returned to base weeks – if not months – ago and heads were about to roll. Not long afterwards the CO was posted. "Put back on traffic duty," was the popular theory. His successor was a strict disciplinarian, who soon made his presence felt in every corner of the station. In my innocence I had believed that we in the huts were outside the main influence of camp discipline, possibly because our easy-going hut corporal, Phyllis, did not burden us with it more than was absolutely necessary. In her mid-thirties and accustomed in civvy street to acting on her own initiative, she looked on service rules and regulations as guidelines rather than orders to be strictly obeyed. In particular, she often ignored the rule that decreed we had to be back in the hut by eleven o'clock if we went out for the evening. When I had been meeting Michael she had allowed me a half-hour's extension if he was late picking me up. Others in the hut enjoyed the same privilege if she considered circumstances warranted it. She was especially lenient with the cooks, who worked unsociable hours for much of the time with limited opportunities for going out in the evening like the rest of us.

Some time during the summer Rosie had met and fallen in love with a pleasant young man called Tom, who worked in the armoury below the photographic section. However, there were difficulties. The armourers' shift system did not coincide with the cooks' and without Phyl's relaxed attitude to timekeeping they would have had few opportunities to meet. The romance flourished, and Rosie confided to the hut one evening that she and Tom were both putting in for leave at Christmas. He was coming to spend it with her family and they planned to get engaged on Christmas Day. I had always thought of her as quite a pretty girl, but as she made this announcement her pale cheeks glowed with colour, her dark eyes shone, and she looked positively beautiful. Knowing that the 'exigencies of the service' took no account of personal plans for happiness, we crossed our fingers that nothing would go wrong for them.

Not long after the new CO took over, Jean, one of the two Admin girls in the hut, reported one evening that she had been questioned about hut discipline by a Waaf Admin officer. Looking apologetic and ill at ease she said she had done her best not to land anyone in trouble, but feared there would be repercussions nonetheless. Sure enough, a few days later Phyl was posted, to everyone's great regret. Her replacement, with new broom zeal, set about restoring strict discipline to the hut immediately. When we came off duty on the day of her arrival she was already installed in the end bed by the entrance door. She greeted everyone with a smile that was meant to be friendly but did not reach her hard pale blue eyes. As soon as she had a sufficiently large audience she introduced herself as Cpl Grant and informed us that from now on no one could go out in the evening until she had inspected the hut, which she hoped to find spotless. We had expected a tightening of the reins but nothing as tight as this. Normally the only time the hut was that clean was on domestic night, in preparation for inspection by an Admin officer the following morning. Surely she didn't mean us to take her literally? But she did. A bed pulled out of line, a biscuit stacked slightly askew, a few specks of dust on a locker, nothing escaped her. The atmosphere in the hut changed overnight. There was now no question of elastic timekeeping. Everyone had to be in on time regardless of circumstances and with no exceptions. Rosie was one of the first to suffer under the new regime. Her meetings with Tom were now largely reduced to moments snatched at the end of the evening when one or other of them came off shift. Rosie was very philosophical. "It's not the end of the world." Christmas was coming, their respective sergeants were recommending them for leave and they would have seven whole days together.

So much for dreaming! One evening as Gina, Ruth and I came off day shift Tom was waiting at the bottom of the stairs looking totally miserable. He held out a folded slip of paper and asked, "Are you going to the mess? Will you give this to Rosie for me?"

Ruth took the note, Gina asked, "Is something wrong?"

"I've been posted overseas," he said flatly.

We all groaned. Gina said, "Where to?"

"India, we think."

"When?" I enquired.

"I go on embarkation leave the day after tomorrow."

THE END OF THE YEAR

"Bloody war," said Gina sourly.

Tom was about to go on duty; he would not be able to see Rosie that night. We cycled over to the mess and joined the queue at the counter. Rosie was one of the girls serving up. She greeted us with a smile that died when she saw our faces. Ruth held out the note and said, "It's from Tom."

Rosie's face lost all its colour. She reached over the counter and took the note, thrusting it into her apron pocket without unfolding it, and went on serving up.

When we were seated at the table Ruth said quietly, "It's a pity she'll be on duty when he's free tomorrow. It's domestic night and she'll be stuck in the hut all evening. Phyl would have let her go out to say goodbye, but this one won't."

Looking up the hut next evening I saw Enid, also a cook and Rosie's special friend, polishing Rosie's bed space, leaving her free to do her shoes and buttons. Looking past them I saw Cpl Grant watching them, her face stony. Rosie checked to see that everything was ready for inspection then approached the corporal's bed. We were too far away to hear her words, but her voice was pleading. The corporal said something sharp. Rosie looked desperate and Enid went to stand beside her. I put down the shoe I was polishing and went to give them moral support. Gina and Ruth came with me and one by one most of the hut came to join us. Diane and Jean, the Admin girls, hung back, looking unhappy. However much they might sympathise privately with Rosie, as Admin staff they were officially expected to uphold the rules, not add their support to getting them broken.

Rosie was trying not to cry. "He's outside now. Couldn't I slip out just for a moment? Please!"

Cpl Grant shook her head, "Rules are rules. There is no more to be said." I felt hot with anger and blurted out, "Couldn't you bend the rules for once?" She ignored me, and without looking at anyone directly said, "Go back to your places, all of you," as if we were an unruly class of five-year-olds. Rosie was the first to turn away, tears spilling over and running down her face. Enid put an arm round her shoulders and went with her. The corporal rapped out Enid's surname. "Go back to your own space and get on with your own cleaning. I shall be coming round to inspect in half an hour."

The pettiness of it was too much. To deprive Rosie of her friend's support as well as her chance to say goodbye to Tom was mean and unnecessary. As I turned to walk away I spat out, "Spiteful bitch!" It was an expletive. I was not speaking directly to the NCO but she heard me. She almost shouted my surname. It stopped me dead. I swivelled slowly round to confront her. Her face was set hard and her icy blue eyes glared at me without blinking. I glared back.

"You will apologise for that remark," she ordered.

The hut had gone very quiet. Nobody moved. In the stillness I heard Rosie give way to a sob she could not stifle, and I could feel her pain as if it were my own. I said nothing, my attitude defiant. Cpl Grant spoke again. "You will apologise, or you are on a charge."

I continued to glare at her in silence. I was in the wrong and I knew it. To apologise would have been the sensible thing to do. But anger had made me stubborn. After a few moments she snapped, "Very well. Dismiss!"

I turned and walked away, and as if released from a spell everyone started to move again, talking in subdued voices.

"Why on earth didn't you apologise?" demanded Gina when we got back to our beds.

"Because I'm not sorry." I snapped, still angry. "She made me mad."

"We noticed," said Gina dryly.

On the following afternoon I was marched into Ma Bee's office by a WAAF Admin sergeant. Last time it had only been a corporal. Presumably the charge of using insulting language to an NCO was a little more serious than losing a knife, fork and spoon and

THE END OF THE YEAR

rated a higher rank of escort. I stood rigidly to attention between her and Cpl Grant, both equally poker-straight. Ma Bee tapped the file on her desk and regarded me solemnly. "Two charges in two months."

"Yes, Ma'am," I agreed.

She read out the charge. "Did you use those words?"

"Yes, Ma'am."

"Do you have anything to say for yourself in reply?"

There was nothing I could think of that did not sound like splitting hairs or special pleading. I fixed my gaze on the wall behind her, just above her head, and answered firmly, "No, Ma'am."

There could be no doubt about the verdict. Another 'Guilty' on my service record, not to be mentioned at home. And the punishment? Seven days CB (Confined to Barracks). "Report to the cookhouse at 1800 hours. Dismiss," ordered Ma Bee. Outside her office Cpl Grant hurried away to the Met. Section, where she worked, without the flicker of a glance in my direction. The sergeant disappeared into her own office, and I returned reluctantly to face Flight on the section. I had visions of having to polish the corridor again, or maybe the general room floor. However, this time he appeared to be satisfied that I was being adequately punished for my crime. He dismissed me without comment.

I reported to the kitchens as ordered and was met by an exuberant Enid. "Rosie's gone," she greeted me. "Sarge got her a seven days compassionate and let her off early to catch the evening train."

I grinned, "Wizzo!"

Enid's face became grave. "She was really sorry about the charge. We both were."

"That's OK," I said cheerfully, "I'd rather be here than spending the evening in the hut just now."

She showed me where to leave my cap and greatcoat and gave me my task for the evening. "Sarge says to put you on the bread slicer. This way."

215

She led me into a small room off the main kitchens. The only thing in it was a trestle table piled high with loaves. On one end was clamped a machine that resembled the bacon slicer on our grocer's counter at home. Enid demonstrated how it worked. She pushed a loaf up against an upright metal wheel with a razor-sharp rim, at the same time turning a large handle on the side of the machine. The wheel rotated at speed, and slices of bread fell off to one side as the loaf shrank rapidly in size. "For Gawd's sake don't let your hand get too near the blade or you'll lose your fingers," she warned. She stopped turning the handle and the blade was still. With a quick movement she lined up the slices into loaf shape again, then stood back to watch me have a go. When she was satisfied I'd got the hang of it she said, "I'll get you a stool to sit on," and went off to find one. I gathered I was privileged. Whoever normally sliced the bread had to stand.

This was a busy time for the cooks as all the girls coming off day shifts trooped in for their supper. I sat alone in my side room turning the handle monotonously. The door was propped open and the smell of cooking made me hungrier by the minute. A friendly girl brought me in a big mug of hot, sweet tea.

"That's welcome," I said, "I'm starving."

She laughed. "Supper won't be for another hour. Can you last out?"

"I'll try," I promised.

At steady intervals someone staggered in with a big wooden tray of loaves, which she tipped onto the table. Reloading the tray with the reassembled sliced loaves she staggered out again.

I had got to the stage where my arms ached and I was beginning to lose concentration when Enid bustled in. "Grub up. It's in the kitchen. Come on." I sat with the cooks at a long table and was presented with a fry-up large enough to last me all week, never mind until breakfast next morning. The talk was mostly about Rosie. Tom had managed to see her for a few minutes before she went on duty that morning but he had gone before she knew she had been granted leave. She was going to his home to surprise him. Would they have time to get a special licence and get married? If not, would they get together anyway? The scene in the hut the night before was chewed over in detail. Some of the names they called our corporal would have made her shrivel up had she heard them. My "spiteful bitch" was very mild in comparison.

After supper the pace slackened in the kitchens. Various night shift workers would come in later for a meal but for the time being the cooks were occupied with cleaning up the kitchens for the day. Everything had to be gleaming to satisfy their sergeant. Somewhere a wireless was playing loud dance music and the cooks sang along as they worked. When they brought in the trays of loaves they had time to stop and chat and the rest of the evening passed very quickly. I was expecting to be there until about ten o'clock at least. However, when Enid went off duty at half past nine the sergeant said I could go too and we cycled back to the hut together. This routine was repeated every evening. I enjoyed my seven days jankers, the only snag being that by the end of the week my battledress trousers were getting tight round the waist and the top was pulling at the buttons.

Rosie returned from leave in a muddled state of elation and anguish. She and Tom had got married by special licence and had enjoyed a wonderful few days together, which had made the wrench of parting all the more painful. Cpl Grant, aware that she had handled the matter badly, made an effort to look friendly towards her, but Rosie, like the rest of the hut, was not deceived. Her overtures were greeted coolly and she was left in no doubt of her unpopularity.

At the beginning of December Mother wrote to say that Father would not be able to get home for Christmas, but Nannie and Aunt Evelyn would be coming up. Was there any chance of my getting leave this year? I would have loved to see them, but knew I had no hope of getting Christmas leave, or any other kind, for the time being. After the first charge I had been in Flight's bad books for weeks. Since the second one he had been so glacial I was afraid he might have me posted to get rid of me. I had no intention of applying for leave – I would not give him the satisfaction of turning me down.

I told Mother some plausible fib and resigned myself to being one of the skeleton staff gain. A gloomy prospect. This time I would not have Ruth for company. She had been invited to spend Christmas with some relatives who had recently moved to London. Gina was not going home but she would be no company. She would spend all her time with the station band. And Don was not going to be there either. Being a family man he was being allowed to go home, as he had done the previous year. I had no serious desire to deprive his family of his company, but I caught myself wishing his request for leave had been refused.

In the event the day went better than I thought it would. It was Cpl Small's turn for leave and we had Jenks in charge at his most relaxed and easy-going. As Diane had gone home I joined forces with Jean, the other Admin girl for the midday dinner, which was excellent again. In the evening I tried to persuade her to come to the dance with me, without success. She was a serious-minded girl. On her last leave she had married her boyfriend, home on embarkation leave. She was not interested in dancing with anybody else. Lacking the courage to go on my own, I expected to spend a dull evening in the hut with the four or five girls, including Rosie, who were also not going to the dance. However, one of them produced a pack of cards and suggested we play Pontoon. Rosie, determined as always that no one should die of starvation during the night, produced mince pies as well as the usual toast and jam. We settled down to a lively evening, using one of the beds nearest the stove as a card table. Cpl Grant had gone home and the atmosphere was as happy and relaxed as it had been when Phyl was in charge. We played until Gina came back in the small hours. The stakes were ha'pennies. When we packed up I was sixpence to the good (the price of a lipstick in Woolworths).

Chapter 18

Growing Up

TWO DAYS INTO 1944 Mrs Blake, the redoubtable lady who had been helping Mother in the house for the last twenty years, had a bad fall in the High Road and fractured her hip. "It will be months before she can work again," said my mother's letter, "She is well into her seventies and these things take a long time to heal at that age." In my next letter home I said I was sorry to hear the news and thought no more about it.

By February Flight had thawed out towards me and I was granted seven days leave to go home for my twenty-first birthday. Having assumed the family would all be together for the occasion, I was disappointed when Mother told me Father would not be there. He had written to say how sorry he would be to miss such an important family celebration, but did not explain why he could not come. Neither did the message he wrote inside my card. Mother was very upset about it. "It's a big day for you, " she said, "he ought to be here."

"Perhaps there are important goings on we know nothing about," I tried to comfort her, "Don't you know there's a war on?" It was the question in universal use to explain all frustrations and delays and every disappointment, an ironic joke. She gave an unconvincing laugh, but I knew his absence continued to worry her.

We celebrated my birthday officially with a special dinner on the Sunday. It had to be that day so that Aunt Evelyn and David, who was now a working lad, could be there. Like most people they worked on Saturday mornings. Mother timed the meal for midday as Nannie and Aunt Evelyn wanted to be back home again before blackout. Aunt Evelyn brought a bottle of sherry she had acquired and before dinner David, as the only man of the family present, called for several toasts: "To Yvonne", "Absent Fathers" and – with a sideways glance at the cake on the sideboard - "the Cook". Mother had surpassed herself with the cake. It was small, but it was not only rich and fruity, it was iced! She must have been hoarding the ingredients for months.

Presents had been a big problem, there was so little in the shops. Clothes were out of the question, everything in that line was on coupons. Anything that was not a necessity was classed as a luxury, and the cost of luxuries was exorbitant. Nevertheless the family did me proud. Mother, Father and David gave me an enamelled cigarette case between them, Nannie and Aunt Evelyn gave me a matching lighter. Mother also presented me with a door key and I cut the cake to the strains of the old song:-

"Twenty-one today, twenty-one today.

I've got the key of the door, never been twenty-one before.

Father says I can do as I like, so hip hip hip hooray,

For she's a jolly good fellow, twenty-one today!"

I thought the bit about Father letting me do as I liked was improbable, even if the possession of my own door key did prove I was now officially an adult.

Mother went upstairs to put her feet up after the others had gone; David and I settled down by the sitting room fire to talk. His talk was all about the war. He had discovered that the Fleet Air Arm accepted volunteers at seventeen and a quarter, three months earlier than the Royal Navy, which had been his original choice. He had therefore volunteered to become a pilot. Having passed the initial educational exams and the medical, he had been accepted as a CW (Commission Warrant) candidate, the equivalent of an Officer Cadet in the Army. He expected to be called up in the coming July. "You don't think it will all be over by then, do you Sis?" he enquired anxiously.

"They don't tell the likes of us what's going on," I pointed out, "but it doesn't look like it, does it?"

"No, it doesn't," he agreed cheerfully.

Although I had enjoyed my leave this time, I was still glad to get back to camp; I much preferred service life to civvy street. It was dark when the train reached Bicester North. As I walked down the incline to the road I heard voices and laughter and saw the usual cluster of cycle lamps dimly illuminating the welcome committee. I peered through the dark, looking for Don, but could not find him. It was Bill who had brought my bike. The convoy moved off. Ruth waited while I mounted my bike and we trailed along in the rear. As Don was obviously not there I asked, "Don's not on night shift is he? I thought that was next week." There was a slight pause before she answered, "He's been posted." It was as if I had been struck a violent blow. My bike wobbled and all but crashed into Ruth's. I did not think to ask where he had gone and Ruth kept tactfully silent while I struggled to pull myself together.

When we reached the Crown some minutes later I discovered that this was to be no ordinary welcome back booze-up. The section had clubbed together to give me a party. I fixed a smile on my face, determined to look in the mood.

Cynthia and Dorothy were of course the organisers. The hotel had given us a private room and laid on sandwiches and a birthday cake. It was not iced like Mother's, but was decorated with twenty-one assorted candles. "We can't light them," said Cynthia, "the hotel wants them back. They're the only ones they've got left." Someone had managed to come by a bottle of whisky (a great rarity), otherwise it was drinks from the bar in the usual way.

The whole section was present. Even Gina turned up towards

the end and the night shift had been given permission to put in a brief appearance. Pilot Officer Roland, Roly, arrived soon after we did, followed by Flight, the last person I would have expected to see, and Cpl Small. Roly opened the proceedings with a conventional little speech congratulating me on getting the key of the door and everyone clapped politely. Sgt Finch got up and said, "Since you all know how little Yvonne has to say for herself…" here he was rudely interrupted by derisive hoots of laughter, "…. I would like to reply on her behalf." He then made a hilarious speech about nothing in particular and the party came alive. Roly called for a toast "To Yvonne," glasses were duly raised and the traditional "Happy Birthday" song belted out. My contribution to the speechmaking was, "Thank you very much everybody. Would you like some cake?"

"Whisky, Yvonne?" asked Jenks, who was in charge of the bottle. I had never tried it before and sipped it gingerly. I didn't much like the taste, but I loved the afterglow. It dulled the pain of knowing I would never see Don again. I went back for 'the other half'. "Go easy, girl, if you're not used to it," warned Jenks. But I was beginning to feel genuinely convivial and didn't listen. When the whisky bottle was empty several people bought me drinks at the bar and I downed them all.

It was a great party. Roly and Flight left early, their duty well done, after which everyone let their hair down. We finished the evening in rousing style singing bawdy versions of "She'll be Coming Round the Mountain When She Comes", "The Quartermaster's Store", and other Forces favourites. Even Cpl Small sang along.

My legs, perfectly functional while I was sitting down in the warm, buckled under me when we got out into the cold night air. I staggered into Bill and nearly sent him flying. Riding my bike was impossible. Bill and Charlie more or less frog-marched me back to the hut, nearly a mile from the Crown. No mean feat when they were none too steady themselves and had to cope with their bicycles as well. Ruth and Gina walked back with us, wheeling my bike between them and taking over from the men when we reached the hut. I can't recall Cpl Grant being there. Perhaps she was on nights. Certainly there was no trouble about our coming in late. I believe I needed help getting into bed, but my mind is a blank until I stumbled out to the loo in the early hours to be sick. The loo door banged violently back against the wall when I opened it, waking up the entire hut. I was very unpopular.

Next morning I could not face breakfast. On the section I sat on a stool in the far corner of the general room wishing everyone would stop shouting and banging things about. Cpl Small brought me a load of old glass negatives to clean. He stacked them on the bench in front of me and I said "Yes, Corporal" automatically, as I had been programmed to do, but I did not move. I wondered what happened to all these pieces of glass once we had washed off the emulsion. Many of the negs would be group photographs we had taken with the tripod camera when each new batch of budding aircrew first arrived. Instead of destroying their images, I thought, why didn't we sell prints as mementoes for the boys to send home to their proud families? We could make ourselves some extra money that way. I recalled the holiday snaps I had taken with my Kodak Box Brownie in my childhood. If the films were handed in at the kiosk before midday a notice on the counter promised, "Prints on the pier at 6 o/c." Bicester hadn't got a pier, but we could use – what could we use? I couldn't think. My head was not working properly. Gina came over with a piece of cardboard and propped it up against the stack of negatives, facing away from me. Everyone came to have a look at it and chuckled loudly. The general room seemed full of chatter and noisy bursts of laughter. Flight left his office and came down to see what was going on. He gave a "Humph" of amusement when he read Gina's notice and went away again. I turned the card round to see what the joke was. It read, 'HANGOVER. DO NOT DISTURB'. How very odd, I thought. I had worked hard on the section for over a year without getting so much as a smile from him. And now when I sat doing nothing, thick-headed and uncaring, he had almost laughed! I wished Don were there to share the joke.

I did not mind Gina knowing how much I missed Don; I accepted that Ruth probably guessed, but I tried not to let anyone else see. Especially Cynthia and Dorothy. I had not forgotten the conversation in the Crown the night I heard that this lady-killer was coming back. I remembered their amused pity for the girls who grieved when he was moved on. I had been so sure that I would never be one of them. Idiot! What was it about him that caused so much heartache? I thought about it many times in the following weeks, but never came up with the answer. I only knew that Don had been special.

For some months there had been an atmosphere of vague unrest in the air, put into words one day by Charlie (who else?). "Four and a half bloody years and still it drags on. When are they going to open up the Second Front?" Even I, who loved service life and dreaded the thought of going back home when the war was over, wished that something would happen to break the monotony of our unchanging routine. Later, when my life had changed beyond anything I could have imagined, I forgot I had been getting bored and looked back on our routine with nostalgia.

The coming of the Forward Equipment Unit (FEU) transformed the atmosphere virtually overnight. From a trickle of lorries in February the Unit grew until the roads to the camp were clogged with convoys bringing in hundreds of crates and containers to be stacked on one side of the airfield. It was an open secret – probably shared with the whole of Oxfordshire - that we were stockpiling equipment for the invasion of France. The Second Front was about to be opened up at last. The knowledge acted like a shot of adrenaline throughout the station. I thought of David ticking off the days until he would be old enough to get into uniform and I worried about him. If the Fleet Air Arm did not call him up the minute he was seventeen and a quarter and the war was over quickly he would miss it. And he would be devastated.

In April I received a short letter from Mother that sent me scurrying down the corridor to Flight's office. Father had been sent home from Llandudno with tuberculosis. I wanted an immediate forty-eight-hour pass to go home and weigh up the situation for myself and I was prepared to fight for it if necessary. I had never seen Flight as a sympathetic man, but he surprised me. When I explained my urgency he granted my request without demur. Furthermore he arranged for me to collect my pass that same evening, leaving me free to go straight to the railway station next morning to catch the early train.

This had one disadvantage. By not going into camp first I missed breakfast. I therefore arrived at Paddington Station feeling ravenously hungry and unable to continue my journey. An SP directed me to the nearest Forces canteen where I stoked up on a hearty meal. Thus fortified, I set off for the underground feeling ready to face whatever was waiting for me at home.

There had been no way I could let the family know I was coming. They were still not on the telephone. Proud of my new door key I let myself in when I arrived, calling out to tell them I was there. Mother came out of the dining room and I got a shock. Her face was haggard and grey with worry and fatigue, making her look like an old woman. Being unprepared for the sight of me she had no welcome ready. If anything, she looked annoyed. I said, "I got your letter."

She asked, "Have you eaten? There's not much food in the house." I assured her I had eaten very well at Paddington and she looked relieved. She did not kiss me, as she usually did, but turned away saying, "Come into the kitchen."

For a second I felt rebuffed, then reminded myself that the disease was infectious and kissing could be dangerous. It was my first sad lesson in living with TB. In the kitchen I asked, "Did you know he was coming home?"

"No. He simply arrived on the doorstep."

'HAVE YOU GOT YOUR IRONS?'

"It must have been a hell of a shock for you."

"In a way. But I thought something was wrong when he didn't come home for your birthday. And when I saw a taxi driver carrying his suitcase up the path for him I knew I was right and it was serious."

She sounded matter of fact. I copied her tone and enquired, "Where is he? In the front bedroom?"

"No. David brought the spare bed downstairs. He's in the dining room - but you're not to go in," she ordered hastily as I turned towards the door. "just say hello from the doorway."

The dining room table, now spread with the paraphernalia of a sick room, had been pushed into one corner. Father's bed had been positioned so that he could look directly out into the back garden through the French windows, which stood wide open. Although the room faced south and the sun was shining, a chilly breeze was gusting in. He had heard my voice and lay on his side watching the door and waiting for me. His greeting echoed Mother's warning, "Don't come in, stay by the door." I had not seen him since the morning he came with me to Paddington when I was leaving home. That had been two years ago, a big gap to bridge under the circumstances. Trying to keep my voice light without sounding flippant I gestured towards the bed and fell back on service jargon, "Jolly bad show, Pop."

He smiled, "It's good to see you. How long have you got?"

"Only a forty-eight. I go back tomorrow."

It is difficult to hold a conversation across a room. After an awkward pause I muttered something about coming to see him again later and went back to the kitchen. Mother was standing at the window with her back to me, staring blindly out into the garden. She had put the kettle on to make tea and it was beginning to sing. I went to the dresser to fetch cups and saucers, but could not find Father's special cup. It held half a pint; he loved his tea. Mother turned round, "I'll get Pop's. We have to keep his things separate." The kettle boiled and I made the tea. While it brewed we sat at the table. I asked, "When is he going into hospital?"

Mother took so long to answer I thought she had not heard me. I was about to repeat the question when she said in an expressionless voice, "He isn't."

"Why not?" My voice was unintentionally sharp.

"He's too old."

"Too old? But – " I did a quick mental calculation, "he's only forty-nine. That's not really old, is it?" My ideas on age were changing rapidly.

"No," said Mother, who was the same age. She shrugged wearily, "They don't take TB cases over thirty-five."

"So what treatment do they give people his age?"

"Only bed-rest and fresh air. And they can get that at home without taking up a hospital bed."

She poured out the tea and took Father's in to him, while I tried to take in the implications of what she had just said. Unbidden, a frightening memory came back to me. An elderly neighbour of ours had contracted TB at the beginning of the war. He had remained at home and lived out the last months of his life in a tent in the back garden. At the time it had not made much impression on me. Now it became significant. Was that what would happen to Father? I was appalled. I could not believe the prospect was real. Then Mother came back and I knew by her face that it was. Very real.

We sipped the hot tea; I asked, "Has he got it in both lungs, or only one?"

"Only one."

Thinking of Mollie I began eagerly, "So he's got a fifty-fifty chance," then stopped. Mollie was young and she had been taken into hospital and given proper treatment. Father was not to be given that chance. Fear and anger knotted my stomach and I started to shake. Mother did not come and put her arm round my shoulders to comfort me as once she would have done, and I understood that all demonstrations of affection were now banned, not just kissing. When the spasm had passed she said, "I'd better go and make up your bed."

I jumped to my feet. "Let me do it." I wanted to be by myself for a while. Upstairs I opened my bedroom window and stood gazing out at the garden as Mother had done, but I saw nothing of it. I was remembering how young all the other patients were on Mollie's veranda. If I had thought about it at all I had assumed the older women were in a separate ward. But were they? Were there any older women? Not if the age rule applied to women as well as men, as it most likely did. I had told Father I would go in to see him again, but I could not face it yet. What do you say to your father when you have just learned he is probably going to die? I needed time to get used to the idea first. When I felt I could cope, I closed the window, fetched sheets from the cupboard and made up my bed before going downstairs to put my head round his door again.

I was back in the kitchen with Mother when David came in from work. His solemn face lit up when he saw me. We didn't say much with Mother there and supper was a quiet meal. When it was over Mother left us to do the washing up and went in to sit with Father. She wore her warmest winter coat as the French windows were never closed and the room was cold. David and I put away the dishes and sat in the kitchen smoking, both of us totally wretched. I said, "This is a shaky do," and he nodded. He had celebrated his seventeenth birthday the previous week. I asked him, "Did you go out with the gang?"

"What's left of it. Most of them have been called up."

"Only three more months to wait and it'll be your turn."

He said unhappily, "I shall feel I'm deserting them."

"You don't have to feel guilty. You haven't any choice."

"I haven't got a date yet. I could ask them to postpone it.," he said reluctantly.

"What good would that do?" I asked.

"Not much," he agreed.

"I'll see if I can get some compassionate leave. Even if it's only for a few weeks it might tide them over until Mrs Blake comes back."

"She's not coming back. She's giving up work. Didn't Ma tell you?"

"No. When did she hear?"

"Just before Pop came home."

"I wonder what the chances are of getting somebody else."

"Not a hope," said David. "Mother's already tried."

We put in an appearance at Father's door to say goodnight when he was ready to settle down; Mother came out and sat with us in the kitchen. She looked tired out. I said, "I think I'll say goodnight too." Mother got up at once, David followed and we all made our way upstairs.

I lay tossing and turning in bed for a long time, unable to sleep. I had told David I would try for a few weeks compassionate leave, but knew that would not solve the problem. Mother was not strong enough to cope on her own; she needed long-term help. I cursed the fall that had deprived her of Mrs Blake at a time when her help was so desperately needed. As David had said, the chances of getting someone else, especially with TB in the house, were non-existent. Sick at heart I knew I would have to apply for extended leave and come home.

Chapter 19
Leaving Bicester

"HALT!" I was once more in the WAAF Admin CO's office, standing to attention in front of the impressive desk. The corporal who had marched me in took two paces backwards and came to attention again. The Queen Bee finished reading the file in front of her and looked up. "At ease," she said in conversational tones and I relaxed. Ma Bee put her elbows on the desk and clasped her hands under her chin. "I believe you wish to apply for compassionate leave?" she enquired.

"Yes, ma'am." I had rehearsed my request beforehand but now the moment had come I had forgotten it. Trying to find the right words I gave her a rambling account of the situation at home, Father's illness and why Mother needed help.

She stopped me once to ask for more details of Mother's health, otherwise she listened without interrupting. When I stumbled to a halt she took her elbows off the desk, picked up her pen and enquired briskly, "What is the name and address of your father's doctor?" Having entered the information in the file, she announced her decision in much the same tone of voice she had once used to sentence me to seven days confined to barracks. I was granted twenty-eight days compassionate leave. If at the end of that time the situation was unchanged I would be given a temporary discharge from the Service for six months, after which the position would be reviewed again.

The formalities having been disposed of she gave me a warm smile and wished me luck. Then looking beyond me she said,

"Carry on, Corporal," and returned to the file. The corporal called her squad of one to attention. I obeyed smartly, about-turned on command and we marched out.

The contrast between the military formality of the proceedings, so appropriate when I was on a charge, and the informality of my request struck me as ludicrous, but I did not feel like laughing. I had asked for leave and been given the prospect of a discharge. Even with 'temporary' in front of it, it sounded so final. I would no longer be a Waaf. The corporal said, "Report to Admin at 1800 hours and you can collect your travel warrant and ration cards. OK?"

Everything was happening too fast. Life was going out of control. It was a measure of my mental confusion that I answered, "OK," instead of "Yes corporal." and hastily corrected myself. She smiled, as Ma Bee had done, said, "Good luck!" and hurried away.

The time was 1530 hours. The teams were out waiting to collect the cameras as the planes landed and the section was very quiet. I went down to see Flight, and was relieved to learn he had already heard from Admin, I had nothing to explain. Nevertheless he looked uneasy. He said awkwardly, "I'm sorry about this," and relaxed visibly when I merely answered, "Thank you, Flight." Perhaps he had been afraid I would burst into tears. Sgt Finch, when I went over to the hangar to tell him I was going, and why, said warmly, "I'm very sorry to hear this. I hope it won't be as bad as you fear. Take care of yourself." When the teams returned I told Gina I was leaving and she passed the word around for me. I was surrounded by good wishes, but somehow nothing seemed real. I felt I was acting a part.

At the end of the shift I cycled over to Admin. The sergeant was matter-of-fact. "For the present you may leave your kit in the hut. I would advise you to pack it in your kitbag and lock it away in your locker. If you are not going to return at the end of twenty-eight days we will send for you to come and collect it." She handed me a chitty. "Return your bike to the stores, get this signed and bring it back. Your papers will be waiting for you."

The walk back from the stores seemed much longer than I expected, as did the walk to the mess for a meal. To accommodate the FEU, the Waafs had recently been turned out of their own relatively small and friendly mess, and we now had to eat with the airmen in their vast, echoing hall. The place still felt unfamiliar, and none of the cooks I knew were on duty. I sat alone in the noise, ate my meal, which was not nearly as good as those Rosie and her fellow cooks had produced, and left as quickly as possible. It was not until I was walking back to the hut that the situation really hit me. I had had to hand back my bicycle, a perk that was only granted to those who belonged on the station. I was now an outsider.

I was aware that my news had gone ahead of me as soon as I entered the hut. Although no one openly commiserated with me, sympathetic smiles followed me as I walked down the hut to my bed space. Jean came down to enquire if I had got my pass OK. She gave me her service number and said if I had any Admin problems while I was away, write and let her know and she would try and get them sorted out. Rosie brought me a jam sandwich to eat on the train as I was once more going to miss breakfast in the morning. Cpl Grant and I ignored each other as we had done since the night she put me on a charge.

Ruth, Gina and I exchanged numbers and home addresses to enable us to contact one another after I had gone. "It'll seem funny without you," remarked Gina and Ruth said, "Aye, it will."

"Not half as funny as not being here," I replied. That was the nearest we came to expressing any sort of regret at my going, and was about as much sentiment as I could handle at that moment. Next morning there was no time for anything more than, "Good bye, I'll keep in touch" before I set off to catch the train.

This time Mother was clearly expecting me. As soon as I walked in she emerged from Father's room and began to scold. "You shouldn't have done this. We'd have managed."

"How?" I demanded.

She ignored the question, demanding in her turn, "Why didn't you tell us what you intended to do before you went back?"

"Because I knew you'd say I shouldn't do it and tell me you could manage," I retorted. "I suppose David told you?"

"Just as well he did, or I'd have had no food in the house."

In the kitchen I handed over my ration card. Her eyes widened when she saw it was for four weeks. I said nothing about the possible extension of six months, hoping that a miracle would occur and it would not be necessary.

It was Father who said, "I'm glad you're here."

"Thanks, Pop."

"Your mother's pleased too, even if she doesn't show it. You mustn't take too much notice of what she says. She's tired."

Although Father had not been given a hospital bed, he had not been abandoned by the medical profession as we had at first feared. In fact the local TB clinic in the High Road kept the whole family under surveillance. Mother and David had been given the BCG vaccination against the disease and as soon as they discovered I was at home, I was given the same treatment. It was the clinic who had given instructions that everything Father used, from bed linen and clothes to his teaspoon, should be kept isolated in his room and dealt with separately. A nurse dropped in at frequent intervals to check on his sputum cup. This was a china cup with a lid into which he had to spit all the phlegm he brought up when he coughed. There were two nurses who took it in turns to make the visit. Sometimes they came together. The senior nurse was dark-haired and buxom with a hearty laugh. She looked about the same age as Mother. The other nurse was younger with light brown hair, merry blue eyes and an Irish accent. They were friendly, efficient and always a tonic to our spirits.

When he first came home Father was suffering from shock, having only just been told what was wrong with him. He was also worn out by the journey from Llandudno and worried sick about the future. He had no energy and was content simply to lie in bed and rest. However, after a very short time he began to feel less drained. After I came home and he no longer had to watch Mother working herself to exhaustion, he banished his worries to the back of his mind and concentrated on fighting the TB. His first problem was to find something to do. "I can't just sit here all day doing nothing," he told the nurses. "I'm getting bored."

"Therapy, that's what you need," said the buxom nurse.

"Not making raffia mats?" protested Father.

"No, leatherwork," she replied.

Hospitals and clinics were still able to obtain leather for use in therapy, although it was unavailable for commercial purposes. In due course Father was able to purchase everything necessary - tools, instructions and, of course, the leather itself - to make a purse. Father, the ex-engineer who loved working with his hands, settled down to work with every sign of contentment.

Mother and I rapidly established a routine for running the house. Mother made herself responsible for anything to do with Father, even his washing. I did whatever Mrs Blake would have done, though I doubt if I did it so well. Sometimes, as I scrubbed the kitchen floor, or stood at the deep stone sink with my arms up to the elbows in suds and dirty clothes, I felt like Cinderella who had been to the ball and now come down to earth with a bump. I particularly disliked doing David's washing. He was working as a laboratory assistant at the Mill Hill gasworks. Some of his duties took him outside into the plant itself. The smell of gas permeated everything. It clung to his clothes, which gave off a very strong odour when they were washed.

Among his other tasks, he was involved in the analysis of various by-products of the process, one of which was benzene. This was stored in a large tank about thirty feet high. To take samples it was necessary to climb up an outside iron ladder, open a manhole cover and lower a sample bottle and dipstick into the tank. When the manhole was opened heavy vapour fumes would be released which could cause dizziness if inhaled. Although he was warned about this he was not told for some time that his predecessor had been overcome by the fumes and had fallen into the tank and died.

Before I was fully awake in the morning I often had a recurring dream. I was out on dispersal fitting cameras. I sat on the grass with a shadowy unidentified partner waiting for the transport to collect us. There was a gentle breeze ruffling our hair, the sun was warm on our backs. From somewhere nearby came the roar of a plane's engine warming up. It was always summer in this waking dream. There was never a bitter wind cutting across the airfield, numbing our hands, or drizzle seeping into our battledresses as we cursed the transport for taking so long to pick us up. When I opened my eyes and saw I was at home, and remembered why I was there, I longed to turn back the clock to my salad days when I had been happy.

As well as ministering to Father, Mother did all the cooking. I did the shopping. I was no stranger to rationing in theory. It had been in force before I went away, and I had heard Mother complaining about it when I was on leave. But food had always appeared on the table at mealtimes and I had never concerned myself with how it got there. Now I was the one who had to do the queuing and deal with ration books and coupons and it was an eye-opener. When I remembered the amount of food dished up for one meal by Rosie and company, and compared it with the scraps Mother had to juggle with, it made me ashamed to have taken her meals so for granted.

I heard from Gina and Ruth once. They wrote jointly, there being insufficient news for two letters. There was hardly enough for one, but they hinted that big changes were in the air, I would find out all about them when I came back, or came to collect my kit, whichever. I was curious and frustrated and yearned to be back with them, taking part in whatever was going on.

One morning there was an official-looking letter for David. He opened it whistling happily, expecting to be give his call-up date. He stopped whistling and his face changed as he read it. The Admiralty informed him that the Fleet Air Arm was no longer recruiting pilots. As he had already been accepted they offered to transfer him to the Royal Navy. Unfortunately, as he already knew, the Navy did not accept recruits until they were seventeen and a half, and he would therefore have to wait a further three months to be called up. He accepted immediately, but having completely recovered from his initial crisis of uncertainty over going away, I think he was more upset over the delay than he was about not becoming a pilot.

Towards the end of my twenty-eight days I received a letter from Admin at Bicester confirming that I had been granted a six months extension to my leave of absence after which, as Ma Bee had already told me, the matter would be given further consideration if necessary. I was instructed to return on a given date to collect my kit. It was time to tell my family what I was doing.

My intention had been to tell both my parents together but by chance I told Father first. I had taken my mid-morning cup of tea outside to sit on the garden seat by the open French windows. Father had finished the leather purse successfully and was now trying his hand at making a wallet with several compartments. As I watched him complete a line of stitching I was thinking that he was a different man since he fell ill. It was a long time since he had been the god I had idolised as a child. He was not the tyrant I thought he had become in my rebellious adolescence. In a way he was not master in his own home any more, the TB clinic was the ruling authority now. He was uncritical and uncomplaining; a model patient, doing everything he was told without demur. I found this rather pathetic, even though I realised he was acquiescent for Mother's sake, determined to make her task of nursing him as easy as he could. For even with me there to help her she still became extremely tired. With David and me she was short-tempered and seemed oblivious of the fact that we too were finding life hard. All her attention was focused on Father.

He knotted off the thread, put down the wallet and looked up. "It's been a great help to your mother, having you at home. When do you have to go back?"

"I've got an extension for another six months. I don't go back until November," I said.

A look of pain passed over his face as he digested this. "I'm very sorry it's necessary. You were happy at Bicester."

The remark caught me off guard and I gulped. Was it an oblique acknowledgement that the life I had chosen for myself was the right one? Or was I reading too much into it?

"Does Mother know?" he asked.

"Not yet."

He rang the little bell on his bedside table. "Yvonne has some news for you," he said when she came in.

I repeated what I had just told Father. As on the day I came home, she was annoyed. "You've kept very quiet about this. Don't we need to be consulted any more?"

I was miserably unhappy at having to leave the WAAF, even temporarily. Her attitude hurt. I said crossly, "I couldn't tell you earlier. The letter only came this morning," aware that I was evading the issue. I could have told them it might happen had I wanted to. I took my empty teacup round to the kitchen, brooding. I ought to have told them. I should have realised a fait accompli would make them feel even less in control of the situation than they felt already. A stray thought came to me: how strange that it was now Father who was the sympathetic one and Mother who was ignoring my feelings.

A few days later I put on my uniform again and returned to camp to fetch my kit. Walking down the incline from Bicester North for the last time I recalled the day of my arrival, the lady who had summoned the old man to give me a lift on his cart, and the drooping piebald horse clopping peacefully into town. Now a convoy of lorries thundered past coming from the camp as I started to walk towards it. I had to keep close to the hedge as they passed for fear of being hit. When the road was clear again a small van going my way drew level on the opposite side of the road. "Want a lift?" called the driver, a Waaf I did not recognise. I crossed over and climbed in beside her gratefully.

The camp was far busier than when I went away. The number of FEU personnel had grown enormously in the last four weeks, as had the amount of equipment stacked on the airfield. But Admin hadn't changed. "You'd better go and get a meal," said the corporal. "Have you got your irons?" I explained that I had only just got off the train and had not yet been back to the hut for my kit. She took a set from her desk drawer and handed it to me. "You can borrow these. But mind you bring them straight back."

The mess was nearly empty and my footsteps sounded loud on the concrete floor as I walked to the counter. An RAF cook came out from the kitchens behind it. "I've just arrived," I told him, "is there any chance of a meal?"

"Coming right up," he said obligingly and went back into the kitchen. I had hardly sat down to wait when he returned with a plate piled high with potatoes swimming in whatever kind of stew they had served for the midday meal. There was also a portion of stodgy rice pudding for afters. When I tasted the food it was nearly cold. I was hungry so I ate it, reflecting that there may have been less to eat at home, but at least Mother's cooking was appetising.

When Admin had received their irons back into safe custody there were various formalities to go through and papers to sign, after which I went over to the section. I climbed the stairs with reluctance. Seeing the old crowd again when I was no longer part of it was going to be hard. I went first to the general room. Several unfamiliar Waafs were milling around. There was a line of cameras on the bench ready for the night shift, so the teams were back. I asked, "Is Ruth or Gina about?" and heard Ruth's voice from the drying room. "In here." The Waafs smiled politely but without interest.

There was no one in the chemical room when I passed the door, but the red light was on above the darkroom doors, showing they were occupied. Ruth was drying group prints of the latest intake of aircrew. "Where is everybody?" I asked when the first greetings were over. "They can't all be in the darkrooms."

"Posted," she said briefly.

"What, all of them?"

"Uh-huh. All the men. There's only Flight and the sarge left, and they're expecting to go any day."

"And Gina?"

"She's still here. Cynthia's gone."

"No! Poor old Dorothy."

"Aye. She's on nights at the moment with one of the new girls. She's not very happy."

Gina emerged from the darkroom with more prints. "You're not coming back," she greeted me. It was a statement, not a question. I must have looked surprised. "Admin told Flight, and he told Sgt Finch, who told us," she explained. "No change at home?" I shook my head. There was a sympathetic pause. Then Gina asked, "Have you heard our latest rumour? They say the OTU is leaving Bicester."

I gaped at her. "So what's going to happen to this place?"

"Nobody knows. Or if they do they're not telling," said Gina.

Ruth started feeding the second batch of prints onto the drum. I said, remembering to keep my voice down, "I suppose I'd better go and see the old man. I'll see you in the hut later."

My interview with Flight was blessedly short. Basically I said goodbye and he said, "Good luck," and I left. Sgt Finch had always been easier to get on with. I went to his office over in the hangar. We talked for some time and as I left he gave me a big wink and said, "All the best. Take care of yourself."

"I will, Sarge. And all the best to you, wherever you go."

I was passed by numerous bikes as I walked back to the hut,

where I met more new faces. Barbara, the ambulance driver, had gone; so had Rosie and Enid and several others. Diane and Jean, from Admin, were still there. So was Cpl Grant. Gina had not come back to the hut. I spent the evening chatting to Ruth, Diane and Jean before going to bed. It was a very tame ending to my time at Bicester. Had the old crowd been there it would have been very different. The day shift would have repaired in a body to the Crown. But that was in the past. Now 'my' Bicester had gone and I no longer yearned to go back there.

Chapter 20

The Home Front

ON THE MORNING of June 6th I was out shopping. I was about to go into the baker's when a woman I had never seen before rushed up to me in a state of great excitement. "Have you heard? We've invaded France. It's on the wireless," she cried, and scurried off to waylay someone else.

I dashed into the baker's. "Did you hear? She says we've invaded France," I informed the shop at large at the top of my voice. Within minutes the High Road was buzzing with the news. Customers told shop assistants who passed it on to other customers. Knots of women began to gather on the pavements and street corners. Some were animated, some looked grave. Many of them had menfolk who they knew would be among the invaders. For them the news was as worrying as it was welcome, though I didn't pause to think of that at the time. I finished my shopping at top speed and ran home as fast as my heavy shopping basket would let me. I let myself in shouting, "It's happened! We've invaded France!" Dumping the shopping basket on the floor in the hall, I dashed into Father's room without warning, forgetting it was out of bounds.

"Did you hear? It's on the wireless."

Mother came hurrying down from upstairs as I turned the set on.

"You know you're not supposed to be in here," she snapped.

"We've invaded France," I repeated, "It's on the wireless."

"Yes, I heard you," she said. "Go and put the shopping away. I'll call you when the next news bulletin comes on."

As I turned to leave the room, feeling deflated, I caught sight of Father's face. He looked grief-stricken. "I hope to God it won't be like the last time," he said, and Mother glanced at him anxiously. In my jubilation it had slipped my mind that he had fought over French soil in the First World War. I knew very little about his experiences there, he never talked about them. What I did know was that according to Mother the war had changed him. They had known each other since childhood so she was in a good position to judge. I had often wondered what he was like when he was young.

When the bulletin came on I stayed outside the French windows and heard it from there. Father listened grimly. "What a bloody waste it all was," he said bitterly at the end. I was shaken. This was the first time I had ever heard him swear. Mother put her hand on his shoulder. "Don't upset yourself," she said gently, "You know it's not good for you." He put up his hand to pat hers and tried to smile for her sake.

During the second half of June a new German weapon appeared in our skies. It looked like a little fighter plane, but was in fact unmanned, being a large powerful bomb with wings. It was propelled by a small jet engine that kept going until it ran out of fuel. When the engine stopped the bomb nose-dived to earth and exploded on impact. Its official name was the V1 – 'V' standing for Vergeltungswaffe, revenge weapon. The press dubbed it the 'doodle-bug', 'buzz-bomb' or 'flying bomb'. The first time I remember seeing one was on a lovely sunny afternoon. Mother and I were working in the garden. Mother was weeding the overgrown flowerbeds, I was mowing the ragged lawn. The air raid warning sounded, we stopped work and listened. There was no sound of approaching planes, the day remained peaceful. I continued pushing the mower over the grass, Mother turned back to the weeds, but kept alert. Suddenly she called, "Stop! Listen! Can you hear anything?" From somewhere in the eastern sky came a spluttering put-put-put sound. It grew louder, a tiny plane was coming our way. Mother shouted, "It's a doodle-bug." She threw down the hoe, I abandoned the mower and we ran for the house. The noise was very near. Mother dashed in through the French windows with me close behind her. She crouched down beside Father's bed and they held hands. I dived under the dining room table. Practically overhead the noise stopped. In the silence I could feel panic rising and clenched my teeth to prevent a scream escaping. A whoosh of air and the crump of an explosion came almost together. From nearby came the sound of falling glass. Our windows rattled but did not break. It was over. Father's face was a sickly grey, Mother's was white. I started to laugh uncontrollably.

The All Clear sounded a few minutes later. An ambulance bell was clanging along the High Road. It turned down the road next to ours and stopped. "That was close," said Mother, "I wonder who got it." I was weak with relief that it wasn't us.

Quite a number of doodle-bugs flew over us in the following months. It was puzzling to know what their target might be. There was speculation that they were programmed to hit the army barracks at Mill Hill. This was particularly worrying because if they missed the barracks they might hit the gasworks. Should this happen during the day David would be in mortal danger. Falling short of Mill Hill, some of them came down in our vicinity. One or two houses in our road were demolished and we lost our front windows again despite the criss-crossed brown paper strips. The effect these bombs had on me was always the same. When the engine cut out I could feel uncontrollable terror mount to screaming point. Our Morrison shelter, which had stood neglected in the sitting room for so long, was finally put to use. Mother had always disdained to use it, and still did so. She continued to sleep upstairs at night as she had done in the Blitz, and David and I still felt obliged to stay upstairs with her. However, at the first rising howl of the siren I was out of bed and downstairs like a frightened rabbit. I flung up the tablecloth, crawled inside the shelter and stayed there until the All Clear gave me courage enough to go back to bed. Mother also came downstairs when the warning sounded, but went in to sit with Father. David followed her, the ban on going into Father's room being temporarily lifted. I admired him enormously for refusing to leave our parents. Try as I might, I could not control the panic that drove me to scramble into the Morrison.

There was one aspect of coming home that I had dreaded so much I hardly dared to think about it. Without treatment it seemed likely, if not inevitable, that Father's condition would gradually deteriorate and he would die. The thought that we would have to stand by helplessly and watch it happen must have haunted all of us, though we never spoke about it. But weeks had slipped by and his condition showed no sign of worsening. As far as we could see he was holding his own against the disease very well. The nurses remarked on it. They brought in a doctor, an elderly man who had come out of retirement to take up practice again for the duration of the war. He examined Father and with years of experience to back his judgement announced that apart from having TB he was very healthy, with the constitution of a much younger man. Mother said tartly that it was a pity the authorities did not take that into account instead of condemning a man because of his age. The doctor departed looking thoughtful.

He returned some days later, again accompanied by the nurses, both of whom were smiling broadly. Mother was summoned into the sick room and I slipped in behind her and stood by the door. The doctor smiled in the general direction of the bed and said he believed that if Father could receive proper treatment he had every chance of making a good recovery. As this was precisely what the family had believed all along, I wished he would stop telling us what we already knew and tell us why they had come. The doctor then spoke directly to Father. "Clare Hall, a sanatorium at South Mimms, is prepared to offer you a bed." He turned to Mother. "It's quite a long way to visit, but it's the best I can do."

Father went white. I thought he was going to faint, and the Irish nurse must have thought so too. She poured him a glass of water from the jug on his bedside table and held it to his lips. Always independent, he took the glass from her hand and drank unaided.

Mother asked, "When can he go?"

"It may not be for three or four weeks," said the doctor, "the clinic will make all the necessary arrangements and let you know."

It was too momentous to take in immediately. We stared at him, unable to react. After they had gone Father sat gazing out through the French windows, too overcome even to speak. Mother stayed with him for a little while then wandered out into the garden to pull up weeds at random. I sat on the lawn smoking a cigarette and watched her. Later, when the wonderful news had sunk in, we could talk and laugh, if somewhat hysterically. When David came home Mother rushed out into the hall to tell him the news. It transformed him. His face beamed, his step became jaunty and he began to whistle. My brother whistled non-stop when his spirits were high. By the end of the evening I was wishing they would return to a normal level and he would be quiet.

"Three or four weeks," the doctor had said, before there would be a bed free. I hoped this was because someone was due to go home. It was a chilling thought that we might be waiting for someone to die. Whichever it was, three very long weeks went by before the clinic informed Father that a bed would be available in two days' time. Mother had spent the waiting period washing, ironing and gathering together everything and anything she thought might be useful to him in the sanatorium.

"If I took all that, there wouldn't be room in the ambulance for me," he protested, surveying the growing mound of articles on the dining room table.

"Take what you want for now. I can bring anything else when I

'HAVE YOU GOT YOUR IRONS?'

come to visit," said Mother gaily.

After breakfast on the appointed day the two nurses came for the last time. Mother was choked with joyful tears, unable to express adequately how grateful we were for all their help and support. Father became quite embarrassed by this show of emotion. His own thanks sounded formal by comparison. The nurses took it all in their stride. "Mind you behave yourself now," said the Irish one, her eyes sparkling with mischief. "Don't you be flirting with the nurses and your wife not there to keep an eye on you." Father smiled awkwardly. Flirting was not his style.

Soon after they left the ambulance arrived. When two men jumped out to open up the back and fetch the stretcher a passing neighbour on her way to the shops stopped to see what was going on; another leaned out of an upstairs window, ostensibly to shake her duster; a third unashamedly came out to her front gate to watch. The men brought the stretcher into the house and I heard Father's voice arguing with them. I gathered he wanted to walk out to the ambulance, not be strapped down and carried out feet first. The men said orders were orders, they would be in trouble if they allowed the patient to walk and he gave in, much to Mother's relief. As they carried him outside two more neighbours came to wish him well. Mother stayed outside to talk to them after the ambulance had drawn away. I left her to it and went back into the empty house. The door to Father's room stood open and I looked inside. The bedclothes had been thrown off carelessly and lay tumbled on the floor. The surplus articles Father had chosen to leave behind looked forlorn on the table. As did the crockery and other things Mother had had to keep in isolation. The bedside table held discarded odds and ends. Thank heavens the nurses had removed the revolting sputum cup.

I knew better than to go in and start tidying up. I lit a cigarette and went into the garden to relax on the seat and think. I took it for granted Father would recover. Mother, who had looked years younger since we were offered this miraculous ray of hope, had stopped snapping my head off at every turn. David could go off into the Navy with an easy mind, and I would definitely be going back into the WAAF. Future prospects for all of us looked good. The big question for me now was – what to do next? My temporary discharge still had nearly four months to run. Briefly I considered applying to go back early, but dismissed the idea. As I had been put into cold storage for the time being it would probably take the Air Force weeks to bring me out again, re-process my documents and organise a posting for me. Had I still been hankering to go back to Bicester if possible, I might have felt differently; as it was I thought I might as well let the system take its course and wait until I was automatically recalled in November.

The main problem was going to be money. The Air Force was not paying me while I was on discharge and the cash I had brought home with me had not lasted long. Mother made me a small allowance out of the housekeeping, but it was hardly enough to keep me in cigarettes. Apart from which, I would feel uncomfortable accepting it from now on. I had come home for a specific purpose: to help Mother nurse Father. As of that morning my help was no longer needed. If I stayed at home I would have to get a temporary job and contribute to the housekeeping rather than take money out of it. I decided to try the Labour Exchange and the local employment agency immediately.

As the doctor had said, South Mimms was a long way to go to visit. The journey involved two buses, with a steep hill to walk up at the other end. The sanatorium was situated at the top. Mother found it exhausting and could not manage it nearly as often as she would have wished. For David the journey was easy. He could cycle there and back in a fraction of the time it took Mother and me.

It did not strike me at the time, but later I thought it strange that although my brother and I had not been allowed beyond the door of Father's room when he was at home, we were encouraged to visit him and sit by his bed as soon as he went into Clare Hall. He was not out on a veranda, but in a large ward with wide doors opening out onto one. These were always kept open, as were all the windows. Being summer, the weather was warmer than it had been when I visited Mollie. Nevertheless every breeze that blew went through the ward and the place only felt warm on really hot days.

Father was the oldest patient there by several years. However, he settled in well. The sanatorium offered several crafts as occupational therapy, one of which was leatherwork. This was right up Father's street. He started by making a simple wallet and progressed to writing cases and handbags with several compartments. Articles made from leather were almost impossible to find in the shops at reasonable prices; he could have sold his output ten times over had he wanted to. Instead he preferred to give away what he had made as presents for family and friends.

Not all the patients stood as good a chance of recovery as Father, despite their youth. Death was a frequent occurrence, particularly among those with TB in both lungs. When a patient was approaching his last days he was moved into a side ward. I was deeply shocked to discover that one of the patients ran a sweepstake, taking bets on who would go into a side ward next. Everyone joined in, even those who were the next likely candidates. I thought this was heartless to say the least, but Father said it was just their way of coping.

Many of the patients were ex-servicemen. For a few months a most attractive young man with blond hair and friendly blue eyes occupied the bed next to Father's. His name was Tony. His story was not an uncommon one. He had been a bomber pilot. His plane had been shot down over the sea. The crew all escaped from the wreckage before it sank and managed to scramble into their inflatable rubber dinghy. But it was many hours before they were spotted by Air Sea Rescue and picked up. They were all suffering from exposure and Tony had contracted TB in both lungs as a result.

He had few visitors, his family lived too far away to come often. Our family therefore 'adopted' him and included him in our conversation as much as possible when we visited. I used to position my chair so that I could sit facing him as well as Father. In fact, of the two Tony had more of my attention than Father did. We got on well and I began to think of him as a boyfriend. Father was well aware of this. As I was saying goodbye to them one day he stared intently into my face and almost imperceptibly shook his head. I refused to believe what I knew he was telling me. But Father was right. A few weeks later he had a new neighbour. Tony was in a side ward and his mother was with him. In the intense way relationships develop in hospital we had all grown fond of him and we mourned him as one of our own.

As if to counterbalance Tony's death I had a joyful letter from Mollie. She and Ted had got married on his embarkation leave a few weeks earlier. The wedding had been a very small affair, only their immediate families had been present. Her father disagreed in principle but had given the bride away with good grace. The day had been perfect. So had their four-day honeymoon. She enclosed a smiling photograph of them both and I prayed nothing would happen to prevent them living happy ever after.

Neither the Labour Exchange nor the employment agency were able to help me with temporary work. July had turned into August before I had a stroke of luck. When I returned home with the shopping one morning Mother was pottering about in the front garden, looking very pleased about something. I was hardly in through the gate when she said, "I think I've found you a job."

"How on earth did you manage that?"

"You know Mrs Gray down the road? She went by some time ago and stopped for a chat. Her husband works in the Borough Surveyor's Department. Apparently since the doodle-bugs started the Enquiries desk has been snowed under with people wanting shelters. They're short staffed and they want someone to fill in on the Enquiries counter until the rush is over."

"Wizzo! How do I apply?"

"She's going to speak to her husband this evening. If you go down after supper you can speak to him yourself."

The Council offices in Church End were spread over more than one site. The Borough Surveyor's Department occupied an old house on the main road. A Mr Bedford presided over Enquiries, and Mr Gray suggested I go down to see him the following afternoon. "It will give me a chance to have a word with him first." It was all very informal. The Enquiries office had once been the front parlour of the house. A counter had been installed across the room on the window side, a row of wooden chairs stood against the opposite wall. Mr Bedford was dealing with a query when I entered and there were two people ahead of me, waiting until he was free. I sat down to wait my turn. This gave me an opportunity to get a good look at him before my interview. He was a tall man aged fifty-something, with receding hair, hard grey eyes and an unsmiling angular face. Later I learned he had been a police sergeant at one time.

When my turn came I stepped up to the counter and introduced myself. Mr Bedford acknowledged me with a nod and looked me over critically before speaking. "Mr Gray tells me you are in the WAAF, but he didn't give me any details. How do you come to be applying for a civilian job?"

I explained about Father as briefly as possible and handed over my papers to prove I was not AWOL (Absent Without Leave). He hardly glanced at them before handing them back. "We're getting more demands for shelters than we can deliver at the moment. I need someone to list the applicants and leave me free to deal with the other queries."

It sounded like a piece of cake. I said formally, "I understand."

Still unsmiling he asked, "When can you start?"

"Tomorrow?" I offered.

"Nine o'clock. Sharp."

I thanked him and promised not to be late. His attitude reminded me so strongly of Flight's at Bicester that I nearly waited for him to say "Dismiss" before leaving.

I was there before nine the following morning. The front door was open and I waited in the hall for him to arrive and open up Enquiries for the day. He came in on the dot of nine. He evidently did not believe in giving the job a minute more of his time than he had to. We exchanged polite good mornings as he unlocked the door. Inside he lifted the flap of the counter for me to go round behind it. "Right," he said, "shelters," and placed a lined pad of foolscap paper on the counter in front of me. "Take their names and addresses, and number each one. Distribution is strictly in order of application. No one gets priority. Got it?"

"Got it." I took out my fountain pen, put the date at the head of the page and wrote "1" at the beginning of the top line, ready for my first customer.

I was astounded at the number of people who had not applied for a shelter during the conventional bombing, but who were now desperate to get one without delay. Writing down their names and addresses and keeping the list in order was, as I had anticipated, a piece of cake. Dealing with the applicants themselves was not. I had every sympathy with their dread of the doodle-bugs and never became inured to their sick dismay when I told them there was a waiting list. Most of them accepted the situation with resignation, but not all. Some, especially those who had put their name down earlier and had come back to enquire why they were still waiting, were convinced that if they pleaded long and hard enough I could be persuaded to treat them as a special case and give them priority. Others, looking along the counter to Mr Bedford, demanded to speak to someone in authority. He ignored them unless they approached him directly, in which case he referred them back to me. When he told me at my interview that he wished to be left free to deal with other enquiries, he had meant exactly what he said. I had accepted the job and he expected me to get on with it.

Every now and then he left the counter and disappeared for fifteen minutes or so. At first I thought he was pursuing enquiries in another office. After a few days I suspected he was skiving off for a quiet smoke. It was during the times when I was on my own that the really troublesome callers showed their hand. Some became abusive. I found a blank stare was the best way of dealing with this (and one that could not be quoted against me afterwards). One man claimed to be a friend of one of the Councillors and intimated that my job was at risk if he didn't get special treatment. With careful politeness I said, "As you wish, Sir," and looked past him to the next person waiting. He left in anger and I thought it wise to report the incident to Mr Bedford.

"If he comes in again, I'll deal with him," he said.

My pride would not allow that. "It's OK. I only told you in case he really is a personal friend of someone and there's trouble later. I can cope."

"Yes," he said.

I took this as high praise and felt I was doing well. However, Mr B returned from one of his walkabouts a few days later to find me bandying angry words with a large blustering man who was refusing to move away from the counter. He was convinced his neighbour, who had received a shelter the day before, had not applied for one until after he himself had done so. He was hellbent on proving that the Council did give some people priority despite their declared policy of first come first served. He was demanding that I produce the lists so that he could find the relevant dates and prove he was right. I tried to explain that I could not help him. At the end of each day the lists were passed to the general office and I never saw them again. He accused me of being obstructive, among other things, and eventually I lost my temper. Three people sitting waiting their turn were following the exchange with great interest, torn between enjoyment of the entertainment and irritation at being kept waiting. Mr B took over with a sergeant's authority and I tried to look pleasant for the next customer. After the blustering man had finally gone Mr B enquired, "Do you get many like him?"

"No, he's the worst yet."

"Good," he said dryly, "we don't want to get a reputation for brawling with the public." I took this as a reprimand, cancelling out his previous accolade.

Up-to-date news of Bicester came in a letter from Ruth. "The rumour we told you about was the real gen. The section will be closed and we are all being posted. I have applied to go somewhere nearer home and Flight is doing his best to see I get it. My family will be pleased to see more of me." And she will be pleased to see more of them, I thought, especially at Hogmanay!

I seldom thought of Michael these days. Very occasionally I fingered his gift of pearls tucked away at the back of my dressing table drawer, still wrapped in the tissue paper they had arrived in. The feel of them brought momentary sadness. I doubted if I would ever wear them. I had never spoken of Michael to my mother and had no idea whether she had ever guessed how I really felt about him. I therefore braced myself for what might be coming when she said one evening, "I saw Mrs C down the High Road today. I hadn't seen her for ages. She's gone to look very old. I heard she was ill for a long time after Michael was killed and she still doesn't look well, poor woman."

Was that the reason why the pearls had not been posted for so long after his death? Perhaps the package had been among his effects when they were sent home and his mother had been too ill to deal with them. Recalling various things Michael had told me about his childhood and his loneliness at home, I was certain he had had no idea how much he meant to his undemonstrative mother. He had been so sure he was a nuisance to his ageing parents. I grieved for all of them, knowing there was no way the past could ever be adjusted or the misunderstanding resolved. I murmured something conventional, but Mother was not paying any attention to me. She was lost in sad reflections of her own. More to herself than to me she said at length, "I'm glad David's not going to be a pilot."

One night in September there was a massive explosion in East Finchley. We lived too far away to be affected by it, but by the following morning rumours were already flying that the Germans possessed a new weapon that could cause greater destruction over a larger area than anything we had suffered before. The really terrifying thing about it was its silence. It had arrived without warning; no planes had been heard overhead; the sirens had not sounded. Unable to believe the rumours, the surveyors went over to East Finchley to check the facts for themselves. There were about half a dozen of them, all but one veterans of the First World War. They came back shaken and awe-struck. In subdued voices they told Mr Bedford what they had seen. The new weapon had made a crater big enough to hold a double-decker bus. The surrounding devastation took them back to the battlefields in France. God only knew how many people had been killed or injured. Fire, Police, ARP and Ambulance Services were all there. Heavy Rescue Squads were still working flat out, searching for anyone still alive and trapped under the wreckage surrounding the crater. Of those at the centre of the explosion there was no trace. They and their houses might never have existed.

The new weapon never acquired a nickname. It was known simply as the V2, the largest rocket ever made. The new terror campaign got under way in earnest in October. The V2 was a terrible weapon. It must have killed and injured many more people than the V1, yet it never caused the same panic and dread as the flying bomb. The moment when the doodle-bug's engine cut out is still remembered with horror by thousands who waited in fear for the bomb to fall to earth, praying it did not have their name on it. In contrast, people became fatalistic about the V2. There was no defence against it, no one ever saw it or knew it was coming, there was no time to feel apprehension or fear. I can remember more than one person saying that if one came their way they would

THE HOME FRONT

rather be directly underneath it than on the edge of the explosion. Then everything would be all over before they knew anything about it.

At the end of September David received his longed-for call-up papers for the Royal Navy. He was ordered to report to the naval establishment at Skegness on the 15th of October. That evening we went up to the Cherry Tree at Totteridge to celebrate. There were only two or three members left of the old gang, all the others having been absorbed into the Services, and as chance would have it they were not there that evening. However, David was delighted to bump into Terry, a founder member of the gang, who happened to be home on leave from the Parachute Regiment. They greeted each other exuberantly, ordered pints and settled down to catch up on news of other members, boys and girls, and reminisce about their youthful exploits. At different times I had heard various tales from David about their rowdy past, but quickly discovered I hadn't heard the half of it.

"Do you remember the night we carried the 'No Entry' sign from Totteridge to Tally Ho!" asked Terry. They rocked with laughter.

"We must have been mad, it's miles," said David when he could speak.

"And what about the night we knocked the bobby's helmet off!" chortled Terry.

"You did what?" I demanded.

"We'd been thrown out of a dance in the church hall, and we went back and gatecrashed," crowed David.

"They got the local bobby to come and throw us out again," Terry recalled.

"And he followed us and we hid behind a wall in the dark and Smithy tipped his helmet off with a piece of wood." chortled David.

There was more in similar vein. "We had some good times," remembered Terry happily.

"Bloody good," agreed my brother with satisfaction.

Their conversation moved on. Terry was talking about the Parachute Regiment and my attention wandered. It was a good job their gang days had not lasted any longer, I reflected, or the whole lot would have ended up with criminal records by the sound of it. What would Father have said if he had known what they were getting up to? Had he been the same at their age? It was hard to imagine him acting so daft. But then, as Mother had told me once, I didn't really know him.

When David left the Gas Company on the Friday prior to his going away, he was given a rousing send-off in the pub at lunchtime. His high spirits lasted throughout his last few days at home. So did his non-stop whistling! On the morning he left, Mother rose early to cook him a special breakfast and tried her best not to fuss over him while he demolished it with gusto. Since Father went to Clare Hall the prohibition on demonstrations of affection had been lifted and at the moment of parting he gave me the cheerful hug of a comrade-in-arms, nothing sentimental. The hug he gave Mother was longer and he kissed her fondly, promising to write as soon as he had settled in. She restrained herself from showing too much emotion and let him go with a smile that died as soon as he turned his back. We stood at the front gate watching him march jauntily up the road and there were tears in her eyes. He reached the corner and turned to give us a last cheery wave before turning into the High Road in the direction of the bus stop. She stood there for several minutes before coming back into the house. I thought she would weep, but she didn't. I suppose that came later. She sat at the kitchen table without moving, lost in anguish. When I put my arm round her shoulders to comfort her, I don't think she was aware of it. David was her baby, all six feet two inches of him, and he had gone away to war. Nothing I could do or say was going to alleviate the pain of that.

The clamour for shelters had died down and with little to do behind the Enquiries counter I was bored. I knew my recall to the

WAAF must be imminent, I had enough money to tide me over for a few weeks, so I gave notice and left. When I said goodbye to Mr Bedford he wished me good luck for the future and actually smiled! I felt quite honoured.

I received two letters around this time, one from Gina and the other from Paul's Mother, readdressed from Bicester by someone in Admin. It was brief and to the point. She had not heard from Paul for several months and she was worried. Had I had any news of him? It made me aware that I had not heard from him since I left camp. Now I too was worried. If he was dead the Air Ministry would have notified his Mother as next of kin. If he was alive, why the long silence? I thought of all sorts of reasons why he had not written, each one more dramatic than the last. I told Mother about the letter, referring to Paul casually as 'one of the boys we met at the Tower in Blackpool'. She said the simplest explanation was that the invasion of France had disrupted the postal services. If she wondered why the mother of a casual acquaintance was writing to me for information about her son, she made no comment.

As a matter of fact, I was wondering much the same thing myself. I would have expected her to write to the girlfriend, not to me, a stranger. Was Paul no longer 'sort of' engaged? Or had his mother become so desperate that she was forced to admit her anxiety and write to anyone who knew her son, hoping for scraps of news that may have filtered through to them if not to her? I was sorry that I had no comfort to offer when I replied.

Gina's letter told me she had been posted to Medmenham, the big photographic printing depot near Marlow on the Thames. Reporting restrictions had apparently been eased since the invasion of France. She said they worked in shifts rounds the clock. The numerous darkrooms were located in a series of connected Nissen huts. Falling rain made a drumming sound on the roof which she found depressing. She did not mention a station band. I assumed there wasn't one. That alone would be enough to depress her without the rain.

'HAVE YOU GOT YOUR IRONS?'

I had been thinking more and more about my return to the Air Force and wondering where my own posting might take me. I hoped it would not be to a depot, especially Medmenham, which sounded dreary. Basically I still wanted what I had wanted when I left Blackpool – anywhere with planes, preferably an operational station. I had loved being at Bicester, but this time I wanted the tension and excitement of being where the real action was. Having no knowledge of what was happening in the Air Force since the invasion, I assumed there were still operational squadrons based over here. It did not occur to me that all the real action might now be based in France. My chief anxiety was that I might be sent somewhere too far away for me to visit Father. David's departure had left gaps in our family visiting rota. If I could no longer visit him either, I knew Mother would struggle to go more often to make up for our absence. She still found the journey to South Mimms and back extremely tiring and my fear was that she would wear herself out and end up in the same state of exhaustion she had been in when I first came home.

The expected brown envelope dropped onto the mat the week after I left the Enquiries office. I tore it open with eager fingers and read my orders quickly. Disappointment vied with relief. There were to be no planes, either training or operational, but I need not have worried about being unable to visit Father. I was being posted to Whitehall.

Chapter 21
Whitehall

MY NEW BILLET was a block of flats. In peacetime they had been highly desirable residences, but having been commandeered by the Air Force they were now, at the end of 1944, as impersonal as any Nissen hut, and shabby with it. Accompanied by an Admin clerk I lugged my kitbag up the stairs to the flat that was to be my home and was shown into what had probably been the dining room. It now held five iron beds of familiar pattern, with biscuits and bedclothes stacked on them with equally familiar precision. One bed had two clean sheets and a bolster case on the end. I assumed correctly that this one was mine and dumped my kitbag beside it. "Are we all photographers in here?" I enquired.

"No, you're the only one. The rest of your section are in a different block. There wasn't a bed free there for you." My spirits sagged. One of the things I had most been looking forward to was the camaraderie born of sharing a billet with girls from my own section. I untied the top of my kitbag and pulled out my second uniform, anxious to hang it in the locker before the creases became too set.

"Leave that for now and I'll take you to the mess. Have you got your irons?" asked the Admin clerk. The question cheered me. However strange this posting might feel in comparison with Bicester, it was reassuring to know that basically the Air Force had not changed in the months I had been away. I dug in my kitbag and produced the implements with a flourish, wondering if I would have been put on a charge on my first day back if I had answered, "No, I left them at home."

The photographic section lay deep underground, off one of the labyrinth of tunnels that run beneath Whitehall. The Cabinet Rooms were situated nearby and the Prime Minister, Winston Churchill, dressed in his famous siren suit, could occasionally be seen making his dogged way to or from his office first thing in the morning.

It was a much larger section than the one at Bicester. A line of small darkrooms, like booths, ran down one wall of the large general room. Each one was furnished with a bench on which stood an enlarger and the dishes needed for developing and fixing prints. In the centre of the big room was an enormous table on which these prints were sorted once they had been dried and glazed. What happened to them after that was not our concern.

When I first reported to the section I had no idea what to expect. Within minutes I realised that the place was in fact a printing depot - exactly the sort of posting I had not wanted. However, it was manned by a cheerful mix of airmen and Waafs in about equal numbers; the atmosphere was lively with the usual banter and laughter and I settled in quite happily. We worked from 0800 hours to 1800, if I remember correctly. There was no night shift.

A week or so after I arrived I found myself working at one of the glazing drums beside a corporal called Pat. I had not spoken to her before although I had seen her around. She was tall and slender with red hair and hazel-green eyes. Her manner was friendly, she laughed easily and I took to her at once. In the course of our introductory exchange of gen I told her I was odd one out at the billet and asked if she thought I had any chance of getting moved in with the rest of the section. "I don't know," she answered, "I'm not in the billet. I live at home, in Addiscombe."

"How come?" I asked in surprise.

"They're short of billets, so one or two of us who live fairly near applied to be billeted out and Admin jumped at it."

I gave this information serious thought. I had gone to see my father at South Mimms on my day off and was dismayed by the amount of time I had to spend waiting for tube trains and queuing for buses there and back. Living at home would halve the journey time and reduce the cost of fares. Apart from which, I could not settle down in the billet. It would be good to get away.

On my next day off I went home to see how my mother felt about having me billeted on her. She was finding the house dismally quiet since David and I had departed and agreed at once. My application to Admin was granted so quickly the shortage of beds in the official billets must have been acute. I packed my kitbag for the last time and said goodbye to kit inspections and domestic nights forever – unless I got posted again! I placed my irons carefully on my wardrobe shelf, just in case I needed them at some unforeseen moment in the future.

I had been so immersed in my family's affairs during the previous months that it is doubtful if I would have been able to recapture my old carefree enjoyment of service life wherever I had been sent. As it was, with one foot in civvy street and the other in the WAAF I soon felt more like a civilian who happened to be wearing uniform than a true servicewoman. The only time I really felt I belonged to the Air Force was on payday. Pay parade was held in another big room on the section. At one end stood a table on which the money was stacked in neat piles. Behind the table sat the paying officer with the pay sheets in front of him. A clerk from the accounts section sat beside him. At the start of the parade we were lined up in the corridor and marched in to stand to attention four – or was it six? - deep in front of the table. Having "right dressed" to straighten up the lines we were given the commands "At Ease" and "Stand Easy". The clerk then called us out one by one in alphabetical order. As each name was called its owner came smartly to attention, marched up to the table and came to attention again. He or she saluted the officer, confirmed their surname and added the last three digits of their number. The clerk counted out the money due and pushed it towards the officer, who entered the amount on the pay sheet before handing it over to the rigid figure in front of him. The recipient saluted once more, took one pace backwards, did a military left turn and marched off parade.

As my surname in those days began with 'G' I had a boring wait before I was called, with nothing to do but watch the rats scampering along the pipes that ran round the walls near the ceiling. It was all a far cry from the Borough Surveyor's office, where a friendly girl from the accounts department came round on Friday mornings delivering little brown envelopes to the weekly paid staff. I had never queried the RAF system before. Now it seemed to me as I stood there waiting my turn that it wasted an awful lot of time.

Nearly everyone left the section to visit the outside world at lunchtime. When I went there in November it was the only time we saw daylight except on our weekly day off. The sun was not up when we started work and it had set before the shift ended.

A favourite lunchtime haunt was St James's Park, not five minutes walk away down Clive Steps and across Horse Guards Road. When it was too cold to sit about, a brisk walk took us to the bridge over the lake. Leaning over the parapet we threw scraps from our packed lunches to the hungry ducks jostling in the water below. Greedy seagulls dived and swooped above them, shrieking excitedly and stealing the food in mid air. When summer came and the weather was hot, most of the section could be found sprawled on the grass by Duck Island, soaking up the sun before we had to return to our underground world for the afternoon.

Whitehall itself was to be avoided at that time of day. There were too many officers about and each one had to be saluted. It was technically a chargeable offence not to salute an officer, although I never knew anyone get more than a reprimand for failing to show respect for the King's uniform. It must have been as boring for the officers as it was for us ORs (Other Ranks) as every salute they were given had to be acknowledged by a salute in return.

Christmas 1944 was so unremarkable that I cannot remember much about it. I know I had the day off and Mother and I spent it at home on our own. We did not go to visit Father, probably because the bus service was too infrequent that day. Nannie and Aunt Evelyn did not join us as Nannie had a bad bout of flu. I think we listened to the King's broadcast in the afternoon, otherwise it was no different to any other day off. I don't even remember exchanging presents, though I suppose we did.

In early January Mother received one of the best presents she could have wished for – a long newsy letter from David. Apart from brief notes telling her he was on this or that 'ship', as the naval training camps were called, she had had no real news of him since he left home. He was clearly very happy in the Senior Service. His high spirits fairly danced off every page. He must have whistled himself dry when he wrote it. He said he had made some jolly good shipmates. They all found some of the naval discipline irksome and had fallen foul of authority on one or two occasions. One particular Petty Officer had given them a lot of trouble. (And vice versa, I was willing to bet!) This did not seem to worry him unduly. He treated it as a joke. On a more serious note, he had been offered a place on a meteorology course, one of the few left open to new recruits, and it promised to be very interesting. His letter took me back to my own early days in the WAAF when each experience was fresh and life was exciting. Compared with those days it had now become exceedingly tame. The great adventure was over. It had ended on the day I left Bicester.

There was no doubt that by living at home Pat and I lost out on much of the camaraderie shared by those who lived together in the billet. My days off were usually taken up with shopping, helping in the house or going to visit Father. But occasionally Pat and I planned our days off to coincide and met in town to explore the City or window-shop in the West End. Wearing uniform on these jaunts entitled us to buy extremely cheap theatre tickets from the kiosk in Trafalgar Square and eat in Service canteens. The one in St Martin-in-the-Fields served cinnamon toast to which we both became addicted. It made a tasty change from our usual drab diet.

At the end of his training David came home on leave prior to joining his first real ship. Mother was beside herself with joy at seeing him again, firmly putting to the back of her mind the thought that from now on he would be sailing into danger. Father was immensely proud when he turned up at Clare Hall in uniform. For myself, although the possibility of danger would always lurk in the background, I could not help feeling relieved that the war had lasted long enough for him to join in.

As the history books have recorded, Germany capitulated on May 7th, 1945. The next day, May 8th was designated VE (Victory in Europe) Day, a national holiday, the official day for celebrating our success. Jubilant crowds milled about Downing Street and the House of Commons to cheer Mr Churchill every time he appeared, smoking one of his huge cigars and giving his famous 'V for Victory' sign. There was riotous dancing in Trafalgar Square. Pat and I joined the thousands surging up the Mall to shout for the King and Queen to come out on the balcony at Buckingham Palace. Wild cheering greeted their every appearance. We stayed until we were hoarse and hungry and then went our separate ways home. We did not stay to see the lights switched on at dusk. Double summertime had extended the light evenings until long past suppertime and we couldn't wait. 'Dimout', a modified blackout, had been in operation for some time, but the return to full lighting was the signal that life was beginning to return to normal.

The euphoria did not last long. Behind the cheers lay the grim knowledge that although we had beaten the Germans only half the war was over. We still had to beat the Japanese. Within days the young men on the section were sent on embarkation leave before being posted either to India or the Philippines. It was understood this latter group was going to Okinawa, a hellhole from which they would be lucky to return.

A number of hastily arranged weddings took place, girlfriends being as determined as the men to live life to the full while they still had the chance. I marvelled at the ease with which so many couples could sort themselves out at short notice with no apparent third-party complications. I also envied them. "There won't be any single men left if this war goes on much longer," I grumbled to Pat. She, like me, was unattached and likely to remain so for the foreseeable future.

The Allied troops advanced swiftly across Germany, releasing the men in the prison camps as they went. POWs were arriving back in England every day. I hoped Paul was amongst them. Our scrappy exchange of letters followed by a year of silence had left us out of touch. I did not even know for certain if he was still alive. I presumed his mother would have let me know if she had been notified of his death, but I could not be sure. Either way, I did not expect to hear from him again. However, one evening in June there was a letter waiting for me on the kitchen dresser when I got home. I recognised the writing immediately and exclaimed in surprise, "It's from Paul!"

Mother was doing something at the stove. She asked over her shoulder, "Who?"

Ripping open the envelope I said, "You know – the POW." The letter was rather longer than his others had been. I read it through quickly, then read it again more slowly. I had often said in the past that I wished he would sort himself out. Well, now he had.

Mother said, "Is he all right?"

"He's fine," I said dryly. "He and his girlfriend got married last week!"

Not knowing what the emotional situation had been between me and Paul, Mother waited for me to give her a clue as to how I was feeling before speaking again. So how was I feeling? I wasn't sure. Glad he had survived, naturally. Shaken, both by his unexpected re-entry into my life and by his news. Hurt? No. I had always known he had a girlfriend in the background. Mostly I felt irritated that he had only now told me her name. Jacky. "If they get an opportunity," I told my mother, "they hope to visit London one day. He wants to know if they can come and see me."

Deciding that my heart was not broken, Mother said, "I hope they let us know before they come, or I may not have anything in to offer them."

I wondered to myself how his new wife felt about his writing to me so soon after the wedding, and whether they would actually turn up in Finchley. For the record, they did, some months later. They came to tea on one of my days off. Paul was again the friendly soul I had known at Blackpool. I thought Jacky was a nondescript sort of girl. Pleasant enough, if rather withdrawn. Paul did not say much about his time in captivity, except to explain his long silence. For the last year of the war the prisoners had been marched from camp to camp, going deeper and deeper into Germany. They had not received any mail or been able to send any. He said being completely out of touch with home was one of the hardest things they had had to bear. Now he was back he was anxious to keep in touch with everybody, including me. I could see by the look on his wife's face that she did not feel the same urge, especially where I was concerned. They left in a flurry of goodwill, with Paul promising to write and keep me up to date with their news. Hardly to my surprise I never heard from him again.

We had another piece of good news in June. I came home to hear Mother singing in the kitchen. Something she had not done for a very long time. It was doubly surprising on this particular evening because she had been planning to visit Clare Hall that day. Usually she returned home dog-tired and rather depressed - definitely not in the mood for singing. I flung my cap at the hallstand and started down the hall to join her in the kitchen. But she had heard me come in. The singing stopped and she hurried out to greet me, "Pop's coming home!"

"When?" I asked, delighted.

"If he passes his final check-up, some time in August."

"So it's not definite?"

"As good as. His lung's fully healed and there's no sign of trouble in the other one."

"Great!"

Physical and emotional exhaustion overcame her after supper and she went to bed early. I went up to my own room to smoke and think about the future. For the last five years Mother had run the household very successfully on her own, making decisions without reference to Father when she had to. How would she feel about relinquishing the reins when he returned? For, unless he had changed, I was in no doubt she would have to.

His return would not make much practical difference to me, so far as I could see. My life was governed by the Air Force for the present. But what of the future? When he went away I had been within a week or two of my seventeenth birthday, chafing against his restrictions and full of resentment at having been dragooned (as I saw it) into going back to school to do the commercial course. I was now twenty-two. Would he still try to organise my life for me as he had done then? I had an uneasy feeling that he might. And I would be faced with the same dilemma as before: either do as he wished or risk upsetting the family, as I had done when I defied him over the Civil Service entrance exam.

Pat was thrilled for me when I told her the news at lunchtime next day. We were strolling through St James's Park towards the bridge over the lake. I did not mention my misgivings for the future, but then I didn't have to. She knew enough about my family's relationships to appreciate the situation. When I said, "I'm not looking forward to living at home again when I'm demobbed," she knew exactly what I meant. She said, "Neither am I."

I knew as much about her family as she did about mine. Her mother was a forceful lady, with whom Pat did not get on easily.

Her father was a scientist, a quiet man, but strict in his way.

We reached the bridge and sat down on a nearby seat to eat our sandwiches and watch the ducks. Pat asked, "Will you go back to shorthand typing after the war?"

"I suppose so. I don't want to, but it pays good money and I don't know anything else. What will you do?" Pat had been at art school before she joined up and had no experience of the business world.

"If I can get a full-time grant I'd like to go to college and study commercial photography."

"I didn't know ex-service bods could get full-time grants." Although I knew some of the boys had been attending evening classes at the Regent Street Polytechnic by courtesy of the Government, I had never given much thought to further study, taking it for granted that I would go back to office work when I was demobbed.

Pat said, as if she had only just thought of it, "Why don't you apply as well? Perhaps we could do something together."

The idea took my breath away. I felt enthusiasm begin to bubble up inside me. Then it subsided. Would my father let me do it? His overall ambition for me had always been that I should have a job with a secure future. He would not consider photography secure. I voiced my doubts to Pat.

After a few moments thought she said, "If you had a definite plan, and could tell him how much the grant would be and so on, do you think you could persuade him?"

"I don't know. It 's worth a try." As I munched my sandwich I mulled over her suggestion. David had always been positive about what he wanted to do, and Father had accepted it, whatever it was. If I presented him with a cut and dried plan, would he accept that too? He might. When I was younger I had had no plan; that had been half the trouble. But the other half had been that I was his daughter, to be protected. David was his son, who had to stand on his own two feet like a man, and that was never going to change. I said, "He's bound to ask what my future prospects would be. What could I say? I haven't a clue."

"Tell him it depends on how well you do on the course," said Pat, obviously a good strategist where fathers were concerned.

I chuckled, then asked seriously, "Have you any idea what you want to do?"

"Eventually," she said, "I'd like to set up my own portrait studio and specialise in children and animals." I gawped at her, impressed. She had more ambition and initiative than I had realised. "Of course," she went on, "I'll have to work for other people first to gain experience."

We munched in silence for a while. Then Pat said, "If we could get a little flat somewhere we could both leave home."

"Oh, my God!" I exploded, "I shall think myself lucky if I can get him to agree to the course. He'll never let me move into a flat."

"Neither would my father if I was on my own. But if there were two of us - " She let the sentence hang.

"I think I'd better concentrate on the course first," I said.

We accepted that if the Allies took as long to beat the Japs as we had taken to beat Germany it might be years before we could put our plan into action. When the war ended abruptly a few weeks later it took everyone by surprise. Everyone, that is, except the men behind the atom bomb. The general public had no idea such a weapon existed.

Years later my brother wrote an account of the end of the war from the viewpoint of an Able Seaman (Met). His ship, the SS "Otranto", a pre-war cruise liner adapted for duty as a troopship, had spent some time steaming round the coast of Australia, calling in at Perth, Sydney and Brisbane before turning towards its real destination. He wrote:

"As we neared the Philippines, we started picking up quite a lot of shipping moving in and out of Manila. In the early hours of 6th August 1945 we dropped anchor in Manila Bay to join an enormous fleet of warships, transports, and merchant vessels being assembled for the invasion of Japan. We were looking forward to getting a few hours ashore in Manila. Our journey up from Australia had been hot and uncomfortable. Apart from the normal ship's crew, there was our entire MONAB (Mobile Operational Navy Air Base) of 400-plus and all our equipment. Bulldozers, trucks, lorries, jeeps and heavy breakdown vehicles packed the areas below decks normally housing aircraft. The ship's company slept in hammocks in any odd corner they could find.

"Within a few hours of our arrival, the news was flashed to all ships in the harbour that a new, very powerful bomb had been dropped on Hiroshima. Every ship erupted with cheering." Over the years since then there has been much debate as to whether we were right to use such a dreadful weapon, but David goes on, "No one was in any doubt about the morality of it at that moment; all they could see was the end of the war and the saving of countless thousands of lives."

They put to sea again the same day and joined a small force of destroyers, minesweepers and a cruiser heading for Hong Kong. They were at sea when the Allies dropped the second bomb, this time on Nagasaki. The Japs called for a ceasefire while they negotiated terms for peace, but they had not formally surrendered when the small fleet arrived on the Colony. David was on one of the first patrols to be sent ashore. They were under orders not to fire unless they were under threat. Making their way along Nathan Road, they came face to face with a Japanese army patrol marching towards them. They took cover where they could, guns at the ready, prepared to defend themselves if necessary. But the ceasefire held. The Japs passed by without a glance, ignoring them completely.

The treaty was finally signed on 14th August. Oddly, David does not say anything about VJ Day on the 15th. Back home the celebrations were even wilder than those on VE Day in May. This time the war was really over and we had won. Our menfolk were out of danger. In due course they would be coming home.

In Hong Kong the Meteorology staff made the Royal Observatory their headquarters. David remained there until 1947, when he was posted back to England to be demobbed. He had his sights fixed on a career in the Forestry Commission. He lived at home for a few weeks while he sorted himself out and arranged his immediate future. That done, he took off for Herefordshire on his first training assignment and never lived at home again.

As soon as the war ended Pat and I started making enquiries about grants and looking round to see what photographic courses were available. I did not tell my parents what I was doing until Father brought up the subject of my future one evening. He had come home as expected, but was not yet ready to return to work. He therefore had plenty of time to sit and think and plan for the future. My future. He said, "You will need to go on a refresher course for shorthand and typing before applying for a job. Why don't you go down to the commercial college and see what they have to offer?"

I took a deep breath and plunged in. "Pop, I don't want to go back to office work, I want to stay in photography."

He looked startled, but said nothing. Keeping my voice level I told him about the grant I had applied for. I also said my friend Pat was doing the same thing, but I did not mention our aspirations concerning a flat. He frowned and I thought he was going to try and make me change my mind. Hastily I played my trump card – my promise to return to secretarial work if necessary. Still he said nothing and I feared he was about to refuse his consent. But to my surprise and relief I found I had an ally.

Mother had been happy for Father to take up what they both regarded as his rightful position as head of the house, but she no longer took a passive back seat if she disagreed with any of his decisions. She said now, "It might be an advantage for her to have more than one skill to rely on. And if the Government is paying for the training she has nothing to lose."

Father did not look happy, but said reluctantly, "Very well. As long as it is understood that you will go back to your real job if you're out of work." I promised gladly, almost unable to believe he had given in without a fight.

Being the same age and having by chance served in the WAAF for roughly the same length of time, Pat and I were demobbed within a few months of one another in 1946, a year earlier than David. Our applications for grants had been successful, but we realised at once that we were not going to have enough money to rent a flat until we were earning reasonable salaries. We were not too downhearted. In fact in a way I was relieved. With Mother's help I had won Father's agreement to the photographic course. I was not at all certain she would back me over moving into a flat. If I was going to have to fight for it, I was quite content to postpone the battle until later.

We had secured places together on an eighteen months course at a photographic college in Bolt Court, just off Fleet Street. Its specialist subject was colour photography, which was just becoming popular. We met outside the College on our first morning and went in together, our spirits high.